YOU CAN'T KILL THE SPIRIT

YOU CAN'T KILL THE SPIRIT

PAM McALLISTER

First of the Barbara Deming Memorial Series:
Stories of Women and Nonviolent Action

NEW SOCIETY PUBLISHERS
Philadelphia, PA and Santa Cruz, CA

Inquiries regarding requests to reprint all or part of *You Can't Kill the Spirit* should be addressed to:

New Society Publishers
4527 Springfield Avenue
Philadelphia, PA 19143

This book is the first of the Barbara Deming Memorial Series: Stories of Women and Nonviolent Action.

ISBN 0-86571-130-5 Hardcover
    0-86571-131-3 Paperback

Printed in the United States of America on partially recycled paper.

Cover design by Mary Shapiro
Book design by Tina Birky

To order directly from the publisher, add $1.50 to the price for the first copy, 50¢ each additional. Send check or money order to:

New Society Publishers
PO Box 582
Santa Cruz, CA 95061

New Society Publishers is a project of the New Society Educational Foundation, a nonprofit, tax-exempt, public foundation. Opinions expressed in this book do not necessarily represent positions of the New Society Educational Foundation.

Appreciation is gratefully acknowledged to the following authors and publishers whose works are quoted in this volume: From "Like a Mountain" by Naomi Littlebear, 1976. From "A Song for Gorgons" by Barbara Deming. From "Furusato" by Ishigi Astu. English verse by Ewan MacColl in *Songs for Peace*, compiled and edited by The Student Peace Union, NY: 1966. From "Bread and Roses" by James Oppenheim, 1912. From "Beloved Comrade," words by Lewis Allen. MCA Music, NY: 1945. From "Singing for Our Lives" by Holly Near. Hereford Music, 1979. (This song was written after Supervisor Harvey Milk, a gay man who believed in coalition and unity, was murdered in San Francisco.) From "Follow the Drinkin' Gourd" by Paul Campbell (based on a traditional Underground Railroad song). Folkways Music Publishers, Inc., NY: 1951. From "It Isn't Nice" by Malvina Reynolds. Schroder Music Co., 1964. From *Ma, can I be a feminist and still like men? Lyrics from life* by Nicole Hollander. St. Martin's Press, NY: 1980.

For my parents, Helen and Arden McAllister,
who brought me safely to the crossroads,

Julia, Anna and Emily
who gave me a push
down the road "less traveled by,"

and Barbara Deming
who walked with me a little way.

CONTENTS

ACKNOWLEDGMENTS

I AM DEEPLY GRATEFUL to the many family and friends who helped me make this book a reality. Barbara Smith recognized burnout when she saw it and sent me the application form for the Berkshire Forum's Radical Writer's Retreat along with a note of encouragement. Betty and Herman Liveright accepted me into the one month's residency at the Writer's Retreat in April 1986 where the first impulse for this book pushed its way past two years of grief and fear. Susan Mitchell and the other Forum staffpeople nurtured the creative space, and the three other writers in residence intimidated and inspired me with their fierce, nonstop typing and helped me renew my courage. For this support I will be forever grateful to Linda Backiel, Marge Grevatt and Rob Okun.

My parents, Helen and Arden McAllister, read the entire rough draft (my mom writing her comments in green ink, my dad in blue) and cheered me on with a sort of amazed enthusiasm. My sisters Lois and Anita and friend Evie kept me laughing and feeling loved.

A number of friends read portions of the book manuscript and took the time to review their reactions and suggestions with me. Their careful readings improved the book significantly. Deep thanks to Diane Berg, Ruth Dreamdigger, Nancy Eckel, Norman Taylor and Jack Wilson.

I am indebted to Lance Bradley who heals by listening and to Karen Ziegler who is able to find the best in me and helps me find it too.

I want to thank my friends at New Society Publishers for believing in this book. I especially want to thank David Albert, my editor, who kept saying "This is going to be a *great* book!" even while he was marking up page after page for revisions. I thank T. L. Hill and Ellen Sawislak for their feedback on several chapters, Mike Holderness for calming my computer-anxiety with clear instructions, Barbara Hirshkowitz for work on production, and Tina Birky for her wonderful design work and attention to detail in copyediting.

A number of people took the time to share their special insights and personal experiences to help me shape the stories in this book. I am especially grateful to Magdalena Kobayashi for reviewing the section on the Japan women's peace movement; Jane Meyerding for telling the story of her blood-pouring action; Holly Near for her thoughtful feedback and help with the chapter on singing; and Edith Adamson, Ed Hedeman and Norman Taylor for their help with the chapter on tax resistance.

I would like to acknowledge my housemate, Loreine Kendrick, who deflected numerous phone calls so I could work uninterrupted, and my cat-companion, Emily, who has truly earned the title Beloved Distraction.

Finally, I am thankful to all the women who have dared, are daring, to experiment with nonviolent action—sometimes in grand, life-*risking* ways, sometimes in quiet, life-*changing* ways—whose spirit has shaped this book and whose stories are recorded here.

PUBLISHER'S NOTE

"THE MEANING OF HISTORY lies in the telling," or so I was always taught in school. I'm sure now that those who felt it necessary to drum this message into me meant it as an exaltation of the historian's art; that the interpretation of history, events as they are filtered through the historian's eyes, is what gives the passage of time its value.

We know of course that events can be retold in a host of different ways, and from a myriad of perspectives. But there is something suspect, even sinister, when the events to be retold, despite the differences in the perspectives of the historians, seem to have so many common elements: the major actors are all (or virtually all) male, their actions almost always result in the death of others—often in large numbers—and the results are measured in their short- or long-term effects upon a dominant church, state or class or in the way goods and services are exchanged. Rare indeed are the histories which retell the events which have led to increased cooperation between people, to a greater shared understanding of our commonalities or potentialities as human beings, or to a firmer understanding of our place in a fragile ecological order.

Let no one imagine that history as it is written is benign. The models of our collective past which are presented to us from an early age, the choice of events to be retold (and by inference what events are not worth retelling) shape our orientation toward the world as we experience it. Historians are not always conscious of their real power; in recasting our past they do nothing less than cast our future.

But there is another kind of history, or perhaps a better word is *heritage*. In traditional English law, heritage is that portion of an inheritance which devolves upon us by right and upon which the "executors" or "administrators" of a will can lay no valid claim. In a more common understanding, what actually constitutes our heritage as a species may be forgotten, indeed it may even seem to be lost. But, as Barbara Deming, to whose life and work this series is dedicated, knew all too well, it is never far from us if we simply "remember who we are."

What Pam McAllister offers us in the *Barbara Deming Memorial Series* is a talisman, a key to reclaiming and invoking our almost-forgotten heritage, specifically a heritage borne by women, in these troubled times. It is a heritage birthed in conflict which yet affirms the human person and the human personality in the midst of conflict. It is a heritage of struggle which nonetheless asserts that we are all, when all is said and done, oppressors and oppressed "earth of this earth, and bone of its bone" (to quote Deming), and that we sacrifice the rememberance of our commonality only at our gravest peril.

This is the heritage of nonviolence which the stories of women contained in this series offer to all of us. As tales of hope, as a heritage which prefigures the options and possibilities of untold stories yet to come, they make us at New Society Publishers proud to publish the *Barbara Deming Memorial Series: Stories of Women and Nonviolent Action.*

David H. Albert
for New Society Publishers
Santa Cruz, California
1 May 1988

From Aphra Behn to Adrienne Rich it has been suggested that among the most subversive and powerful activities women can engage in are the activities of constructing women's visible and forceful traditions, of making *real* our *positive* existence, of celebrating our lives and of resisting disappearance in the process.

—Dale Spender
Women of Ideas
(And What Men Have Done to Them)

INTRODUCTION:
A LITTLE BIT OF GANDHI WITH
A TOUCH OF ETHEL MERMAN

Treasure hunt of a lost wanderer

THE MORNING AFTER US FORCES BOMBED Libya, I sat
on the edge of a little clearing where a birch wood met some young
firs. I had been awarded residency that April 1986 at a writers'
retreat in the mountains, and there, far from my city apartment,
I had discovered morning mist and bird songs. There too, I had
heard news of the bombing. It seemed to me that morning—the
Doomsday Clock at five minutes to midnight and counting—that
I was paralyzed by what was happening in the present and even
more terrified of the future. In that moment my world was
unbearably fragile. One thing seemed clear: there are no hiding
places.

I lay belly down on the earth floor. Inches from my face a
magnificent spider's web caught my eye, caught and held the new
sunlight. I thought of Grandmother Spider, healing spinner
goddess of the Shawnee, Hopi and Piman peoples. Her silvery
threads hold the stars in the sky and she watches over lost
wanderers. Lost wanderers like me. What threads would hold my
earth to my sky a little longer?

In the shadow of the spider's web that morning an answer shaped
itself in my mind. I needed to find the stories of women who had
responded in life-affirming ways to a death-filled world, the legacy
of women's courage that is my rightful inheritance.

After that day I began to hunt the stories of women's courage
and nonviolent creativity as children and pirates hunt buried
treasure. And, as children and pirates know, true treasures beckon
from troubled waters, from places of doom and danger. I soon
learned that the stories of courage I sought would always be found

in the context of oppression and injustice, so I looked for them in the steel blue shadows of Argentina's Plaza de Mayo during the rule of the right-wing junta, in the dust of a squatters' camp outside Johannesburg, and just beyond the glow of the burning cross set on fire by hooded Klansmen on a Mississippi lawn. Barbed wire and banned books became the North Stars that guided my search. I trusted that the stories of women's courage would awaken my creative imagination and breathe new life into my commitment to nonviolent action.

"Oh Gawd, not nonviolence!"

At a party, a discussion began about the anthology I had edited in 1982. One woman there had not heard about it, so she asked the title. I told her, "*Reweaving the Web of Life: Feminism and Nonviolence.*"

"Nonviolence! Oh, terrific," she spat. "Just what we *don't* need . . . another book telling women to be passive."

On other occasions the retorts have been equally misinformed. "So whadda-ya gonna do, just stand there and watch your grandmother get mugged?"

For the record, no—the nonviolence I advocate is not about passivity, and no—I do not intend to stand by and watch anybody's grandmother get mugged.

The notion of power has for so long been equated with the ability to show muscle that when it comes to conflict resolution our stunted imaginations rarely get past the bloody nose or the bombs bursting in air. Fed a constant diet of action, adventure and violence, we come to expect these things. We're also primed to crave revenge or, at the very least, some really juicy karmic retribution. I recognize the dilemma especially as it is presented in a feminist context: in our eagerness as women to develop our strength, we're leery of any stance that could be construed as an expression of passivity or vulnerability.

I could explain that violent resistance and nonviolent resistance are both active stances as opposed to passivity, which is inactive, but the words don't convey the spirit. *Nonviolence* sounds limp and apologetic—*violence* takes center stage with the wimpy *non* as a sideshow—and *pacifism* sounds too much like passivity.

Quite early in life I recognized that nonviolence has an image problem. In the little blue lockable diary I kept as an eleven year old, I listed my heroes: Mahatma Gandhi, the leader of the nonviolent national liberation movement in India; Martin Luther King, Jr., the leader of the nonviolent civil rights movement in the United States and . . . Annette Funicello, Mouseketeer extraordinaire.

I eventually outgrew Annette but I never outgrew the impulse that inspired me to name her beside Gandhi and King. That impulse named my truth as something more complex than the sainted martyrs seemed to represent. And now I see this was a hint of confusion to come, for just a year ago I whispered to my therapist that I really didn't know if I wanted to be more like Gandhi or Ethel Merman.

What strange creature has my psyche conjured?—half a skinny, loin-clothed Gandhi walking bravely to the sea; half a fleshy Ethel Merman belting out "Everything's Coming Up Roses." The two play themselves out in me. In the company of my serious, politically aware activist friends, I feel my brassy Ethel Merman growing restless, feel myself getting campy and loud. And with my get-it-while-you-can, life-is-a-cabaret, I've-got-rhythm-who-could-ask-for-anything-more friends, I suddenly crave the centeredness I feel when my eyes are on the prize and my feet are on the path of truth and justice.

Last winter I went to see the statue of Gandhi, realistically rendered by sculptor K. E. Patel and newly erected in Union Square—a corner of Manhattan steeped in the memory of massive nonviolent labor demonstrations. Poor Gandhi, so lovely, so lonely, so real—portrayed leaning into a great stride, sandaled right foot forward, walking stick in hand, thick glasses resting over boney cheek bones, mouth set in a grimace of determination. That day he looked cold. For a moment I almost saw goose bumps on his naked legs. I felt embarrassed for this saintly figure who seemed so out of place, dwarfed by the surrounding store signs— Mays, Wendy's, Seaman's, Grand Discount House. On the metal fence surrounding the statue was a block-lettered sign, NO PIGEON FEEDING IN THIS AREA. THANK YOU. This was a noisy corner crowded with 14th Street people: street vendors, shoppers, students, prostitutes, young lawyers, drug addicts and homeless people who call Union Square home. Beneath the statue a man and a woman, confused tourists, argued loudly about whether they were that moment standing at Union Square or Washington Square. Oh, Gandhi.

Surely, I thought as I stood with the cold statue, Ethel Merman could handle this scene better than could Gandhi—the saint who never got up on the wrong side of the bed, never swore, never even had an angry thought about his oppressors but always reserved such feelings for the injustice itself—and about whom Albert Einstein wrote, "Generations to come will scarce believe that such a one in flesh and blood walked upon this earth." Clearly those advocates of nonviolence who follow in Gandhi's footsteps are supposed to be calm and patient people. Ethel and I, on the other hand, are not at all calm and patient. We have too many rough edges, too many earthy desires, too many emotions barely contained, too many contradictions. (Secretly I fantasize writing an autobiography titled *Notes of a Pissed-off Peacemaker*.)

But as I looked again at Gandhi in mid-stride, no longer flesh and blood but stone, I thought about the real Gandhi. I remembered reading that he was sarcastic and witty, plagued by self-doubt and blessed with a flexibility that allowed him to change his mind, a characteristic which is loathed by most image-makers and leads to volumes of confused analysis by his critics. Gandhi shared many of the prejudices and limited understandings of his time and place, as well as some of his own unique obsessions and inconsistencies. In other words, Gandhi was as mortal and complicated as the rest of us.

The Gandhi that requires Ethel Merman for completion the way yin needs yang is the Hollywood and headline Gandhi, a distortion, a lie to which I've been as susceptible as anyone else. When Gandhi is portrayed as a one-dimensional sainted martyr, as beyond our reach as Jesus, nonviolence, by extension, is rendered beyond our reach, inaccessible, unuseable. By making it seem like something only saints have done, the history of nonviolent action has been buried just as surely as women's history and the history of oppressed peoples have. When this happens, all of us are deprived of the tools of liberation.

I looked up at the statue and reconsidered. Gandhi, I decided, could handle himself just fine on this busy corner. Indeed, this was precisely where he belonged, where nonviolence itself belonged—with the people—people like the arguing tourists, people like me.

But I'm not the only one confused about the posture and attitude required of advocates of nonviolent action or discouraged by unrealistic expectations. I was once interviewed on a radio talk show in New York City. A listener called toward the end of the program to chide me, saying that an advocate of nonviolence shouldn't be angry. The flustered talk show host quickly reassured the caller that I was really very sweet and not at all angry. I laughed and thanked her for defending me, but then reclaimed my anger and said I felt it was both a sign of health and essential to my life as an advocate of nonviolence. It is evidence of my love for life. Without the anger I'd probably be silent as stone, passive, complacent.

The stories in this book were collected during a winter when mothers and their children in the United States huddled homeless by the thousands on cold sidewalks, vying for space near hot air vents, and shelters turned away aging men for lack of beds. How can I not be angry?

For every *hour* that I spent writing this book, the US government spent $34 million on the military, more than $800 million a day. How can I not be angry?

Every day I worked on the book's revisions, an estimated thirty-seven women were raped in Brooklyn, the New York City borough where I live. How can I not be angry?

I am a woman living in the wilderness of a planet so despairing that Brown University students voted to ask their campus infirmary to stock cyanide tablets they could use in the event of a nuclear war. That the students voiced their despair is healthy; that they have to live with such fear is in itself an atrocity. How can I not be angry?

Why, then, nonviolence?

What has drawn me most strongly to nonviolence is its capacity for encompassing a complexity necessarily denied by violent strategies. By complexity I mean the sort faced by feminists who rage against the *system* of male supremacy but, at the same time, love their fathers, sons, husbands, brothers and male friends. I mean the complexity which requires us to name an underpaid working man who beats his wife both as someone who is oppressed and as an oppressor. Violent tactics and strategies rely on polarization and dualistic thinking and require us to divide ourselves into the good and the bad, assume neat, rigid little categories easily answered from the barrel of a gun. Nonviolence allows for the complexity inherent in our struggles and requires a reasonable acceptance of diversity and an appreciation for our common ground.

Barbara Deming wrote convincingly of the "complicated truth" in her 1977 essay, "Remembering Who We Are."

> ... how can one any longer make neat distinctions between oppressors and oppressed? Won't it often happen that we would have to name the very same person both an oppressed person and an oppressor? Yes, it will very often happen. Life is precisely that complicated. And to pretend that it isn't that complicated doesn't help. We need rescue from neat distinctions that are illusions. . . .

> ... if the complicated truth is that many of the oppressed are also oppressors, and many of the oppressors are also oppressed—nonviolent confrontation is the only form of confrontation that allows us to respond realistically to such complexity. In this kind of struggle we address ourselves always both to that which we refuse to accept from others and to that which we can respect in them, have in common with them—however much or little that may be.

Barbara wrote about the two hands of nonviolence. She wrote that nonviolence gives us two hands upon the oppressor—"one hand taking from him what is not his due, the other slowly calming him as we do this." In another essay she wrote, "We can put more pressure on the antagonist for whom we show human concern. We put upon him two pressures—the pressure of our defiance of him and the pressure of our respect for his life—and it happens that in combination these two pressures are uniquely effective."

This visual metaphor is particularly helpful in describing the basic attitude underlying the nonviolent sensibility. With one hand we say to an oppressor, "Stop what you are doing. I refuse to honor the role you are choosing to play. I refuse to obey you. I refuse to cooperate with your demands. I refuse to build the walls and the bombs. I refuse to pay for the guns. With this hand I will even interfere with the wrong you are doing. I want to disrupt the easy pattern of your life."

But then the advocate of nonviolence raises the other hand. It is raised out-stretched—maybe with love and sympathy, but maybe not—but always outstretched with the message that (as Barbara wrote), "No, you are not the other; and no, I am not the other. No one is the other. . . ." With this hand we say, "I won't let go of you or cast you out of the human race. I have faith that you can make a better choice than you are making now, and I'll be here when you're ready. Like it or not, we are a part of one another." The peculiar strength of nonviolence comes precisely from the dual nature of its approach—the two hands.

The women at the Seneca Peace Encampment in New York State used the two hands of nonviolence in the summer of 1983. Barbara was with the peace camp women the day they went on a women's history walk past the homes of Harriet Tubman and Elizabeth Cady Stanton and past the site of the first Women's Rights Convention. But during their walk, the women were met by a fierce and frenzied mob in Waterloo. People jabbed the pointed tips of their little American flags like tiny spears at the peace camp women and screamed, "Commie dykes, go back to Russia!" and "All you girls need is a little rape." Barbara saw then the two hands of nonviolence used at the most crucial moment when the women were blocked from proceeding and danger was imminent:

> I saw that a number of women had sat down, then formed a circle together. . . I can remember the reassurance I felt at once, at the sight of those quietly seated figures. Without words they made the statement it was essential that we make. The statement that we posed no threat—had no intention of trying to thrust our way through the mob. But the statement that we had no intention of retreating, either. We knew our Constitutional rights. We had a right to walk here. The two-fold message that gives nonviolent struggle its leverage: We won't be bullied; but you needn't fear us. You needn't fear us; but we won't be bullied.

My response to my world requires such complexity as is embraced by nonviolent strategies. As I have learned and continue to learn more about nonviolence, I have realized that, despite first impressions, nonviolence not only allows but requires me to act from the full range of my feelings and reactions. It is about speaking the whole complicated truth, responding to the fullness of the struggle, and it requires my most bitter words, my most hearty laughter, my deepest compassion, my sharpest wit. Mohandas meet Ethel, Ethel, Mohandas.

Tactical nonviolence

The above discussion of the spirit and sensibility of a nonviolent philosophy of resistance may seem lofty, especially in contrast to its practical applications, which this series will illustrate.

In fact, most of the people who participate in nonviolent action are not in the least concerned with the underlying philosophy, nor would they know to call their actions nonviolent. Most would be surprised to learn that they are quite adept at using *tactical nonviolence* or that they have done so every time they have gone on strike, signed a petition, participated in a boycott, stood silently in a candlelight vigil or joined a demonstration. While bombs bursting in air are given prominence in anthems, headlines and national budgets, and the impulse for revenge is celebrated in folktale and box office hits, nonviolent tactics have been used more often and more successfully than violent tactics ever have. The majority of people who've successfully relied on tactical nonviolence have simply understood it to be a direct, common sense way to protest, intervene in or refuse to cooperate with circumstances they deem unjust.

Nonviolent action is often used by those who would be equally willing to use violent tactics in some circumstances. People who have no qualms about taking up the gun to defend flag or family are the same people who vote to go on *strike* at their workplace (the classic nonviolent tactic) and who can be found on *picket lines* every day (another nonviolent tactic).

Furthermore, tactical nonviolence is the backbone of most national liberation struggles, struggles popularly called "violent revolutions." These revolutions do rely on fighters who are able and willing to use violent tactics and lethal weapons. But these revolutions also rely on countless acts of nonviolent resistance by workers, students, women, elders and children who use a full range of tactics including strikes, physical obstruction, sanctuary, hunger strikes, petitions, slowdowns in factories, mass protest demonstrations, acts of economic noncooperation such as boycotts and tax resistance, civil disobedience, and the development of underground presses and/or secret organizations. In these struggles, even teaching people to read is sometimes a revolutionary act of civil disobedience taken at great risk. Nonviolent actions have especially made sense to unarmed or insufficiently armed people whose adversaries are not only equipped with a range of weapons and military apparatus but are rigorously trained, ready and willing to use violence.

Nonviolent actions were used long before the word *nonviolence* was first used in print in 1923 by Clarence Marsh Case in *Nonviolent Coercion: A Study in Methods of Social Pressure*. For centuries people sought ways to live without causing injury to others and experimented with ways to fight injustice without employing violence, but they had no name with which they could identify or give shape to this commitment as an intentional philosophy. Historians studying nonviolence will find it possible only to identify the occasions when a specific nonviolent action was used, but must leave to conjecture any attempt to identify a nonviolent philosophy or strategy.

Theorist Gene Sharp identifies three basic tactical categories of nonviolent action. The first is *nonviolent protest and persuasion*. With these actions we name what we think is wrong, point our fingers at it and try to help others understand. This category would include such tactics as petitioning, picketing, demonstrating and lobbying. The second category is *nonviolent noncooperation*. With these actions we deliberately fold our hands and turn our backs, refusing to participate in the wrong we have named. This category would include such tactics as boycotts, strikes and tax resistance. The third category is *nonviolent intervention*. With these actions we face the wrong we have named, the wrong we have refused to aid, and we step into the way, interfere, block. This category would include such tactics as physical obstruction, blockades, civil disobedience and sit-ins.

Subversive activity:
women resisting disappearance

A few years ago I received a call from a university professor who said he was teaching a class on the history of nonviolence—you know, all about the contributions of Thoreau, Tolstoy, A. J. Muste, Gandhi, Martin Luther King—but he felt he should include something about women. Trouble was, he just didn't have any substantial information about women and nonviolence, and he wondered if I could help. Had women ever contributed anything toward the history of nonviolence? he asked.

Men like Thoreau, Tolstoy, Muste, Gandhi and King usually get the credit for the development of active nonviolence, but women—around the world and from the beginning of history—have consistently experimented with ways to resist oppression and challenge injustice without endorsing violence. In fact, most of what we commonly call "women's history" is actually the history of women's role in the development of nonviolent action.

Feminist historian Dale Spender has written that the most subversive and powerful activities women can engage in are those activities which celebrate our lives and help us resist disappearance. Mary "Mother" Jones, the great labor organizer, knew this. It is said that every speech she gave was a history lesson: she wanted working women and men to know that their courageous acts were not isolated, that they were part of a tradition of struggle.

I too want to tell stories which will empower us, lift us out of our isolation, sustain us in times of personal despair, heal our brokenness. I want to tell stories that will stimulate our imaginations, incite us to action.

I taught the professor's class. I told stories for over two hours to students whose only knowledge of Susan B. Anthony was that she appeared on an odd-sized coin. That day I limited myself to stories of how women in North America (primarily in the United States) have used nonviolent action in their struggles for social justice. The students were spellbound, abandoning their frantic notetaking after the first half hour to simply listen.

I told about the Lysistrata action in 1600 by the women of the Iroquois nation. They threatened to boycott love-making and childbearing until the men conceded some of their power in decisions about war and peace.

I told about Anne Hutchinson and Mary Dyer and the nonviolent tactics they used in the fight for religious freedom in the Massachusetts Bay Colony. I told about the women fighting against slavery: Lucretia Mott, Sarah and Angelina Grimké, Prudence Crandall, Harriet Tubman, Mary Shadd Cary, the women who worked on the Underground Railroad.

I told about the fight for women's suffrage and the nonviolent actions of Susan B. Anthony, Sojourner Truth, Alice Paul and the suffragists.

I told stories from the civil rights movement, stories about Fannie Lou Hamer and Rosa Parks.

I told about women's anti-lynching campaigns, about Ida B. Wells, and women's labor movements. I told of women's long history of fighting for peace: stories about Jane Addams, Jeanette Rankin, Dorothy Day, Barbara Deming, the women at the peace camps.

I illustrated how, in all of these campaigns, women found creative ways to struggle collectively and nonviolently. The stories opened the door for us to talk, not only about women's history, but about nonviolent action—what it is, how it works, why it's used. In the discussion that followed my storytelling, the students, professor and I seemed to feel ourselves empowered by the rich history of women activists who had created an ongoing global laboratory in which nonviolence theory is continually tested and transformed.

That experience also opened my eyes to the difficulty we have in finding these stories, this history. I was startled that such a learned professor had been at a loss in his search for examples of women's participation in the development and use of nonviolence—especially since his area of expertise was the history of nonviolence.

As I began hunting for more stories I soon discovered why he had had such a hard time. Women's stories have been buried. In 1705, English feminist Mary Astell observed, "Since the Men being the Historians, they seldom condescend to record the great and good Actions of Women." Oh Mary, how true.

Texts on nonviolence make little if any mention of women's use of nonviolent action. *The* classic text on nonviolent action is Gene Sharp's *The Politics of Nonviolent Action, Part Two: The Methods of Nonviolent Action* (Boston: Porter Sargent Publishers, 1973). Sharp lists 198 specific nonviolent tactics with several documented examples to illustrate each one. But in this fascinating volume, so popular with students of nonviolence, women are under-represented to a shocking degree. For example, of the nine instances he cites of the use of mass petitions, Sharp includes none by women, though petitioning is a tactic critical to women's history. Of the ten stories he tells of revenue refusal, he cites no examples of women's use of tax resistance. Of the ten examples of protest meetings, he cites none by women. This is not to say that he leaves out women entirely. He has included a number of examples of women's use of nonviolent action, but they are unnecessarily scarce, made conspicuous by their rarity.

Nor is Sharp the only researcher and theorist of nonviolence to largely disregard women's contributions. *Blessed Are the Peacemakers: The Voices of Peace—From Isaiah to Bob Dylan* edited by Allen and Linda Kirschner and published in 1971, includes passages by such diverse thinkers and doers as Buddha, Pope John XXIII, Thoreau, Linus Pauling, Pete Seeger and Daniel Berrigan, but Joan Baez is the *only* woman deemed fit to be included in what would appear to be the otherwise all-male club.

Of the 535 pages which constitute the important volume *Nonviolence in America: A Documentary History,* edited by Staughton Lynd in 1966, only 46 pages are given to words by women.

The Quiet Battle: Writings on the Theory and Practice of Non-Violent Resistance edited by Mulford Q. Sibley, features case studies in nonviolent resistance from modern-day United States as well as from India, colonial Pennsylvania, ancient Rome, South Africa, Hungary and Norway. However, out of twenty-seven essays only one is by a woman.

In the preface to his 1970 political science text *Twentieth Century Pacifism,* Dr. Peter Brock thanks his wife (who remains nameless) "for typing the greater part of the manuscript of this book" but lists only six references to women in the index of his 274-page book. Of these six women, only three were accorded a full sentence each in the text itself. No wonder the professor who called me for help wondered if women had ever contributed to the history of nonviolence. They have, but you wouldn't know it from many of the books we use.

I found the same problem in other areas of published research and soon learned that if I wanted to know about women's actions, I had to look for resources specifically about women. If I wanted to know about a strike by women workers in Japan or South Africa or Peru, books about the labor struggles in these countries rarely helped. Instead, I had to seek books specifically about women in Japan, South Africa and Peru. I repeatedly found that books which claimed to offer general information were often actually accounts specifically of men's thoughts and actions. I shouldn't have been surprised. After all, throughout most of my formal education, the "history" I studied had been filtered through the voices and point of view of North American white males. Their history was labeled "world" history though it left out most of what had happened to the non-kings, not to mention whole continents like Africa,

Australia, and most of Asia and South America. These places, when they were mentioned, served as props for European explorers, men like Columbus who "discovered" a new world, albeit a world inhabited by people who had settled on the land centuries before, people with long traditions, laws, religions, cultural inheritances, history. But it was new to the European white males and so it became "the new world," a world theirs for the finding, its history theirs for the telling. The stories I heard were told in the conqueror's tongue with the conqueror's emphasis.

All history books are biased, they tell a story from a point of view. While white-male-European history is often passed off as world history, what little "history of nonviolence" seeps into the lessons is similarly distorted and still reflects the white-male-European bias. The danger is that the bias is so often unacknowledged, the point of view mislabeled "universal" or "objective."

I am not particularly more interested in women's nonviolent actions than men's, but I am dismayed that so many wonderful stories have systematically been denied us and deemed less vital, less important than other stories simply because they are about actions taken by people who are not male. The denial and suppression of these stories is no accident given that we live on a planet which is overwhelmingly patriarchal. And if mere oversight accounts for their exclusion from history, it is an oversight which both reflects and reinforces patriarchal ideology. I believe this is why Dale Spender suggested that telling our stories as women and thus resisting disappearance is a subversive activity.

This book is not objective. It is a collection of stories that illustrate and celebrate women's use of nonviolent action, told in the voice of one life-loving white North American woman consciously living in what she believes may well be the last days of life as we know it on this planet.

The gestures of courage are repeated

Stories of resistance have been taken from us, the books burned, the songs stifled or forbidden, the troubadours sent wandering in the wilderness where no one will hear the stories they have to tell. Some stories have been told but the storyteller failed to hold our interest: we didn't pay attention. And now, the one who would destroy freedom of speech grins amiably on our television sets.

What can we do? There is talk that soon some people among us will be rounded up, given numbers, sent away. What can we do? This has happened before. Often. What have others done in times like these? We try to remember but it is difficult. We need our stories, our legacy of resistance.

The storyteller has returned with good news: the gestures of courage are repeated from age to age, a legacy passed on in the dream, the blood, the collective memory. Even if we forget, even if the stories are taken away again, something in us will remember when the time comes. It is a mystery but it's true.

The gestures of courage are repeated from age to age. Consider, for example, the nonviolent tactic of providing sanctuary:

–In 1300 B.C., male babies were condemned to death by law. An Egyptian princess and a Hebrew slave mother crossed ethnic and class lines to conspire to break the law. Women's hands reached through the bullrushes, pulled a baby to safety, sheltered him from the pharaoh's wrath, from the soldiers' blades. This is the ancient art of providing sanctuary, the gesture of creating a safe place in a violent world. The women were brave, clever and creative in their resistance to the insanity of their day.

–In 1844, a Quaker farmer put a candle in her window as a sign that her farm was a stop on the secret Underground Railroad. Late that night she hid a black mother and her baby in a barn until the slave-hunters had passed.

–In 1944 Germany, a Protestant woman watched as Nazis goose-stepped past her house. Every time she heard a siren she held her breath. An entire Jewish family was hiding in her attic.

–In 1984, a young volunteer opened the door of a battered-women's shelter to a dispirited woman and her fussing baby. She found milk for the baby and tea for the mother and led them to a room where they would be safe for the night.

–In 1987, an Iowan church woman pulled over into the parking lot and opened her car door to the frightened, young "illegal alien" from Guatemala she had agreed to carry to the next safe house. She was playing her part in the sanctuary movement, the "underground railroad" of the 1980s.

The gesture is sanctuary, an ancient art of protection and resistance to unjust authority.

It is easy to imagine certain familiar gestures being repeated—generations of women lifting spoonfuls of food to babies' mouths, placing cool hands on damp, feverish foreheads. The gestures are familiar and ancient. Less familiar but just as ancient are the gestures of resistance to oppression and yet they are part of our legacy. There is power in these stories. There is power in remembering them.

You can't kill the spirit!

I have arranged most of the chapters in this book to highlight the drama of women's gestures of courage; gestures which have been repeated throughout time and in many places around the globe; gestures which have sometimes succeeded, sometimes failed, been tried again, copied, changed, adapted to new situations. This is the old way to tell history—this storyteller's way. It is my hope that the stories celebrated in this book will hold special significance for readers committed to nonviolent action who have wandered so long in the wilderness of recorded history looking for their legacy. And it is my sneaking suspicion that these stories, here reclaimed and told anew, will stimulate our imaginations—whether we're new activists or seasoned—and stir us to new action in the great tradition of the women whose stories fill this book.

I believe that it sometimes happens—according to some strange, universal rhythm that moves through our lives, some invisible force—that when the time is right for an idea to take hold, it will do so, not just in one place but in many places. In the early 1980s, when New Society Publishers invited me to put together a collection of writings about feminism and nonviolence, I shrugged and said sure, no problem. From my isolated vantage point I imagined compiling a pamphlet-sized collection of essays. Imagine my surprise when the "pamphlet" turned out to be a hefty 440 pages long! Shortly after the 1982 publication of *Reweaving the Web of Life*, my bookshelf reserved for writings on feminism and nonviolence—which had long held one essay by Jane Meyerding, a book by Barbara Deming and a book by Virginia

Woolf—grew so fast with newly published works that it pushed the bookends to their limits within two short years. The time had come.

Once again, but now from a less isolated vantage point, I sense that the time has come for an idea to grow form and substance—this time for the real-life stories of women's nonviolent actions to emerge. As I write this, I imagine women sitting at desks or in libraries or picnicking in green fields with their books spread open around them, scribbling away, breathing new life into the stories we have managed to retrieve, each of us working on the same project but creating it with our own voices. And we need all of it. In a couple years I expect my bookshelves will reflect this new harvest.

The publishers have felt this pulse stirring, seen for themselves the several hundred note cards I've collected citing specific examples of women's nonviolent actions, and suspect that, once word is out, I'll be inundated with more stories. They have wisely chosen to publish this work as a series, of which this book is the first. There is room, then, to do more than inform and document. There is room to play, entertain, inspire, and to incite to action.

For those readers who wish to use this text as a research tool, I have included source notes at the end of each chapter, a recommended reading list at the end of the book and listings of events by chronology and nation as well as a listing of women activists who are mentioned throughout the book. These impose an order more traditionally employed in history books.

If there is anything I have learned from my research, it is that the spirit which informs our resistance to oppression is strong. It is so strong that it can't be killed. Today, around the world, wherever feminists gather to act collectively, they sing a song composed by Chicana lesbian and feminist Naomi Littlebear. Over and over the women sing their anthem:

> You can't kill the spirit.
> It's like a mountain.
> Old and strong, it lives on and on.

This book of stories acknowledges and honors that spirit. Women's spirit of resistance is indeed old and strong, and there are many more stories to come.

Pam McAllister

Pam McAllister
Brooklyn, New York
December 1987

Sources

Deming, Barbara. *Prisons That Could Not Hold: Prison Notes 1964– Seneca 1984*. San Francisco: Spinsters Ink, 1985.
Meyerding, Jane, ed. *We Are All Part of One Another: A Barbara Deming Reader*. Philadelphia: New Society, 1984.
Spender, Dale. *Women of Ideas (And What Men Have Done to Them): From Aphra Behn to Adrienne Rich*. London: ARK Paperbacks, 1983.

NOTE: If you have details about a women's nonviolent action that may be appropriate for inclusion in this series, you are invited to send a letter, copies of news clippings or other descriptions of the action to our attention. Thanks!

New Society Publishers
4527 Springfield Avenue
Philadelphia, PA 19143
ATTN: BARBARA DEMING MEMORIAL SERIES

1
THE WOMEN ARE WATCHING

ON A COLD, MISTY NOVEMBER DAY in 1984, over 1000 women marched through the streets of New York City in the "Not In Our Name" demonstration in preparation for a civil disobedience action the next day on Wall Street. They sang to the accompaniment of drums and bells, carried huge puppets and banners, chanted and danced. They passed out leaflets to the onlookers and pointed accusing fingers at the headquarters of corporations that manufactured nuclear weapons and at banks that did business with the white South African government. "We don't want war! Don't call a war in our name," the women shouted. "Get out of South Africa! Divest now! Don't do business with apartheid in our name! *Not in our name! Not in our name!*"

Toward the front of the march that day was a small group of women, each of whom carried a tall pole, and on the top of each pole was attached a decorative eye made of cardboard and construction paper. "The women are watching!" the marchers called out. The cardboard eyes looked over the heads of the other marchers, over the heads in the onlooking crowds. The eyes led the way, turning their hard stare toward the headquarters of institutions which had financed oppressive governments, manufactured nuclear weapons, been unfair to their workers, displaced low-income communities, or endorsed racist or sexist policies. The eyes were turned toward these institutions while the marchers chanted, "The women are watching! The women are watching."

Seeing what we are not supposed to see, recognizing what we are not supposed to name, making the invisible visible—these are acts of defiance, courage, resistance. The women who watch do not cast down their eyes or try to spare embarrassment by politely looking away as women have been trained to do. They see what no one is supposed to see. By watching, they say to the greedy and warmongering, "We know who you are. We know what you're doing."

In her poem "A Song for Gorgons," feminist, pacifist, activist author Barbara Deming pondered the myth of the Gorgons, the snake-haired sisters of Greek mythology who personified women's rage. According to the myth, anyone who met their furious stare would be turned to stone. But in Barbara's retelling of the myth, a woman who dares to meet the Gorgons' stare will turn, not to stone, but to her natural self, with her own fury writhing awake. And it is, for Barbara, women's insightful fury that can save us all. Her poem celebrates "The truth-hissing wide-open-eyed rude/ Glare of our faces" with which we can see truth and unmask lies. Women can help men to see the truth too, so that together we can bring an end to the patriarchal world order which distorts *all* our lives.

> I sing this song for those with eyes that start,
> With curls that hiss.
> Our slandered wrath is our truth, and—
> If we honor this—
> Can deal not death but healing.

♀ IN ARGENTINA, the mothers were watching with a wide-open-eyed rude glare that helped bring down a death-dealing kingdom. Ever since the military coup in 1976, their children and their children's children had been disappearing. They disappeared if they raised their fists, raised their voices, raised their eyebrows. They disappeared if they joined a union, sang freedom songs, were seen with the wrong people in the wrong place at the wrong time. And occasionally they disappeared even if they had done nothing at all. Heavy footsteps came at night, muffled screams, and then nothing—no bodies, no proof of torture, no world outrage.

For the bewildered families of the "disappeared" there was neither word of assurance nor word of bad news. With no word there could be no funerals, no closure, no coming to terms, no time to grieve or heal. There was only time to wonder, hope, pray and wait and wait and wait. The mothers' children were silently disappearing and no one was supposed to see a thing. They were to look the other way if they knew what was good for them.

Every day many of the mothers of the disappeared went to the Ministry of the Interior in Buenos Aires seeking information from the officials. The mothers waited in long, barren corridors. When a woman finally met with an official, she was told that her case would be "processed" but that, in all likelihood, her missing child had run off, had abandoned the family, was having a secret affair someplace, or was a terrorist who'd been executed by other terrorists. The officials smirked and told the mother to go home.

Still, the mothers went day after day and waited in the long corridors.

One day an official smirked when he dismissed Azucena De Vicenti. She was a sad and aging woman, well into her sixties. Her suffering was not his concern. But that day Azucena De Vicenti was angry. As she passed the other waiting, anxious mothers on her way out, she muttered, "It's not here that we ought to be—it's the Plaza de Mayo. And when there's enough of us, we'll go to the Casa Rosada and see the president about our children who are missing."

And that is how it all began.

The next Saturday, April 13, 1977, fourteen women left their homes to do the bravest thing they had ever done. At a time when all public demonstrations were forbidden, they had decided to stand together as witnesses to the disappearance of their children. They came separately to the Plaza de Mayo carrying only their identity cards and coins for the bus and wearing flat shoes in case they had to run. Only after several years were they able to look back at that day with a sense of humor, joking about the first lesson they had learned—that even in the heart of the most vicious dictatorship, no one cares if you demonstrate on a Saturday afternoon in a deserted square where no one is around to see you.

After that, the women decided to gather on Thursday afternoons when the Plaza was crowded. From that time on, they walked every week in a slow-moving circle around the square carrying pictures of their lost loved ones. Their numbers grew as daughters, sisters and grandmothers of the disappeared joined the circle. People began calling them "the Mothers of the Plaza" or sometimes "*las locas de la Plaza*"—"the mad women."

The women were watching and making their witness a public act of defiance against the military regime. When they realized that the newspapers were afraid to write about their action, they got together enough money to buy an advertisement. It appeared, against great odds and despite efforts by the military to stop it, in *La Prensa* on October 5, 1977. Above pictures of 237 "disappeared" and the names of their mothers was the headline, WE DO NOT ASK FOR ANYTHING MORE THAN THE TRUTH.

Ten days after the advertisement appeared, several hundred women carried a petition with 24,000 signatures to the congress building demanding that the government investigate the disappearances.

The police repression which followed was severe. Hundreds of people were harassed, arrested and detained during the month, including American and British journalists who tried to interview some of the Mothers. Still, the women refused to hide their actions. Every Thursday, two or three hundred women would gather to walk around the Plaza.

On other afternoons the Mothers held open meetings. Many desperate people came seeking information about loved ones who had disappeared. The Mothers were no longer looking for their individual sons or daughters: they were seeking each others' children and the truth about what had happened to the children of Argentina.

At some point during the fall of 1977, a young man named "Gustavo" began coming regularly to the meetings, seeking information about his disappeared brother and helping the women in whatever way he could. A sweet-faced, blue-eyed blond in his mid-twenties, sincere, friendly, generous and compassionate, Gustavo seemed to be every mother's dream child.

Then in December, two days before another advertisement was to be published, this time in *La Nacion*, nine of the women left a planning meeting by a side door and walked directly into a trap. Five or six men, one of them armed with a machine gun, had been lying in wait for the women. The men had been well informed. They demanded the money the Mothers of the Plaza had collected for the advertisement and forced the women into a car. The women disappeared forever. Two days later three more women disappeared; one of them was Azucena De Vicenti.

There was no doubt that young Gustavo had orchestrated the whole maneuver. His real name turned out to be Alfredo Astiz, later recognized as one of the most notorious kidnappers and torturers in ESMA, the Navy Mechanics School in Buenos Aires, where an estimated 5000 people were imprisoned and tortured, and of whom only an estimated 200 survived. Astiz's nickname at ESMA was "the blond angel."

The Thursday following the kidnapping, only forty women came to the Plaza; even some of these stayed hidden in the shadows. When the Mothers of the Plaza called a press conference, only four journalists dared attend, all of them foreigners.

Throughout 1978 the Mothers tried to maintain a presence in the Plaza, to let Argentina and the rest of the world know that the women were still watching, still watching despite great odds, still watching. But the police violence against them was great and each week a few women were arrested. By the beginning of 1979, the Mothers of the Plaza were finding it almost impossible to endure the violence. Each Thursday they met in the shadows, hurried across the square and quickly formed their small circle for a few minutes before the police closed in. Finally, even that became impossible.

No doubt the military men felt smug then as they chuckled over their afternoon cocktails; it seemed that guns, billy clubs, tear gas and terror could defeat even the Mothers of the Plaza. Little did they know that in churches around the city the Mothers continued to gather.

Every meeting was illegal and dangerous but the women had found a way. They entered the dark sanctuaries as women do in cities all over the world every day. Some lit candles and knelt before little altars murmuring special prayers, and then they found a place in the pews to rest and pray. There was nothing unusual in this.

What the authorities couldn't see was that the women in the churches, sometimes numbering over 100, were passing notes to each other as their heads were bowed. These were "meetings" at which decisions were made without a word spoken aloud.

It must have been a great surprise to the authorities when, seemingly out of nowhere, the Mothers of the Plaza stepped out of the darkened churches in May 1979. Determined to formalize their structure, they held elections, legally registered as an association and opened a bank account with some of the financial support which began to come in from around the world. In 1980, they rented an office on Uruguay Street and opened the House of the Mothers. They even started publishing their own bulletin and within several years counted their membership in the thousands.

The women returned to the Plaza. They wore flat shoes and white scarves embroidered with the names or initials of the relatives they were seeking. They came to the Plaza carrying photos of the "disappeared." Some days after walking the circle, several women would leave the square, take a megaphone down a side street and each tell her personal story. They had learned that it was easier for people to understand the horror of one missing child than it was to grasp the picture of thousands who had "disappeared."

The police met the women in even greater numbers than before and the women continued to face tear gas, nightsticks and arrest. But something had changed. The Mothers of the Plaza were determined that they'd never again retreat into silence and shadows. Their visible courage was contagious. Onlookers who had been too afraid to stop long enough to acknowledge the women now stood still to applaud the Mothers as they circled the square.

Argentina's bloody military regime could not hide from the eyes of the Mothers of the Plaza de Mayo. The women were watching and the world was watching them. With their persistence they inspired women in other countries (such as the mothers of El Salvador and Guatemala) where children were disappearing. And they helped bring the day in December 1983 when the people of Argentina inaugurated President Raul Alfonsin as the head of a democratic government.

♀ "NO MORE HIROSHIMA!"
"No more Nagasaki!"
"Women for peace!"

Over 2000 chanting women marched through Tokyo's commercial district on December 6, 1981, just as they had marched in December 1980. The women marched again in remembrance of the day Japan had bombed Pearl Harbor. They followed a banner which declared, "WE WILL NOT ALLOW THE WAY TO WAR!"

The women were publicly remembering and calling on others in their country to remember with them. Theirs had been the only nation to suffer the wartime devastation of atomic bombings. Even as they marched, the disfigured atomic holocaust survivors called *hibakusha* women were suffering from radiation-caused cancers and from ostracism by other Japanese citizens.

The women were remembering, and they were watching in shared rage and despair the increasing militarization of their beautiful Japan, a nation which had made so much progress in transforming its national spirit from warlike to peace-seeking. Wasn't Japan the only industrialized nation whose constitution, written and adopted after defeat in World War II, renounced war? Hadn't Japan's government boldly affirmed a three-point anti-nuclear principle in 1968 by vowing never to manufacture, possess or store nuclear weapons? Hadn't Japan managed to keep its military spending to under one percent of its gross national product and concentrated its citizens' brainpower on designing and producing non-military consumer products? Hadn't it set an example for other nations of the world that peace could be a financially healthy investment? Was all this to be lost?

The women who gathered on December 6, 1981 were watching. They knew that all the good intentions to maintain a peace-loving Japan were being undermined, that men were preparing for war in the very shadow of Mount Fuji. The United States, which had occupied Japan at the end of World War II had never really left, some said. It had signed a security act with Japan in the 1960s which permitted installation of US military bases and was now spending $2 billion per year to maintain its operations there. And suddenly, in 1981, there was no doubt that Japan's peace consciousness had eroded. A "hawkish" prime minister had come to power and the Liberal Democratic Party was leaning far to the right. There was serious talk of revising the constitution and even of reinstituting a conscription system. The "Self-Defense Force" had grown into the seventh largest army in the world. Twenty-four nuclear power plants were operating in Japan, with more being constructed, all of them producing plutonium which could be used to manufacture nuclear weapons.

Now, too, rumors were spreading throughout the population that the United States had brought nuclear weapons to its bases in Okinawa and to its submarines that cruised Japan's waters, and planned to bring Tomahawk cruise missiles tipped with nuclear warheads to its Iwakuni base on Japan's mainland. For its part, the United States would neither confirm nor deny the presence of nuclear weapons in Japan.

The women were watching. They had been watching a long time, and in the spring of 1981 they intensified their campaign to let their government know they were watching. Women workers took to the streets, collecting 2 million signatures against the increasing militarization of Japan. Many pledged that, even if the prisons should become "filled with mammas and grandmas," they would stop the draft before it started. All spring long, women gathered to voice their concerns—at the Rally to Build Peace with Women's Votes, at the Women's Symposium for Thinking of the Constitution, and later, at the Women's Rally Never to Allow an Undesirable Amendment of the Constitution.

That spring, too, 6000 working women came to Meiji Park, Tokyo in the pouring rain to attend a demonstration with a very long name—the Central Rally of Women for a Ban on Adverse Revision of the Japanese Constitution and for the Establishment of Peace. Women from the Housewives Association, the Socialist Party, the 20,000-member Japan Women's Council, the Japanese Women's Caucus against War, and the Women's Bureau of the General Council of Trade Unions of Japan joined together in a campaign of witnessing to the increased militarization.

The year of intense anti-war activity by women concluded with the December 6 demonstration in Tokyo. They chanted as they marched, "No more Hiroshima! No more Nagasaki! Women for peace! Women for peace!" In an effort to encourage solidarity with women's anti-war movements in other countries, the Japanese Women's Caucus Against War invited London-based peace activist and writer Leonie Caldecott to speak briefly during that day's rally about women's initiatives in the European peace movement. Caldecott spoke on a platform with Japanese peace activists who stood, one after the other, to give sincere, carefully crafted messages.

Suddenly, a group of rough peasant women took the stage. They were dressed in cotton trousers and jackets and wide straw hats. Several of the women held a banner while one of their group spoke. The speech was angry and passionate. The crowd stirred. These were the Shibokusa women who lived at the foot of Mount Fuji, two hours by bus from sophisticated Tokyo.

The Shibokusa women, mostly in their fifties and sixties, had been watching military maneuvers in the shadow of the mountain for many years. They had made it their business to watch and disrupt the military exercises conducted there by Japan's young warriors, warriors not so different from those of an earlier time, a time which had brought immeasurable suffering to Japan. The women remembered.

They had watched the young soldiers parade and practice killing on land that did not belong to them. For centuries, that land at the foot of Mount Fuji had been cultivated by hard-working farmers. They had worked the poor land, managing to grow radishes and beans. The people had also started a silkworm industry there. But in 1936, the Japanese army took over the land and began using it for military drills, and after World War II, the US army moved in. The San Francisco Peace Treaty was signed in 1952 between Japan and the United States, and the farmers hoped that the land would be returned to the people, but the Japanese government continued to use the land for its "self-defense" exercises. The local farmers protested and a few concessions were made, but the state didn't leave. Eventually the men went off to cities to look for work. The women stayed. The women watched, and they helped create a resistance movement in Japan, helped fight for their land rights and against all preparations for war. When others got discouraged, these women sustained the spirit of resistance. They remembered Hiroshima and Nagasaki. They remembered when the land at the foot of beautiful Mount Fuji had been used to grow food.

During an interview with Leonie Caldecott, the Shibokusa women explained:

> We are not clever. Most of us have hardly been educated at all. But we are strong because we are close to the earth, and we know what matters. Our conviction that the military is wrong is unshakeable. We are the strongest women in Japan! And we want other women to be like us.

It is their intention to be a mischievous, bothersome, embarrassing presence at the military base. They create secret paths leading from their cottages to the center of the military exercise areas. In groups of ten or less, they sometimes crawl along the paths startling the soldiers, plant scarecrows here and there, sit in a circle to sing and clap or stand to point and laugh at the soldiers. They always ignore direct orders to go away.

Theirs has been a long struggle. Once, in 1970, 1000 riot police came to evict them from their cottages. The women dressed for death that day. They realized that the struggle was their whole life, the journey was their home.

The people in the nearby town sometimes treat the women with contempt. Of less concern to the women are their frequent arrests.

When they are arrested, the grinning Shibokusa women refuse to give their names or any information. They laugh and say they are too old to remember who they are.

The Shibokusa women, by their own reckoning the "strongest women in Japan," witness for peace with their lives. They are watching, watching, taking care "that the third atom bomb never comes."

> Deadly rain gathers poison from the sky,
> And the fish carry death
> In the depths of the sea,
> Fishing boats are idle, their owners are blind,
> Deadly harvest of two atom bombs.
> Then land and sea folk
> You must watch and take care
> That the third atom bomb never comes.
> —Ishigi Astu, "Furusato"
> (English verse by Ewen MacColl)

♀ THE WOMEN AT THE GREENHAM COMMON peace camp are watching. They are seeing what they are not supposed to see and are making the invisible visible. The women have been at Greenham Common in England since 1981. Now they watch each of the nine gates at the US Air Force base where ground-launched cruise missiles were deployed in November 1983 in preparation for World War III.

Except for the nine miles of barbed wire fence surrounding low-lying bunkers and missile silos, it might be easy to overlook the missile base in the gray mist and the lush green countryside. This is just what the peace camp women don't want to happen, so thousands of women sometimes show up to encircle the base. They hang photos of their mothers or children on the wire fence, create little yarn webs as a symbol that everything is connected in a fragile and precious web of life. They sing and bang pots and pans. One time, 50,000 women "embraced the base." They held mirrors up to the fence to reflect its death-dealing energy back on itself. It was as though the women were answering the myth of the Gorgons by saying to the missile base patriarchs, "It is not *our* glance but your own that will turn you to stone."

Between these expansive media events, small handfuls of women persist. They play host to the constant stream of supporters from around the world who visit the camp every day. Sometimes they do nothing but wait and watch, and sometimes they tear open great holes in the fence with wire cutters, or go over the top of the fence, entering the base either to damage whatever equipment they can or to illustrate just how inadequate the security is at the nuclear missile base. Once, at dawn on January 1, 1983, forty-four women climbed the fence and danced in a great circle on top of a missile silo.

It is very hard to make the threat of nuclear war tangible. It is too big, terrible, unthinkable. Real estate agents complain that property values around the base have dramatically decreased, not because of the ugly barbed wire that grows where silver birches once did, but because of the presence of the peace camp women.

Since the deployment of the missiles, the women have made it their business to monitor and expose the missile system, which is supposed to be very secret, if not invisible. Cruise missiles are small and designed to be launched from mobile launch points. When a nuclear alert is given, the missiles are to be taken from the silos and put in a truck caravan which will carry the missiles to a firing point somewhere in the countryside.

In preparation for an actual alert, the trucks are sent out for practice runs that function partly to make nuclear war, or the thought of it, a matter of routine for the young men hired to do the job. But a caravan of twenty-two trucks is not really invisible even if camouflaged. How, the women wonder, would an enemy know that any movement of trucks from the base is merely dress rehearsal for World War III and not opening night? And is it really safe to have these mammoth fifty-foot trucks designed for US highways traveling along the narrow, winding English roads, trucks presumably carrying a massive cargo of death on a nighttime practice run?

The peace camp women have observed other eerie late-night practice runs at Greenham. Every so often a siren sounds. Nearby, in the prosperous town of Newbury, the wives and children of the US military men are gotten out of bed, herded onto buses and raced to the "safety" of the nuclear bunkers inside the base. The children are terrified, crying, wondering if this is real, if the end has come. The British police who open the gates for the Americans have no such bunkers. There are no plans to protect them in case of a nuclear exchange.

The peace camp women are watching the cruise missiles. Since deployment, women have stood at the gates of the base in nightly vigils, tracking the movements of the missile carriers. They have stood in rain and snow, enduring the abusive taunts of the soldiers, watching for the invisible. When the gates open and a convoy rumbles past, they blow whistles into the night to awaken the women at the other gates, then find phones to alert nearby towns. Other women race for their cars and spend the night charting the course of the convoy, tracking every inch of its movements. The women have painted slogans on the sides of the trucks and published their findings about the convoys' routes and hiding places.

The women see what they are not supposed to see, force the invisible out into the open. The women are watching.

Sources

Not-in-our-name demonstration
tal. "Not In Our Name." *off our backs*, vol. 14, no. 12 (Jan. 1985).

Gorgons
Deming, Barbara. "A Song for Gorgons" from *Reweaving the Web of Life: Feminism and Nonviolence*. Pam McAllister, ed. Philadelphia: New Society, 1982.
Walker, Barbara. *The Woman's Encyclopedia of Myths and Secrets*. New York: Harper & Row, 1983.

Mothers of the Plaza de Mayo
Simpson, John and Jana Bennett. *The Disappeared and the Mothers of the Plaza: The Story of the 11,000 Argentinians Who Vanished*. New York: St. Martin's Press, 1985.
Workgroup Social Defence of Women for Peace. *Social Defence* (pamphlet). Amersfoort, Netherlands: Women for Peace, 1984.

Japan women's peace movement
Astu, Ishigi. "Furusato" from *Songs for Peace: 100 Songs of The Peace Movement*. Student Peace Union, ed. New York: Oak, 1966.
Caldecott, Leonie. "At the Foot of the Mountain: The Shibokusa Women of Kita Fuji" from *Keeping the Peace: A Women's Peace Handbook*. Lynne Jones, ed. London: Women's Press, 1983.
Mitchell, Greg. "Rearming Japan." *In These Times*, August 7–20, 1985.
Japanese Women's Caucus Against War. *Our Movements*. Tokyo.
Japan Women's Council. "Appeal—Total Ban on Nuclearization and Total Disarmament," address. Tokyo.

Women's Bureau: General Council of Trade Unions of Japan. "Struggle
of Working Women Against the Adverse Revision of the Japanese
Constitution, Against Nuclear Armament, For Disarmament,
Against Military Bases, Against War and For Peace."

Greenham Common women

Blackwood, Caroline. *On the Perimeter*. New York: Penguin Books,
1984.

Cook, Alice, and Gwyn Kirk. *Greenham Women Everywhere: Dreams,
Ideas and Actions from the Women's Peace Movement*. Boston:
South End Press, 1983.

Harford, Barbara, and Sarah Hopkins. *Greenham Common: Women at
the Wire*. London: Women's Press, 1984.

Jaffe, Susan. "Arrival of Cruise Missiles Intensifies Antinuke
Campaign." *In These Times*, Dec. 21–Jan. 10, 1984.

Jones, Lynne, ed. *Keeping the Peace: A Women's Peace Handbook*.
London: Women's Press, 1983.

Snitow, Ann. "Holding the Line at Greenham: Being Joyously Political
in Dangerous Times." *Mother Jones*, Feb./Mar. 1985.

2
YOU HAVE STRUCK A ROCK

IT IS SAID that in Pretoria that day, even the babies on their mothers' backs did not cry when the 20,000 women stood for a full thirty minutes in complete silence. Beneath the pale winter sun they stood—black women in the green and black colors of the African National Congress, Indian women in brightly colored saris, Xhosa women wearing elaborate headscarves and ocher robes, white women in quiet colors, beige and blue. They had come to Pretoria that August 9, 1956 to see the prime minister, to deliver a petition and to protest, once again, the extension of the pass laws to women.

Passes, sometimes described as the "African workers' handcuffs" or "badges of slavery," are identity booklets used by the government to control and track each carrier's movements. The failure to produce a pass on demand is a criminal offense and can result in arrest, imprisonment, and deportation to forced labor camps. Pass books are essential to the smooth functioning of the South African police state and the rule of the white minority.

Even before the British defeated the Dutch Boers in 1902 and finally won control of the South African colony, a system of white supremacy was in place. Called *baaskaap* (bossdom), it was a system which required the separate development of the races, and it paved the way for the official institution of *apartheid* (racial separation) in 1948. In order to establish rule over the Asians they had brought as slaves and indentured laborers and over the vast majority population of indigenous Africans, the tiny minority of white colonists used democratic processes among themselves to institute and maintain a brutal, efficient and comprehensive police state.

The women who gathered in Pretoria in 1956 understood that the pass laws were a crucial prop of the white police state. They had seen the men of their communities subjected to harassment and pass raids. Their mothers had resisted pass laws in 1913, and they were bound by honor to bestow the legacy of resistance upon their daughters and granddaughters. Just the year before, in October 1955, women throughout South Africa had renewed their campaign of resistance to the pass laws when 2000 women of all races had headed for Pretoria to protest. That year, the white-ruled government had done everything it could to interfere. It had canceled the buses the women had hired and set up roadblocks. Undaunted, the women had pooled their financial resources and taken the trains. Helen Joseph, a white activist and the secretary of the multi-racial Federation of South African Women, remembered that day, "I saw the train come over the top of the embankment and out of every window of the train there were women's heads and they were waving and shouting and singing, singing the freedom songs. And I knew that it was going to succeed. I knew then that nothing could stop them."

In Pretoria in 1956, the women were proving that "nothing could stop them." Once again, the apartheid regime had made it as difficult as possible, this time by officially banning all processions in the city for the day. But this had not stopped the women. They had simply arranged themselves in careful groupings of two or three and walked slowly up the wide avenue to an amphitheatre ringed with formal gardens and government buildings.

At first there was a silence of waiting as the amphitheatre filled with women. Lilian Ngoyi, Rahima Moosa, Sophie Williams and Helen Joseph, four women representing each of South Africa's racial divisions (African, Asian, Coloured and White), delivered an anti-pass petition with over 100,000 women's signatures to the offices of the prime minister. The prime minister, however, refused to see the women and remained in hiding all day.

The silence of the 20,000 women changed. No longer a silence of waiting, it took on a life of its own—pulsing between them, solid beneath their feet, alive in their breathing together, raging through their veins. And suddenly the women began singing freedom songs, harmonizing with the familiar African anthems, " *Nkosi sikelel' iAfrika* " and " *Morena Boloka,*" and another song with these words:

> You have killed our husbands,
> You have raped our daughters,
> You have caused our children to suffer.
> But now you have touched the women,
> You have struck a rock,
> You have dislodged a boulder,
> You will be crushed.

When the women dispersed, they kept singing for a long time, and their voices echoed over Pretoria. Ever since that day, August 9 has been celebrated as South African Women's Day in honor of the demonstration which was both a culmination of years of resistance and a renewal of the women's commitment to further struggle.

As early as 1913, the women of South Africa had organized to resist the police state. That year, Indian women played an important role in the nonviolent resistance campaign being led by Mohandas Gandhi in the states of Transvaal and Natal. The campaign was initially directed against the Asiatic Registration Bill, under which Indians would be required to be fingerprinted and to carry government registration certificates at all times. Other laws had been passed imposing stiff taxes and immigration restrictions on the Indians. When the Cape Supreme Court ruled that only Christian marriages were valid in South Africa, the Indian women rose up in outrage. With this ruling, the court invalidated Hindu, Muslim and Parsee marriages, essentially rendering all Indian women concubines and their children "illegitimate."

The Indian women were indignant and many of them, including Kasturbai Gandhi and some other women *Satyagrahis* (nonviolent activists) from Gandhi's experimental communities, Phoenix Farm and Tolstoy Farm, courageously joined the resistance. They developed a strategy of crossing state borders without the required immigration permits, and, by doing this, deliberately courted arrest. Some women crossed from Transvaal into Natal; others crossed from Natal into Transvaal. For this crime, a number of the women were arrested and imprisoned, some even condemned to hard labor. This was just as they had planned, knowing that the arrests would call attention to the absurdity and injustice of the travel restrictions. More and more women dared join in the civil disobedience and many marched in Gandhi's "army of peace." The women were especially effective in helping convince the Indian coal miners to go on strike. The resistance throughout the Indian population continued to grow until over 50,000 Indian workers were on strike, several thousand of them jammed into hastily constructed prisons of wire netting. But the state cannot jail everyone. Within a year, the government met all the demands of the Indian community—abolishing the tax and the Asiatic Registration Bill and recognizing the legality of non-Christian marriages. Unfortunately, though it forever changed the lives of those involved, including Gandhi's own, and proved useful in experimenting with the power of nonviolent action, the campaign never actually challenged the legitimacy or morality of the white supremacist rule, nor was an effort made to establish solidarity with the black African population.

It was left to the indigenous African peoples to initiate their own vigorous civil disobedience campaign. In 1913, the same year the Indian women began agitating, 600 women in the Orange Free State city of Bloemfontein marched together to protest the pass laws and presented the surprised mayor with a bag full of passes the women didn't intend to carry. At the head of the delegation was Charlotte Maxeke (1874–1939). She is sometimes called the "Mother of African Freedom" because she was a founding member of the African National Congress Women's League in 1919 and helped organize a number of women's actions.

In 1924, having endured years of protest and noncooperation, the government temporarily gave up the idea of making women carry passes. Hundreds of women throughout South Africa had refused to cooperate, and the jails were filled with those who had resisted the segregationist policies. However, the white-ruled government did not give up its plans for the "separate development" of the races, and increasingly repressive laws were passed restricting the lives of Indians and indigenous Africans. But the people's struggle proved to be as resilient as the government's repression. In the 1950s women joined in the Defiance Campaign Against Unjust Laws, which supported the following actions:

> –White women in the newly formed Black Sash organization wore mourning bands and stood in a silent vigil outside government offices to protest the increased repression. (Black Sash became a multi-racial activist group in October 1963.)

–In Johannesburg, 400 domestic workers went on strike.

–In Pretoria, 4000 women blocked the city streets.

–In Venterpost, 10,000 women signed a petition against apartheid and 500 women took it in person to the government officials.

–In Gopane village in the Baphurutse Reserve, women burned their passes. When police arrested 35 of them, over 200 other women stepped forward, volunteering to be arrested too.

–In Sanderton, Transvaal, over 900 women took part in an illegal procession. All were arrested.

–In Motswedi and Braklaagte, officials who arrived to register the women were stunned to find the villages temporarily deserted.

–In Johannesburg, when passes were issued to domestic workers in the late fifties, women spontaneously started a defiance campaign which had an immediate impact on the city: the *Star* ran a headline, "No Nannies Today." The campaign got the support of the African National Congress Women's League (ANCWL) and the Federation of South African Women (FSAW) who promised to fill the jails with 20,000 women. Two thousand women were arrested for defying the pass laws and were jailed after they refused to pay their fines. However, when their husbands insisted they return home, the campaign was called off.

Winnie Mandela, anti-apartheid activist married to Nelson Mandela (leader of the outlawed African National Congress), was arrested in 1958 for taking part in a women's anti-pass demonstration in Johannesburg. She was imprisoned for two weeks and was pregnant at the time. In her book, *Part of My Soul Went with Him,* she writes about taking the long view of the struggle.

> I was in prison for the first time in 1958, my first pregnancy was there. And I was visited by my children in that same prison eighteen years later in 1976—the very daughter that I had been expecting when I was in that prison the first time, in pursuit of the very same ideals!

Winnie Mandela has been frequently detained, interrogated and jailed. She keeps a suitcase ready so that when she's taken to prison in the middle of the night at the whim of a white officer, she will have a set of clothes, toothbrush and comb with her.

> Detention means that midnight knock when all about you is quiet. It means those blinding torches shone simultaneously through every window of your house before the door is kicked open. It means the exclusive right the Security Branch have to read each and every letter in the house. . . . Ultimately it means your seizure at dawn, dragged away from little children screaming and clinging to your skirt, imploring the white man dragging Mummy away to leave her alone.

She writes about how she was once forbidden to wear traditional African dress and how she began to wear the colors of the African National Congress instead. She writes about what it's like to be under constant surveillance and house arrest, and what it's like to be "banned"—a status which means she can never talk with more than one person at a time or be quoted in print in South Africa. She writes of her daily attitude of resistance to apartheid.

> I can't even go to church without a permit. But I will never go and ask a magistrate if I can go and worship God. . . . That would be accepting that their powers superseded those of God. I will never ask for permission from a human being to go to church.

"I am a living symbol of whatever is happening in the country," she writes. "I am a living symbol of the white man's fear."

> When they send me into exile, it's not me as an individual they are sending. They think that with me they can also ban the political ideas. But that is a historical impossibility. They will never succeed in doing that. I am of no importance to them as an individual. What I stand for is what they want to banish. I couldn't think of a greater honor.

For Winnie Mandela, as for thousands of other South African women who are giving their lives to the struggle today, the fierce legacy of resistance is their strength. They have not forgotten that day in 1956 when their mothers and grandmothers stood 20,000 strong and knew themselves to be solid as rock and sure as dislodged boulders, determined to crush apartheid. The day is at hand. *Amandla ngawethu! Power to the people!*

THE WOMEN COME OUT of their kitchens, out of their houses, out from the shadows—in South Africa, Cuba, Australia, the United States. The earth doesn't rumble, but shifts slightly as those who've been kept apart come together, that which had been kept silent is spoken, sung, screeched. The women are not called "courageous," though they are. They are not called "healers," though they are. They are called "strident." The strident women, courageous healers, inform the oppressors that now they have struck a rock, that that which has oppressed the people will be crushed.

♀ DURING THE LAST YEARS of the Batista regime in Cuba, the streets were littered with the mutilated bodies of dead boys. Government retaliation after any civilian uprising was effectively designed to terrorize the entire population, force silence and complicity. William Soler was only fourteen when government soldiers seized him on January 2, 1957 in the city of Santiago. The next day his body was found in an empty lot. He had been tortured.

It seemed with this last death the hearts of the Cuban women burst wide open. It was impossible for them to stay hidden in the shadows any longer. On January 4 at 10:00 in the morning, William Soler's mother (whose own name was not recorded in the accounts) walked slowly out of the Church of Dolores. Behind her another woman stepped out of the church, and another and another. In all, forty women whose sons had been killed by police or government soldiers walked out of the church in silence. They were dressed in black, the mourning color in Cuba. Each prayed silently, clutching her rosary beads, crying. Someone had made a white banner with black letters, *"Cesen los asesinatos de nuestros hijos."* "Stop the murder of our sons." They held the banner high and continued down Calle Aguilera in silence.

They walked past the city park, and other women joined them. The 40 grew to 200. They walked silently through the city's shopping district and more women joined, many simply walking out of the stores. The 200 grew to 800. The women carried rosaries and handkerchiefs and their shoes made clicking sounds on the narrow cobblestone streets. The 800 grew to 1000 as still other women stepped into the silent procession of mourning women. Men watched from the doorways, some overcome with emotion.

Suddenly a jeep loaded with soldiers appeared, blocking an intersection. The soldiers demanded that the procession disperse. Almost as if nothing had happened, the women stopped and waited in determined silence, their grief stronger even than their fear of the machine gun pointed at them. Frustrated, the soldiers leaped out of the jeep and began roughly pushing the women. "Go home!" the soldiers shouted as they pushed into the block of women, but the women could not be provoked. They simply stepped aside to let the soldiers pass through, then closed ranks again. The soldiers had struck a rock and they were at a loss. It was clear that nothing would move these grieving, angry women. The silence of 1000 women was eerie and awesome.

After the soldiers left, the women began to disperse without a word. Some of the women continued to city hall where they delivered a petition demanding an end to the killing and a return to civil law. The "mothers' protest march" in Santiago signaled the beginning of the end of the Batista regime. More and more Cubans were empowered and inspired by the women's public grieving to initiate other acts of resistance.

♀ FOR MANY YEARS, women throughout Australia watched the parade pass every April 25 on Anzac Day. An "Anzac" is a soldier in the Australian and New Zealand Army Corps. "Anzac Day" is Australia's Memorial Day, a day set aside to honor the veterans of wars and to remember the dead. The date specifically commemorates April 25, 1915, when thousands of young Anzac soldiers died on the shores of Gallipoli. By the end of World War I, over 60,000 Australian fighters had been killed in battle.

Every Anzac Day, women stood on the sidelines with the children and waved starry little national flags and cheered the veterans who'd survived the various wars. After the parade, they gathered in the parks and listened to men give speeches and watched men lay wreaths on the shrines of remembrance.

As with memorial days in other countries, however, Anzac Day had become not so much a day to remember and mourn the sacrifices of war or renew commitments to peacemaking, but a day of boasting, flag waving, beer drinking and bravado, a day to justify the old wars and to celebrate current military budgets.

The anguish of war was disguised by the rousing music of marching bands, pipes and drums, by the cheery waving of the Boy Scouts and Girl Guides and by the neat, clean dress uniforms, ribbons and medals of the veterans. The truth of Anzac Day seemed to have gotten lost—lost, that is, until some women began to remember.

It began very quietly and innocently enough in the capital city of Canberra in 1978. Twenty women standing on the sidelines of the Anzac Day parade held aloft a banner—"WOMEN AGAINST RAPE"—as the veterans marched by. No one seemed to notice.

By 1981 feminists had decided to make Anzac Day a major annual event. Their intention was to honor the forgotten victims of war—women, especially those who had been raped in wartime. When word spread about the women's plans, supporters of the Returned Servicemen's League (RSL) panicked and felt the memorial celebration slipping from their control. Rumors began to circulate that the women were planning to slash the drums, spray-paint the veterans and pour porridge down their tubas. There was even a rumor that the women planned to lie down on the march route. When the Minister of the Australian Capital Territory (ACT) heard this, he amended a local traffic ordinance to include a ruling that anyone likely to "cause insult" during the Anzac Day parade would be guilty of an offense. Suddenly, the feminists' concerns expanded to include the right of free speech, and their circle of allies widened.

On April 25, 1981 a crowd of over 300 women and a handful of supportive men assembled on a street adjacent to the Anzac Day parade route in Canberra. A black banner with white lettering stretched over their heads, "IN MEMORY OF ALL WOMEN OF ALL COUNTRIES RAPED IN ALL WARS." As the women began to march toward the parade route, they were suddenly confronted by seventy uniformed police officers. Immediately, the women sat down in the street. Beneath the glaring lights of the television cameras, sixty-one women were arrested and taken to jail. As they waited long hours to move through the bureaucratic process, they began to sing in their cells. Their friends, waiting outside the jail, heard the singing and raised their voices in a loud chorus of support.

After the arrested women were released, they and their friends walked together to the Stone of Remembrance beneath their banner. There they conducted a ceremony of their own and presented the flowers they had carried all day.

The publicity generated by the women's actions resulted in increased media attention to the issue of rape. One rape crisis center reported that twenty-one women called to discuss their wartime rapes after the Anzac Day parade. Several men called as well, needing to talk about the wartime rapes they had committed.

On Anzac Day morning 1982, after a year of organizing, over 500 women again marched to the Stone of Remembrance before the official ceremony. There they gave their own Anzac Day speeches, drawing the connections between rape and war. They laid a wreath on the tomb and held high their banners and posters written in twenty-five languages. After their ceremony, the women retired to the hillside overlooking the official ceremony and stood proudly in prominent view of the crowds with their banner, "IN MEMORY OF ALL WOMEN OF ALL COUNTRIES RAPED IN ALL WARS."

Throughout the continent that day, feminists in other cities participated in their own Anzac Day actions. In the west coast city of Perth, women added three wreaths to the "official" ones. The women's wreaths all bore the inscription "LEST WE FORGET ALL WOMEN FROM ALL COUNTRIES RAPED AND MURDERED IN MEN'S WARS." Several men were offended and ripped the inscriptions off the women's wreaths, but the women promptly replaced the inscriptions with extras they'd brought just in case.

In Adelaide, women braved threats of violence by supporters of the Returned Servicemen's League but were prevented from laying a wreath at the Cross of Sacrifice. They did manage to place small red crosses in the gardens by a government building and to issue a statement that Anzac Day glorified the negative aspects of masculinity.

In the southern city of Melbourne, police officers prevented women from presenting a wreath with a sash that read "FOR ALL WOMEN RAPED IN ALL WARS." The women were told that the inscription was "offensive."

Despite some setbacks, it was clear to everyone that things were changing. The Australian feminists were forging a new kind of Anzac Day. No longer waving little flags from the sidelines, the women had begun to move in a new direction.

♀ WOMEN STEP FROM THE SHADOWS to find each other, to reclaim the night, reclaim half of the sky, reclaim the language and the power to name. They bring with them their weaving, their best curse words, their babies, their bells and drums.

In November 1980 and again in 1981, women from the northeastern United States gathered in what came to be known as the Women's Pentagon Action. Their Unity Statement began with the words, "We are gathering at the Pentagon . . . because we fear for our lives. We fear for the life of this planet, our Earth, and the life of the children who are our human future." In the middle of the historic statement were the words, "We women are gathering because life on the precipice is intolerable." And the statement ended with the hopeful words, "We know there is a healthy sensible loving way to live and we intend to live that way in our neighborhoods and our farms in these United States, and among our sisters and brothers in all the countries of the world."

It was an action conceived and carried out in four stages. In the first stage, the women walked together by the thousands in the slow pace of *mourning*. They walked in silence between the still, cold tombstones of the war dead at Arlington National Cemetery. When the women passed the gates of the cemetery and headed for the Pentagon, they marched to the slow beat of a bass drum. A fifteen-foot high mourning puppet from the Bread and Puppet Theatre led the way. (The first year the mourning puppet was draped in black, the next year in white.) The women began to moan, wail, keen. When they reached the Pentagon Parade Grounds, they knelt and constructed a cemetery of their own, commemorating the violent deaths and needless suffering of women. Some of the hand-painted tombstones bore women's names: "Karen Silkwood," "Mary Dyer," "Anne Frank," "My Mother Roberta, Self-Induced Abortion, 1964." Others honored the nameless women: "the Radiation Victims," "the Raped Women," "the Native American Women," "the Salem Witches," and "the Mother of the Soldier My Son Killed in Vietnam."

Suddenly the drumbeat changed to a faster, more insistent beat and the fiery red puppet took the lead for the second stage. The ritual moved easily, naturally, from the expression of mourning to a release of pent-up *rage*. The women began to ululate or howl and they shouted, "We are angry, we are angry." They waved posters that read "WE WILL NOT LET YOU DESTROY OUR PLANET!" They stomped the ground in a dance of rage. They clenched their fists and made harsh noises with homemade instruments—pebbles in coffee cans. Over the heads of the demonstrators, white bird puppets atop high poles rent the sky, swooping, flapping their long, gauzy wings in fury, stirring the air. The windows of the Pentagon were filled with curious employees.

The rage evolved into the third stage of the women's demonstration—*empowerment*. Yet another huge puppet appeared to lead the way. (The first year this puppet was gold, the second year black.) The empowerment puppet held a basket of scarves and the women helped themselves as they began to encircle the Pentagon, a building one mile in circumference. As they circled, they read the Unity Statement and sang songs from the civil rights and women's movements—"We Shall Not Be Moved," "Song of the Soul," "You Can't Kill the Spirit." By using the scarves to connect woman to woman, the circle finally closed around the war building, and the women gave an exultant whoop of victory.

The fourth stage—*defiance*—began. Women who had taken workshops on nonviolent civil disobedience began the work of blocking three of the five major entrances to the Pentagon. Some of the women sat on the steps, linking arms and letting their bodies become limp as soon as officers approached to arrest them. Other women, led by the Spinsters, a Vermont affinity group of feminist activists, began spinning webs of multi-colored yarns across two of the entrances to express their conviction that all life is connected. They decorated the webs with flowers, feathers, leaves and bells. Police came out with pocketknives to destroy the webs and clear the entrances, thus unwittingly but brilliantly playing their part in the women's pageant. They helped to demonstrate that the web that connects all life is today being torn apart, our connections to each other, the animals, the earth, severed.

The women who chose not to participate in civil disobedience acted as support people for the women being arrested. They sang. They shouted, "The whole world is watching." They talked to Pentagon employees and any passersby or tourists curious enough to stop and listen. The second year some women from Ithaca, New York created a model community in a corner of the River

Entrance parking lot. The village, made out of large cardboard boxes, illustrated the women's vision of institutions they'd like to see built in their communities with the money currently being spent on preparations for war and death. There were institutions such as a women's shelter, a peace academy, a food co-op and special housing for lesbian mothers.

Both years the women arrested at the Women's Pentagon Action were subjected to handcuffs and leg irons and were chained together at the waist. They also received unusually harsh sentences, many spending thirty days in jail. Some of those jailed fasted or worked together on writing a "Why We're Here" statement.

In 1981 at the Arlington Jail, a number of the arrested women staged a sit-in to force the prison to keep the bathroom door unlocked. This was to avoid the humiliating process of asking a jailer to open it with a key every time they needed to use the facilities. They sat in front of the door singing "You can't kill the spirit, She's like a mountain./ Old and strong, she goes on and on . . . ." They stared down the sheriff who threatened to bring in 100 US marshalls to keep the bathroom door locked. The door stayed unlocked.

Sources

Women in South Africa

Fischer, Louis. *The Life of Mahatma Gandhi*. New York: Collier Books, 1962.

IDAF Research, Information and Publications Department. *To Honour Women's Day: Profiles of Leading Women in the South African and Namibian Liberation Struggles*. London, International Defence and Aid Fund for Southern Africa in cooperation with the United Nations Centre Against Apartheid, 1981.

Lapchick, Richard E., and Stephanie Urdang. *Oppression and Resistance: The Struggle of Women in Southern Africa*. Westport, CT: Greenwood Press in cooperation with the United Nations, 1982.

Luckhardt, Ken, and Brenda Wall. *Organize or Starve! The History of the South African Congress of Trade Unions*. New York: International, 1980.

Mandela, Winnie. *Part of My Soul Went with Him*. New York: W. W. Norton, 1984.

Mehta, Ved. *Mahatma Gandhi and His Apostles*. New York: Penguin Books, 1977.

Women's Intl. Resource Exchange. *Resistance, War and Liberation: Women of Southern Africa*. New York: WIRE, 1984.

Cuban mothers march

Sharp, Gene. *The Politics of Nonviolent Action: Part Two—The Methods of Nonviolent Action*. Boston: Porter Sargent, 1973.

Anzac Day in Australia

Morgan, Robin, ed. *Sisterhood Is Global: The International Women's Movement Anthology*. Garden City, NY: Anchor Press/Doubleday, 1984.
cad. "Australian Women Protest All Wars." *off our backs*, vol. 12, no. 10 (Nov. 1982).

Women's Pentagon Action

King, Ynestra. "All is Connectedness: Scenes from the Women's Pentagon Action, USA." *Keeping the Peace: Women's Peace Handbook*. Lynne Jones, ed. London: Women's Press, 1983.
Johnson, Lynn. "Weaving A Web of Life: Women's Pentagon Action, 1981." *Win Magazine*, vol. 18, no. 2 (Jan. 15, 1982).
"Demonstration: The Talk of the Town." *The New Yorker*, Dec. 8, 1980.
Breslawski, Lynne. "We Are Gathering Because Life on the Precipice is Intolerable." *New Women's Times*, Jan. 1981.

3
PLAGUING THE PATRIARCHS, DISTURBING THE KINGS

THE FIERY SUFFRAGE ACTIVISTS, dressed in their most beautiful gowns and fanciest hats, were indistinguishable from the other fashionable London "ladies" filing into Covent Garden one evening in December 1913. Unlike the other women, however, the suffragists weren't thinking much about the opera they were about to see, *Jeanne d'Arc*. Nor were they resting their gloved hands on the arms of gentlemen escorts: their gloved hands were clutching hidden megaphones and suffrage leaflets.

The battle for the vote had been long and bloody and there was no end in sight. Emmeline Pankhurst, the fifty-five-year-old leader of the militant Women's Social and Political Union (WSPU), was that very minute enduring her sixth imprisonment and hunger strike of the year. Nor was she the only one. Many women had been jailed and a great number of those, brutally force-fed that year. In June, Emily Wilding Davison, wearing the purple, green and white of the WSPU flag, had deliberately thrown herself beneath the King's horse at the annual Derby and had died, a martyr to the suffrage cause, two days later. Thousands of women, clergy, trade unionists and students from all over Britain had joined in her solemn funeral procession carrying purple irises. During the year, too, many attempts had been made to petition the parliamentary government, but the women had been betrayed at every turn.

A new plan had been proposed—the suffragists would take their demand for justice to the throne of the monarch. Not surprisingly, however, this was easier said than done. King George and Queen Mary were heavily protected from contact with the people. On the women's first attempt, suffragists had tried to present a petition to the King when he was on his way to open Parliament in Westminster but they had been blocked. Another time, when the King had visited

Bristol, a women who tried to present a suffrage petition had been struck with the flat of a sword by one of the King's royal guards.

This night, the King, Queen and their entire Court were to be at the opera, and the elegant suffragists entering Covent Garden were quite sure they'd finally manage to get the King's attention.

Upon entering the theater, three women gracefully stepped into a private viewing box that had been secured for them directly across from the Royal Box. As they settled into their seats, chatting gaily and adjusting their long skirts, they managed to lock and barricade the door of the box without attracting attention.

A hush fell over the theatergoers as the lights went down and the orchestra began to play. Joan of Arc came alive on stage, filling the arena with her courage and passion. Little did the theatergoers know there were such strong women offstage as well as on.

At the close of the first act, just as the orchestra was filing out and the applause was dying down, the three suffragists jumped to their feet and, with the use of a megaphone, addressed the startled King. Shouting over the turmoil of the audience below, they informed the King that women were fighting that day for human liberty just as Joan of Arc had fought centuries before. They told him that suffragists were being tortured just as the maid of Orleans had been tortured—in the name of the King and the church and with the full knowledge of the government.

The theater was in an uproar. Genteel Londoners were shocked by these brazen women. In the moments before the door of the box was broken down, the women with the megaphone got in their last words, protesting that the leader of the suffrage cause was, that very night, being held in prison and tortured through force-feeding by the King's authority.

It didn't take long for the three women to be ejected from the theater, but there was more to come.

Just as the audience thought it was safe to settle back into their seats, forty women who'd been sitting quietly in an upper gallery suddenly rose to their feet and flung suffrage literature onto the heads of the audience below. The theater remained in utter confusion for almost an hour before Joan of Arc could resume her battles on stage.

> I know that I am a slave, and you are my lord. The law of this country has made you my master. You can bind my body, tie my hands, govern my actions: you are the strongest,

and society adds to your power; but with my will, sir, you can do nothing.

—George Sand, *Indiana*

For centuries, ruling-class men have cornered the market on positions of power, holding the keys to the kingdom and the copyright to the Book of Rules. But for just as long, women have been disrupting the kings' courts; confronting the fathers who know best; invading the men's dinner parties, opera outings, and conferences, and generally giving the patriarchs a hard time. Women do this in order that their point of view be heard in a world which otherwise disregards their concerns.

♀ ON JUNE 23, 1976, in the city of Tel Aviv, eleven women stood trembling outside the main entrance of the Hilton Hotel with large posters hidden inside their clothes. None of them had ever done anything like this before. Even veteran women's movement leader Marcia Freedman, who had been elected to the Knesset in 1973, was nervous. The women were about to infiltrate and disrupt the national convention of the Society of Gaenecologists and Obstetricians. What woman wouldn't tremble!

In 1976 the women's movement in Israel, though young and cautious, had already tested its muscle. Consciousness-raising groups were thriving in Haifa, Tel Aviv, Jerusalem and on two kibbutzim. Women in Tel Aviv had published an anthology of feminist literature in Hebrew, and the first edition had sold out quickly. Feminist issues had been brought to light and were being discussed on radio, television and in the newspapers. Universities were offering seminars on feminist literature and politics.

Only a year before, in June 1975, women in Haifa had staged their first demonstration. They confronted, of all things, the powerful (and, feminists claimed, virulently anti-woman) Rabbinical Court. In Israel at that time, all laws regarding marriage and divorce, though technically passed by the government, were administered in accordance with ancient rabbinical laws. There was no civil marriage, and divorce could only be obtained through appeal to the Rabbinical Court where women were not allowed to testify. Life and death decisions about women's lives were being made by men who began every morning with the prayer, *Baruch atah Adanai elchaynu melech ho-alam, she lo asanee ishah.*

(Praised be the Eternal our God, Ruling Spirit of the universe, who did not make me a woman.)

It was before the closed doors of the Rabbinical Court that women gathered to speak truth. Megaphones were passed through the crowd of demonstrators so that any woman could give voice to her grievances. Even some of the women onlookers who had stayed carefully on the edge of the crowd responded to the call for testimony as one after another demanded a change in the system.

Spurred on by this success, feminists from Haifa, Tel Aviv and Jerusalem were eager to try their hand at planning a national demonstration. One appropriate focus for such a demonstration would be the government's failure to act on the abortion bill. The previous year, the women of Israel had launched a campaign to make abortions safe and legal. A petition to this effect had resulted in 30,000 signatures.

At issue were two abortion bills which had come to a preliminary reading in the Knesset. One, drawn up by a government committee, recommended abortion on approval but did not specify whose approval should be sought. The other, drawn up by Marcia Freedman, recommended that the abortion decision be left to the woman with no conditions specified within the first three months of pregnancy. For a short time, debate had raged in the Knesset while outside, women had used the opportunity to advance the idea that women and men should have a right to decide the fate of their own bodies.

The bills had been sent back to the committee for redrafting. Nothing more had been heard from the redrafting committee. The debate had been silenced. Perhaps, the women thought, it was time to act, to put pressure on the Knesset to open the debate again.

But before the women could plan an abortion-related demonstration, another move by the government claimed their attention. In January 1975, a civil rights bill had been introduced in the Knesset, recommending that a clause be added to the Israeli Declaration of Independence which would cancel all laws which discriminated on the basis of sex, excluding only that legislation aimed at protecting pregnant women. Inside the Knesset, the bill passed easily with only the religious parties voting against it. However, the morning after the vote, Prime Minister Rabin suddenly announced that the government would not support the bill. The bill was sent back to the committee with little chance that it would ever be acted on.

Women in Tel Aviv turned their full attention to planning a mock funeral for the civil rights bill. Following Israeli funeral customs, they sent out notices of the demonstration in the form of somber funeral invitations. On October 21, 200 women joined in the mock funeral, none but the organizers realizing that the demonstration was unlicensed. The demonstrators were therefore stunned when their peaceful protest was abruptly and forcefully disrupted by the police. A number of women were injured and four women were arrested. Thirty others went with the arrested women to the police station where they staged a spontaneous sit-in. The next day, the story was splashed across the front pages of the newspapers. Throughout the country, women's movement activists and supporters were jubilant and ready for more action.

That December in Tel Aviv, during the feast days of Hanukkah, 500 women and 40 men walked in a candlelight procession for women's freedom. The marchers sang, chanted and carried banners. Though the peaceful procession generated no press coverage, it may have inspired the prime minister's decision to set up a committee to investigate the status of women in Israel.

In February 1976, the abortion bill was finally reintroduced in the Knesset. This revised version represented a merging of the two previously proposed bills. When the bill passed the first reading in the Knesset, the women relaxed—too soon. An open letter was published in all the newspapers. Signed by five eminent members of the Secretariat of the Gaenecological Association of Israel, the letter outlined the doctors' objections to the bill, suggesting that it granted women too much freedom and stating their intention to refuse to perform abortions even if the bill became law.

This seemed to the women a rather high-handed and hypocritical move on the doctors' part, in light of the estimated 45,000 to 80,000 illegal abortions performed every year in Israel. This, the women noted, conveniently resulted in unreported and untaxed income for at least several hundred of the country's 600 gynecologists. No wonder the doctors wanted abortion to remain illegal.

That's when the women decided to invade the Hilton Hotel and confront the gynecologists face-to-face. Eleven women met before the action. Everyone was nervous and they wisely decided to take this into account: they planned in advance such details as who would start the chanting, what slogans would be used and when.

An inside contact let the eleven women in through a side entrance of the hotel and, before anyone could stop them, they burst into the hall, unrolling their posters and chanting, "My body belongs to me! My body belongs to me!"

The gynecologists, momentarily disoriented, began to clap in rhythm with the chanting as the women mounted the stage. But the mood changed abruptly when the chairman of the session denied the women's request that they be allowed to address the convention for ten minutes. As if remembering who and where they were, the gynecologists stood up and shouted for the women to leave. Again, Marcia Freedman politely asked the chairman to grant the women permission to speak and promised that they would then leave peacefully, but again the request was denied. Three hotel security guards appeared and began pushing the women off the stage.

Suddenly everyone was pushing and shouting. A vase filled with roses was knocked off the podium. One doctor picked up a pitcher of water and threw it at Marcia, drenching her but injuring another doctor in the process. The turmoil continued for a full thirty minutes. The women never stopped chanting.

When the conference chairman saw that he couldn't get the women to leave, he asked the doctors to temporarily leave the hall until the situation could be gotten under control. As the delegates filed slowly out of the auditorium, the women began a new chant, "The gynecologists are afraid of women!"

Eventually, the police were called and the women were placed under arrest. At this, the eleven women sat down and decided to use passive resistance during the arrest procedure. While the police waited for reinforcements, the women calmed each other and each picked up one of the roses that were now strewn about the stage.

Outside the hotel, news had spread of the women's action. Radio and television reporters were primed; television cameras were ready to roll. As each limp woman was carried out of the hotel, she clutched a rose and gave the clenched fist liberation salute.

The women never stopped chanting even as they were carted off to the police station. At each traffic light a curious crowd closed in on the paddy wagon which fairly vibrated with the women's shouts—"Free choice! Legal abortion! My body belongs to me!"

In the days that followed, the news media analyzed every angle of the story—the women's action, the pros and cons of abortion, women's rights in general—and the members of the Knesset found themselves debating, not only freedom of choice issues, but violence against women and other feminist concerns as well. And for a long time, people throughout the country talked about "the Hilton Affair."

♀ LEST WE IMAGINE that Jewish women only began confronting the patriarchs in the mid-twentieth century, open the Bible. There, in one of the first stories in the book of Exodus, is the story of women consciously choosing to disobey a king.

According to the scriptures, the Hebrew midwives, among them two whose names were recorded, Shiphrah and Puah, were called before the king of Egypt about 1300 B.C. In one sense these were powerful women; daily they held the mysteries of life in their hands. Pharaoh hoped they would also be willing to call forth death.

"When you attend the Hebrew women," he commanded them, "watch carefully. If the baby is a girl, you may let her live; but if it is a boy, kill him."

These were cruel times for the Hebrew people. They were slaves of the Egyptians, forced to do hard labor, constantly bent under the rule of men carrying thick, heavy whips. However, though their lives were unbearable, they were a people of such strength that they were considered a threat to national security. If war broke out, the king feared, the Hebrew people might take up arms against the Egyptians. And so he ordered genocide.

The midwives refused to participate in the genocide of their own people. They conspired to disobey the king, recognizing the law of life, the law of their God, as having higher authority than the law of the king.

When Pharaoh realized that the women were not complying with his orders, he summoned them again, this time demanding to know why he had been disobeyed.

There seemed little point in trying to reach the conscience of a man who could order the murder of infants. It was more important, the women decided, to cover and continue their resistance, and so they disguised their efforts by claiming, "The Hebrew women are not like the Egyptian women. They are hardy and give birth before we can reach them!"

Though the king intensified his diabolical scheme, he had to do it without the compliance of the Hebrew midwives. The Bible says that God was kind to the midwives who broke the law of their land and that the Hebrew people increased in number and grew even stronger, though they were enslaved.

♀ OVER 3000 YEARS LATER, on Thursday, October 6, 1983, another handful of women—twentieth-century lesbian feminists living in the shadow of the bomb—acted to stop the genocidal impulses of a more technologically advanced but no less brutal patriarchal order.

US Vice President George Bush and West German President Karl Carstens were the guests of honor at a banquet in the Franklin Plaza Hotel honoring the 300th anniversary of German settlers' arrival in Philadelphia. Several blocks from the banquet thousands of protesters, many of them Quakers and Mennonites of German ancestry, held a peace rally in front of the Museum of Art to reclaim the predominant pacifist legacy of the early settlers. This legacy that was not only being ignored in all the festivities but undermined. Indeed, Philadelphia peace activists suspected that the occasion was actually being used to celebrate German-American unity in the coming deployment of 572 US-made cruise and Pershing II missiles in Germany. One woman at the peace rally carried a banner which summed up the concerns: "THEY BROUGHT A PEACEFUL IDEAL. WE ARE SENDING WEAPONS."

For seven members of the Philadelphia Women's Encampment, the peace rally wasn't enough. The women decided to crash the party. On the evening of the banquet, two women dressed up in German folk costumes complete with aproned skirts and *lederhosen* (kneesocks). When they showed up at the door, each carrying a bunch of helium balloons, everyone assumed they were part of the evening's program. The women nodded and grinned their way through the sophisticated crowd to the beat of an oompah band, stopping now and then to pose for pictures.

When they were situated just below the apex of the majestic atrium ceiling, the women stopped. Each took a deep breath and let go of her balloons. As the partygoers gaped, the balloons floated up to the ceiling. To everyone's amazement, a banner, which had been attached to the balloon strings but previously hidden, unfurled and hung suspended over the crowd. It read, "WOMEN SAY NO TO EUROMISSILES!"

Meanwhile, another intrigue was unfolding elsewhere in the crowd. Having spent the early part of the evening fussing in front of their mirrors, several other feminist anti-war activists dressed in semi-formal evening gowns found it relatively easy to gain entrance to the celebration. Indeed, they were escorted by police officers themselves. When other protesters outside the gates tried to hand them anti-war leaflets, the activists-in-disguise kept in character and pushed the literature away.

Once inside, they tried to maintain their composure as they strolled through the elegant crowd of 2000 people and prepared for the next stage. The women staged their action on a busy landing, since they didn't have the $35 tickets required to enter the party's inner sanctum, where the most important officials were to be. They didn't realize that the US Vice President was not yet in the inner sanctum, but was, instead, waiting in a room quite near the place they had chosen for their action.

Nodding silently to each other, the women suddenly opened their purses and whipped out dark purple shawls, each one embroidered with the words "NO NUCLEAR MISSILES!" With their shawls draped over their shoulders, the women formed a circle and abruptly sat on the floor in the midst of the astonished crowd. Then they started keening. Occasionally one of the women would speak above the wailing, "We mourn for all the potential victims of a nuclear holocaust in Europe."

The FBI, CIA, police and security officers were momentarily stunned, not to mention confused. These women didn't look anything like the terrorists they were busily guarding against, and if these "ladylike" protesters could have slipped by, who could guess the security risk other seemingly gracious people posed.

The security personnel took so long to coordinate their actions that the women actually had time to complete their prepared ritual and start all over again before the arrests began.

Sources

London action

Pankhurst, Emmeline. *My Own Story*. London: Virago, 1914/1979.
Mackenzie, Midge. *Shoulder to Shoulder: A Documentary*. New York:
Alfred A. Knopf, 1975.

Israeli actions

Rein, Natalie. *Daughters of Rachel: Women in Israel*. New York:
Penguin Books, 1979/1980.
Daube, David. *Civil Disobedience in Antiquity*. Edinburgh, Scotland:
Edinburgh University Press, 1972.
The Holy Bible. Exodus 1:8–22.

Philadelphia action

Kulp, Denise. "Drawing Connections Between Women & Activism: The
Philadelphia Women's Encampment." *off our backs*, vol. 17, no.
2 (Feb. 1987).
Schaffer, Michael D. "Protesters Say Missiles Betray Immigrants'
Ideals." *The Philadelphia Inquirer*, Oct. 7, 1983.

4
WE FIGHT FOR ROSES, TOO!

IN THE LAWRENCE, MASSACHUSETTS STRIKE of 1912, women textile workers carried banners that proclaimed, "WE WANT BREAD AND ROSES, TOO!" These words captured the workers' longing, not only for the basic necessities of life, but for the things beyond the necessities that make life worth living— for beauty, dignity, a sense of self-worth. For life's roses. Recognizing that the women's concise slogan captured the full spirit of their struggle, James Oppenheim wrote the song "Bread and Roses" which includes this verse:

> As we come marching, marching, unnumbered women dead
> Go crying through our singing their ancient song of bread.
> Small art and love and beauty their drudging spirits knew.
> Yes, it is bread we fight for,
> But we fight for roses, too.

Bread and roses. That's what hard-working women the world over fight for.

♀ ONE EVENING IN 1888, Annie Besant and her new friend Herbert Burrows attended a meeting of the socialist Fabian Society in London. They were stirred by that evening's speaker, Clementina Black, whose topic was "Female Labor." Black, secretary of the Women's Trade Union League, was urging the formation of a consumers group whose participants would pledge to buy products only from shops certified "clean" from the taint of paying unfair wages. During the spirited discussion which followed the lecture, someone mentioned that Bryant & May Ltd., a match factory, paid its workers pitiful wages while it awarded its shareholders extravagant dividends. Everyone agreed that someone with social consciousness should investigate the situation.

Annie Besant couldn't resist the challenge. Ever since she had escaped her disastrous marriage to the Reverend Frank Besant in 1873, she had been involved in social reform, establishing for herself a reputation as a "free thinker." With fellow radical Charles Bradlaugh, she had co-edited a periodical called *The National Reformer* and lectured widely on behalf of the National Secular Society. Indeed, she had become a proponent of militant atheism, touring with the lecture "The God of Christianity versus the God of Freethought." Her friend, Bernard Shaw, once called Besant "the greatest orator in England."

In 1877, she and Bradlaugh republished a controversial birth control pamphlet. They were taken to court and convicted of obscenity. Shortly after being sentenced, Besant lost custody of her daughter to the husband she despised. This terrible blow did nothing to stop her activism. In 1885, Besant joined the Fabian Society which had as its goal the establishment of a socialist state in Great Britain through a process of evolutionary change. Her outrage at the sufferings of hard-working people was heightened in 1887. On November 13 of that year, the day which became known in London's labor history as "Bloody Sunday," police violently quelled a demonstration of workers at Trafalgar Square. Over 100 demonstrators were seriously injured and hospitalized: two died of their injuries. Besant, who was in the crowd that day, was deeply affected by what she had witnessed. Shortly after Bloody Sunday, Besant joined with another journalist, W. T. Stead, in publishing a new, weekly paper, the *Link*. Their masthead carried a quotation by Victor Hugo: "I will speak for the dumb. I will speak of the small to the great and of the feeble to the strong. . . . I will speak for all the despairing silent ones."

After the discussion at the Fabian Society meeting about Bryant & May, she saw an opportunity to use her new publication, to "speak for all the despairing silent ones." She wanted to expose the working conditions at the match factory and to generate public concern. She was in a position to do something. Annie Besant spent the next few early summer days of 1888 using her journalist's skills to interview the match workers and investigate their working conditions.

Bryant & May was located in London's East End. By the end of that year, Jack the Ripper would kill and mutilate six, possibly seven, East End women, bringing the neighborhood a grisly notoriety. But the East End already had a colorful folklore as well as its share of urban tragedy. Like New York City's Lower East Side, it was a stepping-off place for immigrants. Its crowded tenements had housed Huguenot weavers in the 1600s, Irish dockworkers in the 1700s and early 1800s, and Jews fleeing persecution in Russia by the thousands in the 1880s.

The East End was an area vulnerable to epidemics, especially the bubonic plague in the 1660s and cholera in the 1800s. Factories in the East End, including a "chemical works" and a sulphate manufacturer, spewed poisonous clouds into the air and turned the Thames into an open sewer. Others, like the manure manufacturing factory, simply stank. The water supply was both inadequate and impure, and some sections of the East End were occasionally without water for whole seasons. And it was crowded. Living space was at times so precious that large cupboards were rented out as rooms. It was here in the East End that Annie Besant went to interview the workers at the Bryant & May match factory.

Most of the workers were young women who were paid wages ranging from five to eighteen shillings a week, while the average weekly wage in London was twenty-nine shillings. The poorest East Enders expected to spend no less than three shillings, sixpence (half a shilling) every week on food and at least two shillings, three pence on rent. Despite the low wages, the company expected each employee to contribute toward the cost of the equipment on which she worked and to pay a sixpence fine for any error, such as dropping a tray. Besant interviewed one pale sixteen-year-old match factory worker who lived with her sister. They subsisted on bread, butter and tea for days at a time, the young worker explained, and looked forward to an occasional bit of marmalade.

Nor were low wages the only hardships faced by the matchworkers. The factory air was thick with phosphorus which literally ate away at their faces, disfiguring the women with a disease workers called "Phossy-Jaw." Many of the women also suffered from early baldness, the result of having to carry heavy loads on their heads.

"It is time someone came and helped us," one of the young match workers told Annie Besant.

With Burrows' help, Besant gathered the facts and presented them in the *Link*. In her article titled "White Slavery in London," she described the appalling work conditions she had found at Bryant & May and called for a boycott of the company's matches.

"Who will help?" she asked her readers.

> Plenty of people wish well to any good cause; but very few care to exert themselves to help it, and still fewer will risk anything in its support. "Some one ought to do it, but why should I?" is the ever re-echoed phrase of weak-kneed amiability. "Some one ought to do it, so why *not* I?" is the cry of some earnest servant of man, eagerly forward springing to face some perilous duty. Between those two sentences lie whole centuries of moral evolution.

After publication of her exposé, Besant was promptly threatened with a libel suit, but Bryant & May didn't follow through. Instead, the company came down hard on the workers. They asked the "matchgirls" to sign a petition certifying that Besant's statements were untrue, exaggerated at best, and that, in fact, the workers at the Bryant & May factory were well treated. When no one would sign the paper, one young woman was singled out as the leader and threatened with immediate dismissal. She pushed the paper away. Even with the threat of losing her job, she would not sign the company's page of lies, nor would the other workers.

The women at Bryant & May wondered what would happen next. They didn't have to wonder for long. The next day the company acted on its threat and fired the young worker who had pushed the paper away. As soon as the other women heard the news, 1400 workers threw down their work, stood up and walked out. (The male workers, being better paid than the women and working in supervisory positions, didn't join the strike. Having no one to supervise, they were eventually sent home for lack of work.) Not knowing what to do, the women marched out of the factory and headed for Fleet Street where the *Link* office was located. When they got to Fleet Street they began calling in unison for "Annie Besant! Annie Besant!"

Besant saw them from her office window and, unsure of what had happened and reluctant to "speechify to matchgirls in Fleet Street," asked that three of them come into her office and talk to her. The women explained that they were being punished for having told her their story but, one of the workers explained, "You had spoke up for us, and we weren't going back on you!"

Besant was inspired by the courage and faith of the match factory workers. Mindful that this would be one of the first significant strikes in Britain's labor movement involving a large number of women, she and Herbert Burrows worked hard the next two weeks to support the action which would come to be known as the "London Matchgirls' Strike." While the women carried rough homemade banners and attracted large crowds with their rallies, Besant and Burrows sent out an appeal for money. Generous donations came in, and the money was used as strike pay. They wrote articles, addressed clubs, held meetings. They solicited and won the support and assistance of the Women's Trade Union League. They joined in a procession of the striking workers through the city to the House of Commons where the women told their story to members of Parliament. "The girls behaved splendidly, stuck together, kept brave and bright all through," wrote Besant in her autobiography.

Besant sent letters to Bryant & May shareholders who had received dividends ranging from 20 to 38 percent.

> How would you like to start your work at half past five a.m. and reach home again at seven p.m., having been on your feet nearly all the time, and after doing this for five days, with an additional half day on Saturday, to take home 11/2d [eleven shillings, two pence] as a reward? And if you did not reach the average, but only got 5/6d [five shillings, sixpence] and had been at work for fifteen years, might you not say like my poor friend said to me the other day, "I'm most tired of it."

Everyone involved with the strike worked, as Besant later recounted, "'til the whole country rang with the struggle."

Finally, the London Trades Council consented to act as arbitrator and, with this help, a satisfactory settlement was reached with Bryant & May on July 16. The workers, newly empowered, returned to their jobs with all fines and deductions abolished. They had won a number of concessions including better wages, though it would be many years before they would be protected from the poisonous, cancer-causing white phosphorus they had to work with. In addition, they formed the Matchmakers' Union which grew into one of the strongest women's trade unions in England in subsequent years, with Besant as secretary and Burrows as treasurer.

One final note: Besant petitioned for a "matchgirls' drawing room." As she envisioned it, this was to be a home for working women who had no real homes and "no playground save the streets." She wanted it to be a pleasant refuge with a piano, some light literature and tables for papers and games—not, she warned, an institution with rigid rules of discipline and prim behavior, but a home fostering an atmosphere of friendship and freedom, a place for the roses of life such as art and beauty, to which these women were entitled. Within two years, a donor made Besant's dream come true and opened a home for the "matchgirls."

THE THEORY OF NONVIOLENCE is based on the premise that all power ultimately depends on the consent and/or cooperation of those over whom the power is wielded. This is not to blame the victim. It is a recognition that there is great revolutionary potential in the collective withholding of cooperation. The strike, then, might be understood as the basic metaphor for nonviolent direct action. In her essay "New Men, New Women," Barbara Deming wrote about the concept of *strike* and of *reverse strike:*

> We act out respect for ourselves by refusing to cooperate with those who oppress or exploit us. And as their power never resides in their single selves, always depends upon the cooperation of others—by refusing that cooperation (if there are enough of us), refusing our labor, our wits, our money, our blood upon their battlefields, our deference, we take their power from them. The strike, in a great variety of forms—this is all that is needed to depose them (if, again, there are enough of us, enough of us who recognize that this is so). The strike, and what Danilo Dolci has named the reverse strike: carrying out by ourselves the work we think should exist, doing this in our own way, and doing it of course whether or not we are given "permission."

In almost every corner of the globe, women have experimented with the collective power of the strike, using a variety of tactics in a range of circumstances. In 1818 in Valencia, Venezuela, hospital laundresses went on strike to demand the back pay they were owed. In Iran in 1890, royal harem women organized a successful tobacco strike to break the British monopoly of Persian tobacco production. Twenty thousand women silk workers went on strike in Shanghai, China in 1923, demanding a ten-hour day. And in 1972 in Italy, when their demands for improved salaries and better work conditions were ignored, the cashiers in one Naples department store went on a "smile strike." By refusing to smile, they were withholding that aspect of cooperation the store needed most to maintain its friendly façade.

> In the black of the winter of nineteen nine,
> When we froze and bled on the picket line,
> We showed the world that women could fight
> And we rose and won with women's might.
>
> Hail! the waistmakers of nineteen nine,
> Making their stand on the picket line,
> Breaking the power of those who reign,
> Pointing the way, smashing the chain.

♀ CLARA LEMLICH WAS SORE ALL OVER. Her body was bruised and aching after the beating she'd taken two days earlier on the picket line in front of the Leiserson factory in New York City's Lower East Side. She'd just gotten out of the hospital in time to attend the meeting in the Great Hall of the Cooper Union Building, which was overflowing with garment workers ready for action. But what a disappointment it was turning out to be. Two hours of long-winded speeches by well-meaning people was more than enough, even if one of the speakers was a big name—Samuel Gompers, the president of the American Federation of Labor. Clara only half listened to the cautious rhetoric. She was thinking back over the events of the past eleven weeks.

It had all started on September 25, 1909, when she and 100 other workers had walked out of Leiserson's. They were angry. Some of the shop's more experienced workers were being laid off on the pretext of there not being enough work, but they'd been lied to. The work was actually being sent to another, cheaper shop Leiserson's had opened downtown.

This was on top of the deplorable everyday working conditions endured by the workers at Leiserson's garment shops. Day after day, the women and girls (some as young as eight years old) entered the factories at 7:30 in the morning and worked until 6:30 at night sewing "waists" (women's blouses) and "shirtwaists" (tailored blouses popular at the turn of the century). Very few women took home more than $6.00 per week after a full seven days of work and the youngest girls made as little as $1.50. Out of their low wages, workers had to pay for the needles they used and for the boxes they sat on for chairs and were charged for electricity.

There were constant fines as well. If a foreman thought a worker had taken two or three minutes too long on a bathroom break, a fine would be deducted from the week's pay. There were fines for damaged work and errors, and anyone who arrived five minutes late in the morning was sent home for a half day without pay. Such punishment and arbitrarily imposed fines could be disastrous, not only for the worker, but for the family that depended on her. Most of the garment workers were Jewish or Italian immigrant teenagers, many of whom provided the main financial support for their families. A small family living in a dark and crowded tenement building in the Lower East Side could expect to pay at least $1.50 per week for rent and no less than $3.00 for food. This left very little for clothes, shoes, medicine, household and toiletry needs or educational materials, books and entertainment. And many of the workers sent whatever they could save to their relatives in Europe. But the long hours and low wages were not the workers' only hardships.

The shops were stifling in the summer and freezing in the winter. There was rarely any ventilation or clean water. And a number of shops were clearly firetraps. Anyone could see that. That September, the workers at Leiserson's had decided to stick together to fight their stingy, mean-spirited employers. They called a strike.

Nothing about this action was easy. The day after the walkout, the company had started recruiting other workers—scabs, strikebreakers—and had hired thugs to beat up the picketers. The police hadn't helped. They arrested any picketer who spoke to a scab.

Three days after the workers at Leiserson's walked out, workers at the Triangle Waist Company went on strike. They had been tricked too. One of the company men had talked sweetly to the women and had told them that the company wanted to help them start a union. He asked which women had already sought union membership. One hundred fifty women raised their hands. It was a trap. That same evening, the women who had raised their hands were told that, because of a lull in the trade, they wouldn't be needed for awhile. The very next day the company advertised for more workers. The women realized they'd been tricked and returned to picket the Triangle Waist Company.

It was an ugly strike. The company hired prostitutes and pimps to beat up the strikers. As terrible as this was, it received no publicity until November 4 when Mary Dreier, president of the New York Women's Trade Union League, came to the picket line to witness police brutality and was arrested in the confusion. The police officers and judge were profusely apologetic and embarrassed for having mistakenly arrested an educated, middle-class woman, but their mistake resulted in a publicity boost for the strikers. The next morning, a headline on page one of *The New York Times* charged, "Arrest Strikers for Being Assaulted." Mary Dreier was interviewed. She articulated the freedom of speech issue at stake on the picket line:

> Whenever we spoke to the girls, the police would come up and abruptly order us to stop talking and when we asserted our legal rights in the matter, persisted in their refusal to allow us to talk. As to the incident this morning which resulted in my arrest, I am glad of the chance to tell the facts.

With the newspapers beginning to report on their working conditions and wages, the mood of the workers moved decidedly toward a general strike.

Clara Lemlich sat thinking of these things as the men's speeches droned on and on that eventful evening of November 22, 1909. Couldn't they feel the tension in the room? the readiness? the terrible ache for action? the need to give voice to misery and rage? Clara's blood was boiling. Years later she would recall the spirit that informed her life in those days, "Ah—then I had fire in my mouth. . . . What did I know about trade unionism? Audacity—that was all I had—audacity!"

Clara stood up and interrupted a speech to ask if she might address the workers. The moderator, as surprised as everyone else, promptly decided that the young striker had as much right to the platform as he did and granted her request. Several thousand people strained to see Clara—the young woman union organizers called "a pint of trouble for the bosses"—as she made her way to the podium. Her blood racing, Clara spoke in Yiddish with such an impassioned eloquence that even those who spoke only English or Italian understood the spirit of her speech.

"I am a working girl," she said, "one of those who are on strike against intolerable conditions." The workers nodded. Many of them recognized Clara as a fiery orator and an organizer of the Leiserson strike. She knew what she was talking about. "I am tired of listening to speakers who talk in general terms," she said. "What we are here for is to decide whether we shall or shall not strike. I offer a resolution that a general strike be declared—now!"

The mass of workers rose to their feet as one body, shouting, waving their hats and handkerchiefs for a good five minutes. When at last the crowd settled down, the moderator asked if anyone wanted to second Clara's resolution. And again, the people were on their feet, everyone in the Great Hall seconding the motion.

The moderator cried out, caught up in the emotion of the moment, "Do you mean faith? Will you take the old Jewish oath?" he challenged them. Two thousand people raised their hands and shouted fervently, "If I turn traitor to the cause I now pledge, may this hand wither from the arm I now raise."

Messengers ran with the news to where other garment workers were meeting. They too endorsed the call for a general strike.

The next morning thousands of women waistmakers went to work, not sure of quite how to proceed. One worker, Natalya Urosova, described what that morning was like in the shop where she was working:

> . . . there was whispering and talking softly all around the room among the machines: "Shall we wait like this?" "There is a general strike." "Who will get up first?" "It would be better to be the last to get up, and then the company might remember it of you afterward, and do well for you." But I told them, "What difference does it make which one is first and which one is last?" Well, so we stayed whispering, and no one knowing what the other would do, not making up our minds for two hours. Then I started to get up. And just at the same minute all—we all got up together, in one second. No one after the other; no one before. And when I saw it—that time—oh, it excites me so yet. I can hardly talk about it. So we all stood up, and all walked out together. And already out on the sidewalk in front, the policemen stood with the clubs. One of them said, "If you don't behave, you'll get this on your head." And he shook his club at me. We hardly knew where to go—what to do next. But one of the American girls who knew how to telephone called up the Women's Trade Union League, and they told us all to come to a big hall a few blocks away.

And so, on November 23, 1909, the women from over 500 shops walked out in what would be called "The Uprising of the 20,000" and "the first great strike of women."

Pauline Newman, a teenager working at the Triangle Shirtwaist Company, later remembered that day:

> Thousands upon thousands left the factories from every side, all of them walking down toward Union Square. It was November, the cold winter was just around the corner, we had no fur coats to keep warm, and yet there was the spirit that led us on and on until we got to some hall to keep warm and out of the wind and out of the cold at least for the time being.
>
> I can see the young people, mostly women, walking down and not caring what might happen. The spirit, I think, the spirit of a conqueror led them on. They didn't know what was in store for them, didn't really think of the hunger, cold, loneliness, and what could happen to them. They just didn't care on that particular day; that was *their* day.

The union organizers were amazed. They had hoped at least 3000 workers would participate in a general strike. They never dreamed over 20,000 would walk off their jobs. Picket lines were hastily established in front of the 500 shops, and meetings were conducted in Yiddish, English and Italian in over twenty-four meeting halls. Within four days almost half of the strikers had returned to work with union contracts.

For the rest, the winter was as Dickens had described the period of the French Revolution, "It was the best of times, it was the worst of times." It was the best of times because of the spirit and solidarity; and because the separate and totally alien universes of rich and poor touched briefly in a way they rarely had before or have since. It was the worst of times because the strikers suffered.

Some women were beaten even before they took their places on the picket line. One sixteen-year-old worker showed up at the union office covered with bruises inflicted by her father who'd punished her for being on strike. The union found her another place to stay.

Out on the picket lines the women were cold, hungry and subjected to public humiliation, brutal beatings and arrest. The bosses hired thugs to beat up the women. The newspapers reported the violence:

Gangs of men used their fists against girl strikers. Two strikebreakers hurled a picket to the ground and then stamped on her. A group of thugs pounced on a strike committee chairman while he was collecting funds and injured him so badly that he had to remain in bed for three weeks. Another assailant jumped upon a 19 year old girl, smashed her side and broke one of her ribs.

McAlister Coleman, a young reporter for the *New York Sun,* described the scene he had witnessed on the picket line:

The girls, headed by teen-age Clara Lemlich . . . began singing Italian and Russian working-class songs as they paced in twos before the factory door. Of a sudden, around the corner came a dozen tough-looking customers, for whom the union label "gorillas" seemed well-chosen.

"Stand fast, girls," called Clara, and then the thugs rushed the line, knocking Clara to her knees, striking at the pickets, opening the way for a group of frightened scabs to slip through the broken line.

As is often the case with violent tactics, the employers' brutality backfired and, instead of frightening the picketers away, strengthened their resolve and won support for the strike by heightening public sympathy for the workers.

The women were arrested over and over again. Esther Lobetkin, a seamstress who had only recently arrived from Russia, must have found New York a strange place, but she was committed to the struggle. She was arrested on the picket line many times. Often after an arrest, the police would punish the strikers by not letting them sit on the benches. "One of our girls got so tired she went to crouch down to rest herself," Esther remembered, "when one of the officers came over and poked her with his club and says, 'Here, stand up. Where do you think you are? In Russia?'" But such heartlessness did not deter Esther from walking into the lion's den day after day. Each time she was arrested she made it a special point to call from the back of the patrol wagon to the other strikers, "Don't lose courage, we'll win yet!"

The police taunted the picketers with sexual innuendos, calling them prostitutes because they were walking the streets. Seventeen-year-old Yetta Ruth, a spokesperson for her shop, was shocked by her treatment after arrest. "While I was at the station house on 20th street," she said, "the officers treated me in such a manner that a girl is ashamed to talk about." She was accused of living with a number of men and was asked to mend one officer's torn pants. Another policeman winked at her and grinned when he said, "Come along, Yetta."

The judges were even worse. Magistrate Olmstead stared down at some bruised and bleeding women who'd been carrying signs reading, "WE STRIKE FOR JUSTICE." He bellowed, "You are on strike against God and Nature, whose firm law is that man shall earn his bread in [*sic*] the sweat of his brow. You are on strike against God!" Another judge, one Justice Cornell, sentenced some of the young strikers to the workhouse on Blackwell's Island. Many strikers were charged with vagrancy or disorderly conduct and fined. One magistrate told the women, "You have no right to picket. . . . Every time you go down there you will get what is coming to you and I shall not interfere."

The union organizers sent strikers out to tell the world what was happening and to ask for help. They spoke at churches, colleges and clubs. Twenty-five-year-old Polish immigrant Rose Schneiderman was sent off to Massachusetts to raise money for the strikers. She won over the students at Radcliffe, Wellesley and Mount Holyoke Colleges and brought back $10,000, most of which was used to post bail for the strikers.

Sixteen-year-old Pauline Newman was sent to canvass New York State. She couldn't believe it when International Ladies' Garment Workers Union Secretary John Dyche pulled her aside one day and said she'd be going to Buffalo that night. She had never been out of the city since she'd arrived on the boat from Lithuania in 1901. She didn't even own a suitcase. That didn't matter. Dyche brought her his own suitcase, took her to the station and gave her a one-way ticket to Buffalo, telling her to remember how desperately the strikers needed money. He knew she could do it. Newman remembered:

> I got to Buffalo on the coldest day of the year. It was snowing, hailing, and windy. . . . I didn't know where the Labor Council was. The trolley-car conductor told me where to get off, and there was the red-brick building that matched the address I had. I walked up one flight—dark stairs and a locked door. Another flight, the same thing. The third floor door was unlocked. I opened it, hoping to find someone there. The room was empty and chilly, but I sat down and must have dozed off. When I woke up a

young machinist was standing over me. He brought me
coffee and sandwiches, lighted the stove, and I began to
come to life. That night at the meeting of the Central Trades
and Labor Council I spoke and began to collect the money
we so badly needed.

Meanwhile, back in New York, affluent and middle-class
volunteers in the Women's Trade Union League (WTUL) were
working hard in support of the strikers' cause. The League had
been formed in 1903 "to organize women locally into trade unions
and to assist already organized workers to secure better
conditions." Some of the wealthiest society matrons in New York
City joined, including Anne Morgan—daughter of J. P. Morgan,
Alva Belmont and Mrs. Henry Morgenthau. Many of the wealthy
reformers who joined the League were interested in being allies
to working-class women and in promoting both women's suffrage
and unionization, though there was little talk about actually
challenging or confronting the systemic basis of class oppression.
Nevertheless, the League proved indispensable to the strikers in
1909 when it took on such tasks as fundraising, providing bail
and provisions for the strikers, public speaking, media outreach
and picketing.

On December 3, the League organized a march of 10,000
strikers to City Hall. At the head of the parade were three women
strikers and three women "allies" from the WTUL. A number of
the marchers carried signs informing Mayor McClellan,
"PEACEFUL PICKETING IS THE RIGHT OF EVERY WOMAN." When
they reached City Hall, a representative group of strikers handed
the mayor a petition and told him about their terrible suffering at
the hands of "New York's finest." The mayor promised to take
up the matter with the police commissioner.

Wealthy, fur-laden League members formed what some of the
strikers called "The Mink Brigade" and began showing up on the
picket lines. They carefully recorded what they saw, making
detailed accounts of the police treatment of the strikers and keeping
tallies of the number of women arrested and sentenced.

Wealthy society matron and suffrage activist Alva Belmont
announced very early that she intended to help the strikers in
whatever ways she could. "Women the world over need protection
and it is only through the united efforts of women that they will
get it," she said. Belmont assisted the League in setting up a

weekly motorcade of rich suffrage activists. Fancy, well-polished, chauffeured cars lent by millionaires were driven through the narrow streets of the Lower East Side, picking up and dropping off the strikers. Honking to call attention to the pickets, the cars carried both fashionable ladies dressed in furs and poor, working women dressed in threadbare coats.

Belmont was outraged by what she learned of the mismanagement and injustices in the judicial system. After spending six hours at the Jefferson Market Courthouse in Greenwich Village, she declared that the city would be better off if more people really knew what was going on in night court. "Every woman who sits complacently amid the comforts of her home or who moves with perfect ease and independence in her own protected social circle, and says, 'I have all the rights I want,' should spend one night at the Jefferson Market court. She would then know that there are other women who have no rights which man or law or society recognizes." But, she promised, "There will be a different order of things when we have women judges on the bench!"

While the strikers were winning the sympathy and curious scrutiny of wealthy capitalists, they were also being feted by the socialists. On December 9, hearty labor organizer Mary "Mother" Jones took to the podium of the Thalia Theater in Manhattan as the guest speaker for New York's Socialist Party. Jones, described the next day in the *New York Call* as "the valiant agitator for the freedom of the workers" and "champion of all oppressed," worked her audience into a fever pitch. Frequently interrupted by outbursts of applause and cheers, she delighted the women workers with a tactical suggestion:

> You make all the fine waists, but you do not wear them.
> You work hard and are poorly paid, and now you have
> been forced to strike for better conditions of labor, shorter
> hours and higher wages.
>
> You ought to parade past the shops where you work and
> up the avenue where the swells who wear the waists you
> made live. They won't like to see you, they will be afraid
> of you!

She gave a great boost to the women that day as she spelled out the logic of their increased involvement as garment workers in the business of labor organizing.

> You must stick together to win. The boss looks for cheap workers. When the child can do the work cheaper he displaces the woman. When the woman can do the work cheaper she displaces the man. But when you are organized you have something to say about the conditions of labor and your wages. You must stand shoulder to shoulder. The woman must fight in the labor movement beside man. Every strike that I have ever been in has been won by the women.

Mother Jones promised the crowd that this would be the last great battle of humankind—the fight of the workers to own the tools with which they toil. She reminded the strikers that they were fighting to see that day when there would be no master, no slave, when, for the first time in human history, all would be free. She brought down the house.

Clara Lemlich and a number of other strikers were invited to tell their life stories on December 15 to some wealthy women attending a luncheon at the exclusive Colony Club. While such meetings seemed to fascinate the women at both ends of the social ladder, some of the workers were resentful of the effort they had to make with the rich women. After all, they wondered, how could the women who paid $2.75 for linen waists at Lord & Taylor understand what it was like to earn only $6 a week making them? How could women who could afford to buy silk hosiery for $1.50 a pair at Bloomingdale's know how crucial the $1.50 could be when it was needed for the family's rent each week? And weren't some of these listeners members of the elite who, that very year, attended the debutante's ball for fashionable young Marjorie Gould at the Plaza Hotel—a party which cost the proud parents $200,000? How could they know what it was like for a mother at the other end of town to be worried sick over the 50¢ she needed each week to buy bread for her children, and the 20¢ for fish? One of the strikers, Theresa Malkiel, wrote:

> They've brought me to their fashionable clubhouse to hear about our misery. To tell the truth, I've no appetite to tell it to them, for I've almost come to the conclusion that the gulf between us girls and these rich ladies is too deep to be smoothed over by a few paltry dollars; the girls would probably be the better off in the long run if they did not take their money. They would the sooner realize the great contrast and division of classes. . . .

Still, there's no doubt that people in the middle and upper classes were hearing things they'd never heard before about their own society. Members of the Manhattan Congregationalist Church, after listening spellbound to Rose Schneiderman tell about her life and the working conditions of the waistmakers, resolved to support the strikers and to urge the public "to find out who are these mean manufacturers . . . that are grinding down the girls."

In mid-December, waistmakers in Philadelphia uncovered a new dirty trick being played by the manufacturers: some of the work not being done by the striking workers in New York was being shipped to workers in Pennsylvania. On December 20, they too walked out and joined New York waistmakers in a general strike.

In Philadelphia, as in New York, wealthy women were drawn to the cause of the waistmakers. Students from Bryn Mawr College and young society debutantes carried placards up and down the sidewalks demanding justice for the women workers. Martha Gruening, a Bryn Mawr graduate student, was arrested for carrying such a placard and sent to jail on the charge of inciting to riot. "It is women of your class," the judge screamed at her, "not the actual strikers, who have stirred up all this strife. Had you and your kind kept out of this, it would have been over long ago."

The Philadelphia strikers tried a new tactic to persuade those women still working to join them. The picketers passed out little cards printed with the words,

> YOU ARE DOING LITTLE MORE THAN STARVING TO DEATH
> ON THE DOLLAR-A-DAY WAGES THAT YOU ARE GETTING.
> WHY NOT STARVE OUTSIDE? OUTSIDE WE HAVE FRESH AIR
> AND STARVATION IS NOT SO DEADLY. INSIDE, IF YOU DON'T
> STARVE TO DEATH, YOU WILL DIE OF TUBERCULOSIS. COME
> ON, GET A LITTLE FRESH AIR.

With the new pressure of the Philadelphia strike, the New York Manufacturers' Association sought a settlement on December 23, offering a number of concessions such as shorter hours (a fifty-two-hour week), higher wages, reinstatement of strikers, and the promise that employers would supply needles and electricity at no extra charge to the workers. But the manufacturers were not ready to grant union recognition. At a mass meeting on December 27, so large it had to be held in five different halls, union organizers asked the strikers to vote on the contract. They overwhelmingly rejected it. They wanted union recognition. The strike would continue.

The new year dawned bright, cold and bitter. There was to be one last grand and dramatic event before the end of the strike. On January 2, 1910, a mass rally was held at Carnegie Hall in support of the strikers. The stage was filled with 370 women who had been arrested during the strike. In the front row sat twenty who had served hard time in the workhouse. Each of the strikers proudly wore a sash across her chest proclaiming "ARRESTED" or "WORKHOUSE PRISONER"—badges of honor. One after the other, speakers stood to tell the story of the strike and of what the women had suffered at the hands of the police. Morris Hillquit, the Socialist Party leader, closed the rally with a rousing cry, "Be of good cheer, your victory will be glorious!" The audience rose to its feet in thunderous applause. It was the last hurrah for the fading strike.

By mid-January the strikers of both cities were facing severe blizzards. And there were other problems. Although some of the League members continued their support by setting up soup kitchens for the strikers, other comfortable society women withdrew their support. They had become impatient with the workers' insistence on union recognition and felt that the manufacturers had offered enough concessions. Strike funds began to get low.

To further complicate matters, a conflict within the black community came to a head. Black women had rarely been hired in the garment factories, and when they had, they had met with considerable racial prejudice from the other working girls and women. Black women had also not been encouraged to join the union, though a handful were members. The manufacturers took advantage of this situation during the long days of the strike and began recruiting black women as scabs.

On January 10, an editorial appeared in a black weekly, *New York Age,* advocating that black women use the strike as an opportunity to break into an area of employment from which they had previously been excluded. This was not a new idea in women's labor history. In the mid-1800s, Susan B. Anthony had been a strong ally of working women and an advocate of equal pay for equal work and the eight-hour day. Observing that union men kept women out of many trades and often opposed women's suffrage, she had occasionally encouraged women to act as strike-breakers if they had no other way to enter or learn a trade. And she had arranged for women to be trained to work in her print shop at a time when union apprenticeships in the print trade were not open to women.

In the wake of the 1910 editorial in *New York Age*, a crisis meeting of the interracial Cosmopolitan Club was held on January 21 in a black community church in Brooklyn. The Club was an organization of black and white progressive community leaders who met to discuss concerns and aspects of "the race question." Mary White Ovington, one of the founders of the National Association for the Advancement of Colored People (NAACP), had also been instrumental in the formation of the Cosmopolitan Club. It was largely under her impetus that the Club met to discuss the relationship of black workers to the strike. At this meeting the Club members passed a resolution which read in part:

> *Resolved,* That the citizens of Brooklyn in mass meeting assembled, protest and urge the women of color to refrain from acting in the capacity of strikebreakers in the shirtwaist making concerns of New York, because we regard their action as antagonistic to the best interests of labor.
>
> We further urge that, in the event of the successful termination of the strike, organized labor exercise a proper consideration of the claims and demands of the men and women of color who desire to enter the various trades in the way of employment and the protection of the various labor unions . . .

By this time the strike was fizzling out. Shops were settling with the strikers, some recognizing the union, others not. On February 6 the Philadelphia strike was settled. In New York the strike officially ended on February 15, although over 1000 workers were still on the picket lines. In some of the shops, workers had to settle for token change. One of these was the Triangle Waist Company where, a year after the strike, on March 25, 1911, a terrible fire would leave 146 women dead.

Despite its limitations, the "Uprising of the 20,000" left the majority of those who'd gone on strike with improved conditions, a shorter work week and better pay. In four months, Local 25 of the International Ladies' Garment Workers Union (ILGWU) had grown from 800 members to almost 10,000. The women involved had experimented seriously with worker solidarity and union organizing. They had successfully withheld cooperation from their exploitative, rich employers. Many had developed leadership skills. And everyone had gotten a taste of the power inherent in nonviolent collective action.

> In the black of the winter of nineteen nine,
> When we froze and bled on the picket line,
> We showed the world that women could fight
> And we rose and won with women's might.

Sources

London matchgirls' strike

Bermant, Chaim. *London's East End: Point of Arrival*. New York: Macmillan, 1975.

Besant, Annie. *An Autobiography*. London: T. Fisher Unwin, 1893/ 1920.

Dinnage, Rosemary. *Annie Besant*. New York: Viking Penguin, 1986.

Lewenhak, Sheila. *Women and Trade Unions: An Outline History of Women in the British Trade Union Movement*. New York: St. Martin's Press, 1977.

Morris, O. J. *Grandfather's London*. London: Godfrey Cave, 1956.

Uprising of the 20,000

"Arrest Strikers for Being Assaulted." *The New York Times*, Nov. 5, 1909.

Eisenstein, Sarah. *Give Us Bread But Give Us Roses: Working Women's Consciousness in the United States, 1890 to the First World War*. Boston: Routledge & Kegan Paul, 1983.

Foner, Philip S. *Women and the American Labor Movement: From Colonial Times to the Eve of World War I*. New York: Free Press/ Macmillan, 1979.

Howe, Irving, and Kenneth Libo. *How We Lived: A Documentary History of Immigrant Jews in America, 1880–1930*. New York: Richard Marek, 1979.

Jones, Mary. "This Is Not a Play, This Is a Fight!" from *Mother Jones Speaks: Collected Writings and Speeches*. Philip S. Foner, ed. New York: Monad Press, 1983.

Neidle, Cecyle S. *America's Immigrant Women*. New York: Hippocrene Books, 1975.

Schofield, Ann. "The Uprising of the 20,000: The Making of a Labor Legend" from *A Needle, A Bobbin, A Strike: Women Needleworkers in America*. Joan M. Jensen and Sue Davidson, eds. Philadelphia: Temple University Press, 1984.

Schulman, Sarah. "When We Were Very Young: A Walking Tour Through Radical Jewish Women's History On the Lower East Side 1879–1919" from *The Tribe of Dina: A Jewish Women's Anthology*. Melanie Kaye/Kantrowitz and Irena Klepfisz, eds. Montpelier, VT: Sinisters Wisdom Books, 1986.

Tax, Meredith. *The Rising of the Women: Feminist Solidarity and Class Conflict, 1880–1917*. New York: Monthly Review Press, 1980.

Wertheimer, Barbara Mayer. *We Were There: The Story of Working Women in America*. New York: Pantheon Books, 1977.

5
INJUSTICE, DEATH AND TAXES: WOMEN SAY NO!

THE WORLD JUST DIDN'T MAKE SENSE to thirty-two-year-old Hubertine Auclert. On the one hand she was considered a French citizen expected to obey the laws of her country and to pay property taxes. On the other hand, she was denied the citizen's right to vote simply because she was a woman. The male rulers couldn't have it both ways, Auclert decided. She began plotting a way to unhinge the system.

On election day in February 1880, Auclert and several other tax-paying women of Paris initiated the first stage of the action. They stomped past a line of startled men and presented themselves for voter registration. They demanded that they be recognized as full citizens of France with rights as well as responsibilities. They demanded an end to the injustice of taxation without representation. The men were amazed: there was nothing wrong with the system's inconsistencies as far as they were concerned! The women were turned away. It was time for stage two.

Taking advantage of the publicity the women had generated, Auclert called for a women's "tax strike." She reasoned that, since men alone had the privilege of governing the people and alloting national budgets, men alone should have the privilege of paying taxes.

"Since I have no right to control the use of my money," she wrote, "I no longer wish to give it. I do not wish to be an accomplice, by my acquiescence, in the vast exploitation that the masculine autocracy believes is its right to exercise in regard to women. I have no rights, therefore I have no obligations. I do not vote, I do not pay."

Auclert was an energetic organizer, activist and writer. In 1876, at age twenty-eight, she had helped found the Women's Rights Society, an organization so threatening to the government it was ordered to dissolve. The women disobeyed the order and met in secret until 1879 when the repressive atmosphere lifted a little and the group was allowed to exist openly. In the years immediately following the tax strike, Auclert founded a newspaper, the *Woman Citizen,* and a group, the Women's Suffrage Circle, as well as helped initiate petitions, demonstrations and boycotts.

"I have been a rebel against female oppression almost since birth," she wrote. She claimed her fighting spirit was inspired by the "brutality of man toward woman which terrified my childhood, prepared me at an early age to demand independence and consideration for my sex."

During the 1880 tax strike, Auclert was joined by twenty other women—eight widows and the rest, presumably, single women. When the authorities demanded payment, all but three of the women ended their participation in the strike. The remaining women continued to appeal the decision. But when law enforcement officers attempted to seize their furniture, Auclert and the others gave in. They decided they had done the best they could to call attention to the injustice.

Bitter and witty, especially when articulating the economic injustice of women's oppression, Auclert later wrote, "If people were paid to bring children into the world, I truly believe that men would find a way to monopolize the job."

AUCLERT WAS NOT THE FIRST WOMAN to organize against the taxation of women without government representation. Mid-nineteenth-century United States saw a number of women's rights tax resisters.

Lucy Stone, like Auclert, had been at odds with patriarchy for as long as she could remember. As a child with an eye for the practical, she had vowed to learn Hebrew and Greek someday in order to determine, first hand, if the Bible passages which seemed to grant men power over women indeed had been properly translated.

After graduating from Oberlin College in 1847, she had become a lecturer for William Lloyd Garrison's American Anti-Slavery Society. She baffled audiences by making connections between racism and sexism, speaking for women's rights as well as for the abolition of slavery. She had also supported the women's dress reform movement by wearing the controversial "Bloomer" outfit—a knee-length skirt and pantaloons.

When Lucy Stone and Henry Blackwell married in 1855, they used the occasion as an opportunity to challenge marriage laws. At their wedding ceremony, they signed and read aloud a statement protesting women's legal status and lack of property rights. The document read in part:

> While acknowledging our mutual affection by publicly assuming the relationship of husband and wife, yet in justice to ourselves and a great principle, we deem it a duty to declare that this act on our part implies no sanction of, nor promise of voluntary obedience to such of the present laws of marriage as refuse to recognize the wife as an independent, rational being, while they confer upon the husband an injurious and unnatural superiority, investing him with legal powers which no honorable man would exercise, and which no man should possess.

To emphasize further the idea that a wife was an "independent, rational being," Stone retained her own name after the ceremony. This horrified many people and confused others, but it also inspired some women to become "Lucy Stoners" and keep their birth names after marriage.

In 1858, shortly after they had moved to Orange, New Jersey, Lucy Stone decided to publicize the injustice of government taxation of women who, because they were denied the vote, were without representation. Twelve years earlier, in 1846, Henry David Thoreau had spent a night in jail for his refusal to pay the Massachusetts poll tax, an action he had taken in opposition to the US war with Mexico. Now Lucy Stone decided to use the same tactic to publicly draw attention to women's oppression as voteless taxpayers. When she refused to pay her taxes, the government held a public auction and sold a number of her household goods.

LYDIA SAYER HASBROUCK had become radicalized in 1849 when she was denied admission to Seward Seminary for wearing the practical new "Bloomer" costume. In 1856, after lecturing for feminism, dress reform and temperance, she edited *Sibyl*, a feminist "Review of the Tastes, Errors and Fashions of Society."

Like Lucy Stone, Hasbrouck's radicalism led her to become a tax resister, refusing to pay local taxes in protest against the denial of her right to vote. A tax collector, so the story goes, managed to steal one of Hasbrouck's Bloomer outfits from her house and advertise it for sale, the proceeds to go toward the taxes she owed.

ABBY KELLY FOSTER had always been an active worker and speaker for women's rights, but, in 1873, at the age of sixty-three, she was newly inspired. She had just heard about Julia and Abby Smith, two sisters in neighboring Connecticut, who were refusing to pay the taxes on their farm in order to protest the denial of suffrage to women. This was just the sort of nonviolent direct action that appealed to Abby. Her husband, Stephen, agreed. That year, they refused to pay their taxes on their beloved "Liberty Farm" in order to give voice to the urgency and justice of women's suffrage.

When they refused again in 1874, the city of Worcester, Massachusetts took action. The farm was seized and put up for auction to the highest bidder.

Letters of support for the Fosters' tax resistance poured in from the progressive leaders of the day. Boston abolitionist Wendell Phillips wrote, "Of course I need not tell either of you at this late day how much I appreciate this last chapter in lives full of heroic self sacrifice to conviction." Lucy Stone and Elizabeth Cady Stanton sent words of encouragement. William Lloyd Garrison, a pacifist abolitionist, wrote, "I hope there is not a man in your city or county or elsewhere who will meanly seek to make that property available to his own selfish ends. Let there be no buyer at any price."

Unfortunately, Osgood Plummer, a politically conservative neighbor, bid $100 for the farm, but he retreated when Stephen Foster chided him. Later, Plummer wrote a letter to the local newspaper explaining that he had only wanted to teach the Fosters a lesson about obeying the law.

With no other bidders, the deed to Liberty Farm reverted to the city. For the next few years, Abby and Stephen lived with the fear and uncertainty of losing the farm, but they continued their tax resistance until Stephen's ill health became an overriding concern. In 1880, the Fosters ended their protest and paid several thousand dollars to save the farm. The point had been made.

HALFWAY AROUND THE WORLD, in September 1878, Kusunose Kita, a forty-five-year-old woman from Shikoku, Japan, began to resent her situation. Since her husband's death six years earlier, she had been expected to assume her husband's property tax responsibilities but not been allowed to assume his political rights. She wrote an angry letter to government authorities.

> I do not have the right to vote. I do not have the right to act as guarantor. My rights, compared with those of male heads of households, are totally ignored. Most reprehensible of all, the only equality I share with men who are heads of their households is the onerous duty of paying taxes.

Her complaint was made public and picked up by the newspapers, and Kusunose Kita became an overnight celebrity throughout Japan. Ueki Emori, the male leader of Japan's popular-rights movement and a champion of women's rights, read Kusunose's letter and thereafter sought her input on ideas of equality for women. For a few years, Kusunose Kita was upheld as a symbol of Japanese women's ability and courage to speak for themselves. She became known as *Minken Baasan,* "Grandmother Popular Rights."

IN 1911, THE WOMEN'S TAX RESISTANCE LEAGUE of London published a little pamphlet entitled *Why We Resist Our Taxes.* Like their nineteenth-century sisters in France, the United States and Japan, the land-owning women of London recognized a raw deal when they saw one. They too were subject to taxes but deprived of the right of suffrage. "The government of this country which professes to be a representative one and to rest on the consent of the governed, is Constitutional in its relation to men, Unconstitutional in its relation to women," wrote Margaret Kineton Parkes, author of the pamphlet. Parkes did not mean all women, however. She hastened to reassure the reader that the tax resisters were not in the least radical but only fair-minded, concerned with votes only for women householders, certainly not for all women. The League, she claimed, was about passively resisting the unconstitutional government ruling England. Because they had been granted the municipal vote, women tax resisters were more than willing to pay local "rates," and they promised they'd have equal willingness to pay "imperial taxes" as soon as they were granted the parliamentary vote.

The London tax resisters devised a new way to reach beyond those already enlightened members of the public who attended suffrage meetings. They began making suffrage speeches at public auctions, a tactic that had unexpectedly good results. Many people were converted to the suffrage cause once they had the chance to hear the argument from the resisters themselves. The auctioneers not only permitted the women to make their speeches, but sometimes actively invited the speeches and even addressed the cause in their own words. One auctioneer who openly supported the tax-resisting suffragists ended his remarks by saying: "If I had to pay rates and taxes and had not a vote, I should consider it a great disgrace on the part of the Government, but I should consider it a far greater disgrace on *my* part if I did not protest against it."

Since the granting of suffrage, women's tax resistance has most often been undertaken to protest a government's military spending or its involvement in a specific war—such as the US war in Vietnam. For part of her life, Barbara Deming was a war tax resister. In her essay "On Revolution and Equilibrium," she explained the rationale for this form of nonviolent noncooperation.

> Words are not enough here. Gandhi's term for nonviolent action was "satyagraha"—which can be translated as "clinging to the truth. . . ." And one has to cling with one's entire weight. . . . One doesn't just say, "I don't believe in this war," but refuses to put on a uniform. One doesn't just say, "The use of napalm is atrocious," but refuses to pay for it by refusing to pay one's taxes.

Very few war tax resisters go to prison, even for a day. Those few that do are determined never to contribute a penny to the military budget. For others who avoid such harsh punishment, the point of resistance is to protest a specific war, or to make it as difficult as possible for military expenses to be taken for granted. Still, as we will see, the more extreme the war tax resistance, the more dramatic the story.

♀ AT 6:30 ONE JUNE MORNING in 1959, Juanita Nelson threw on the new white terry cloth bathrobe she'd recently ordered from the Sears-Roebuck catalog and answered her door. Two US marshalls informed her that they had an order for her arrest. What a way to start the day.

Juanita and her husband Wally, who was out of town that day, had not paid withholding taxes nor filed any forms for eleven years, so it was, in one sense, no big surprise that the government wanted to see her. "But even with the best intentions in the world of going to jail," she later wrote, "I would have been startled to be awakened at 6:30 a.m. to be told that I was under arrest."

She explained to the bright-eyed government men that she would be glad to tell the judge why she was resisting taxes if he'd care to come see her. Then she proceeded to explain why she would not willingly walk out of her door to appear in court.

> I am not paying taxes because the overwhelming percentage of the budget goes for war purposes. I do not wish to participate in any phase of the collection of such taxes. I do not even want to act as if I think that anyone, including the government, has a right to punish me for an act which I consider honorable. I cannot come with you.

The government men were not moved. They called for back-up assistance while Juanita considered her situation. Should she get dressed? Would getting dressed be a way of cooperating? Quickly she called a friend on the phone to let others know what was happening to her, and just as quickly she was surrounded by seven annoyed law enforcement officers. There was a brief exchange about her still being in her bathrobe, and one uncomfortable officer asked her whether or not she believed in God. She answered in the negative. ("He did not go on to explain the connection he had evidently been going to establish between God and dressing for arrest," Juanita later reported.) Suddenly, a gruff, no-nonsense officer said, "We'll just take her the way she is, if that's the way she wants it." He slapped some handcuffs on her and lifted her off the floor. In maneuvering her into the government car, he apparently tried his best to expose the nakedness under her bathrobe while another officer tried to cover her.

As the car carried her into the heart of Philadelphia, she tried to think. "My thoughts were like buckshot," she wrote of her experience, "so scattered they didn't hit anything or, when they did, made little dent. The robe was a huge question mark placed starkly after some vexing problems. Why am I going to jail? Why am I going to jail in a bathrobe?" The only thing she was sure of at that moment was that, until her head cleared, she would refuse to cooperate with her jailers. When the car stopped, she was yanked from the back seat, carried into the federal court building, dragged up a flight of stairs and thrown behind bars.

This was not the first time she had been locked up. She had once been sent to the Cincinnati County Jail on a charge of disorderly conduct after she, being black, had tried to gain admission to an amusement park which was for whites only. During that jail stay she had refused to eat, refused to walk where the guards told her to walk, refused to wear the prison uniform.

While she was remembering all this, several friends stopped by to visit her. (Her phone call had been a good idea.) The first visitors were two men, tax-refusing pacifists like herself. They thought it best, for the sake of appearances, to go to court in the proper clothes. They offered to get some clothes for her, and she agreed—just in case she decided she'd feel more at ease in them.

After the men left, a woman friend stopped by. "You look like a female Gandhi in that robe!" she said. "You look, well, dignified." Juanita grinned.

When they finally came for her, Juanita, still refusing to walk, was wheeled into the courtroom in her bathrobe. The clothes the men had brought were left behind in a brown paper bag. The judge gave her until Friday of that week to comply with the court order that she turn over her financial records or be subjected to a possible fine of $1000, a year in jail, or both. Juanita Nelson went home.

Friday came and went. Many Fridays came and went. The charges were dropped and she heard nothing more. Every now and then, the Internal Revenue Service sends her a bill or tries to confiscate a car, but so far the government has met a wall of nonviolent noncooperation. They should have known when they saw Juanita in her bathrobe: nothing will make her pay for war.

> Most people who take any notice of my position are appalled by my lawbreaking and not at all about the reasons for my not paying taxes. Instead of trying to make me justify my civil disobedience, why do they not question themselves and the government about a course of action which makes billions available for weapons, but cannot provide decent housing and education for a large segment of the population?

LIKE THE ASCETICS OF OLD, Eroseanna (Rose or Sis) Robinson was singularly unburdened by material possessions. She had no bank account, owned no real estate, and when the Internal Revenue Service (IRS) tried to seize her personal property, they found that all she had was an ironing board, a clock, a quilt and some clothes.

Robinson took seriously her membership in Peacemakers (an organization founded in 1948 to promote radical, nonviolent direct action). She had been a war tax resister since the early fifties, filing no statements of income and ignoring the various notices and certified letters sent by the IRS. In 1960, thirty-five years old, single and black, Robinson was a skilled artist and athlete; creative, too, in finding ways to live in the United States without paying for the US military. She tried to keep her earnings below the taxable level and for a period managed to spend less than $3 per week for food. She also arranged to earn a withholding-free income from several different work situations. Even with the little money she made, Robinson regularly sent sums greater than the taxes she owed to groups that worked for peace and social justice.

On January 26, 1960, federal marshalls descended on Robinson at a community center in Chicago and demanded she come with them. When she refused, they carried her bodily out of the center and to the district court where she was seated on a bench before a judge. She refused to accept the services of a lawyer and asked instead that they lay aside their roles as judge and defendant and speak to each other as two people with genuine concerns. When the judge agreed, Robinson talked. "I have not filed income taxes," she said, "because I know that a large part of the tax will be used for militarization. Much of the money is spent for atom and hydrogen bombs. These bombs have a deadly fallout that causes human destruction, as it has been proved. If I pay income tax, I am participating in that course. We have a duty to contribute constructively to life, and not destructively."

After making this statement, she was handcuffed, put in a wheelchair because she refused to walk, and taken to jail.

The next day she was wheeled into court again, where she encountered a different judge. This judge ridiculed her and her supporters who were standing in a vigil in front of the courthouse. He accused her of having an attitude of "contumacious criminal contempt." He committed her to jail until she would agree to file a tax return and show records of her earnings.

Not only would she not agree to file a tax return, she also would not agree to cooperate in any way with the prison system. She would not walk. She would not eat. She did agree to see one visitor one time—her friend Ernest Bromley, a radical pacifist and member of Peacemakers, who had come to see her in Cook County Jail. He wrote while she dictated a message for all her supporters on the outside:

> I see the military system and jail system as one thing. I don't want to give up my own will. I will not compromise by accepting a lawyer or by recognizing the judge as judge. I would rather that no one try to make an arrangement with the judge on my behalf. I ask nothing from the court or the jail. I do not want to pay for war. That is my main concern. Love to everyone.

On February 18, Robinson was again wheeled into court. It was clear that she would not compromise her principles to spare her own discomfort. The judge sentenced her to jail for a year and added an extra day for "criminal contempt."

On March 1, she was moved to the federal prison in Alderson, West Virginia. There she continued her fast, though prison officials began to force-feed her liquids through a tube inserted into her nose. She refused to cooperate in any way with her own imprisonment nor did she try to send letters through the system of prison censorship.

Ten members of Peacemakers, including long-time activist Marjorie Swann, set up their tents just beyond the gates at Alderson and issued a press release on May 14. They explained that they were there to show support for Robinson and that most of them intended to fast just as she was fasting. They invited anyone who wanted to talk to stop by the gate where they were camping. The pacifists propped up signs along the stretch of dusty road—"NO TAX FOR WAR," "PEACE IS THE ONLY DEFENSE," "THOU SHALT NOT KILL," and "ROSE WON'T PAY INCOME TAX."

After fasting for ninety-three days, Robinson was suddenly and unconditionally discharged from prison on May 20. The judge who ordered her release said Robinson had become a burden to the prison medical facilities, adding that he felt she had been punished sufficiently. He didn't mention the picketers camped outside.

When Robinson was released from prison late that Friday afternoon, the first thing she saw was a huge banner held high by her friends—"BRAVO ROSE!"

A NUMBER OF WOMEN have become war tax resisters in reaction to a specific war. Mary Bacon Mason, a Massachusetts music teacher, became a tax resister in 1946 after World War II. She told the government she would be willing to pay double her tax if it could be used only for aid to suffering people anywhere, but would accept prison or worse rather than pay for war. The only possible defense, she said, is friendship and mutual help. Of World War II she said:

> I paid a share in that cost and I am guilty of burning people alive in Germany and Japan. I ask humanity's forgiveness.

IN 1948, CAROLINE URIE of Yellow Springs, Ohio, bedridden and elderly, gained national attention and inspired many people to consider war tax resistance when she withheld 34.6 percent of her tax. She sent an equivalent amount as a donation to four peace organizations and wrote an open letter to President Truman and the IRS:

> Now that the atomic bomb has reduced to a final criminal absurdity the whole war system, leading quite possibly to the liquidation of human society, and has involved the United States in the shame and guilt of having been the first to exploit its criminal possibilities, I have come to the conclusion that—as a Christian, Quaker, religious and conscientious objector to the whole institution of organized war—I must henceforth refuse to contribute to it in any way I can avoid.

EIGHTEEN YEARS LATER, and in response to a new war, another woman from Yellow Springs, Ohio, Doris E. Sargent, wrote to the *Peacemakers* newsletter with a new war tax resistance tactic. She noted that the government had reintroduced a federal tax attached to telephone bills. The money was earmarked specifically

for US military expenses. Sargent proposed a radical response—
that all those who demanded an end to the fighting in Vietnam
ask the phone company to remove their phones in protest. If
everyone who opposed the war were willing to make such an
extreme sacrifice, real pressure could be put on the government.
Then Sargent suggested a less extreme idea—that people keep
their phones and pay their bills but refuse to pay the federal tax.
Phone tax resisters could send a note with their bills each month,
stating that the protest was not directed at the phone company but
at the government which was using the phone tax to support war.
The idea caught hold, and phone tax resistance became a popular
way to protest the war in Vietnam. It is still used today as a form
of war tax resistance.

The war in Vietnam turned many people into war tax resisters.
Pacifist folksinger Joan Baez set an example as a tax resister early
in the war years by withholding 60 percent of her income tax. She
was instrumental in persuading countless others to follow her
example. In April 1965, she explained:

> We talk about democracy and Christianity—and we try out
> a new fire-bomb. We talk about peace and we move
> thousands more men and weapons into Vietnam. This
> country has gone mad. But I will not go mad with it. I will
> not pay for organized murder. I will not pay for the war in
> Vietnam.

IN 1972, LIFE-LONG QUAKER MEG BOWMAN wrote a letter to
the IRS to explain why she had decided once again not to pay her
federal income tax.

> "Do you carefully maintain our testimony against all
> preparations for war and against participation in war as
> inconsistent with the teachings of Christ?" Query,
> *Discipline* of Pacific Yearly Meeting, Religious Society of
> Friends (Quakers).

> The above quotation is from the book that is intended to
> give guidance to members for daily living. The book
> repeatedly stresses peace and individual responsibility.

> It is clear to me that I am not only responsible for my
> voluntary actions, but also for that which is purchased with
> my income. If my income is spent for something immoral

or if I allow others to buy guns with money I have earned, this is as wrong and offending to "that of God in every man" as if I had used that gun, or planned that bomb strike.

When I worked a five-day week it seemed to me that one-fifth of my income went to taxes. This would be equivalent to working one full day each week for the U.S. government. It seemed I worked as follows:

—*Monday for food.* I felt responsible to buy wholesome, nourishing items that would provide health and energy, but not too much meat or other luxuries, the world supply of which is limited.
—*Tuesday for shelter.* We maintain a comfortable, simply furnished home where we may live in dignity and share with others.
—*Wednesday for clothing,* health needs and other essentials and for recreation, all carefully chosen.
—*Thursday for support of causes.* I select with care those organizations which seem to be acting in such a way that responsibility to God and my brother is well served.
—*Friday for death,* bombs, napalm, for My Lai and overkill. I am asked to support a government whose main business is war.

Though the above is oversimplified, the point is clear. I cannot work four days a week for life and joy and sharing, and one day for death. I cannot pay federal taxes. I believe this decision is protected by law as a First Amendment right of freedom of religion. If I am wrong it is still better to have erred on the side of peace and humanity.

Sincerely,
Meg Bowman

"THE ONLY THING OF WHICH I'M GUILTY is financially supporting the war in Southeast Asia against my better judgment until the year 1970," said Martha Tranquilli when she was charged with the criminal offense of providing false information on her income tax forms.

At 7:30 a.m. on July 19, 1974, Tranquilli stood on the steps of the state capitol building in Sacramento, California and addressed the 100 supporters who had gathered. After a short Unitarian service held on her behalf, the aging white woman with a long gray braid told them in her calm, soft voice that she envisioned the day when scientists and workers would join in refusing to pay war taxes or do war work.

> I was very much afraid of going to prison, but I think I have overcome that fear. I plan to read, write letters and meditate as much as possible. I'm going to try my best to make an adventure out of this thing.

One after another, friends and strangers attending the rally came up to embrace Tranquilli and offer words of encouragement. After some spirited singing, they accompanied her to the federal building where she turned herself in to the federal marshalls.

Hers was a media image made to order. "63-Year-Old Tax-Resisting Grandma Goes to Jail" shouted the headlines, and the war tax resistance movement didn't mind the national publicity Martha Tranquilli generated.

Tranquilli was opposed to the Vietnam War and all the suffering the war was inflicting on the people of Vietnam, the people of the United States, and on the earth itself. She had therefore decided to withhold the 61 percent of her 1970 and 1971 income taxes (amounting to approximately $1,100) which she believed would go to pay for the war.

Her anti-war activities dated back to World War II and the bombing of Hiroshima. "I was very much opposed to what Hitler was doing, but when we dropped the bomb, it exploded something in me," she told a reporter for the *Palo Alto Times*.

In 1964, Tranquilli's son Vincent went to Mississippi to work with the Student Nonviolent Coordinating Committee. When he told Martha that they needed nurses, she moved to the town of Mound Bayou to work as a supervising nurse in the local hospital.

It was in Mound Bayou, Mississippi that Martha was tried and sentenced for tax fraud in May 1973. Like other war tax resisters, Tranquilli withheld her taxes by listing unusual dependents. Tranquilli listed seven peace organizations as dependents, including War Resisters League, the Women's International League for Peace and Freedom, the American Civil Liberties Union and the American Friends Service Committee. (Another war tax resister in the 1970s claimed 3 billion dependents, explaining to the IRS that he felt the population of the earth depended on him and on others to refuse to pay war taxes. That case went to court and the tax resister was acquitted by a court of appeals of the charge of willfully filing a false and fraudulent W-4 form.)

Tranquilli was found guilty of tax fraud, but the judge was reluctant to send her to jail and indicated he'd give her a suspended sentence if she would only apologize and promise not to do it again. When Tranquilli refused this offer she was sentenced to nine months in prison and two years probation. The Mississippi Civil Liberties Union helped her appeal the case and, while the appeal was pending, she moved to California. Both the Court of Appeals and the US Supreme Court refused to hear her case.

On July 19, 1974, after making national headlines and being cheered on by supporters, Tranquilli began her stay at Terminal Island Prison in San Pedro, California. She quickly got involved in the life of the prison community, writing for the prison paper and serving on the prison council. She also took a course in theater arts.

In letters to friends, she wrote about what she was learning from her prison experience:

> In my opinion everyone should spend a few weeks in a place like this for its education value. We would soon use our ingenuity to devise a more constructive way to handle these social problems.

> The College of Crime is graduating me March 3rd. I have learned much—how to ripoff Welfare departments, the food stamp agency, a bank and very colorful language to use when caught.

After her release, Tranquilli wrote to a friend: "Be sure to say that I did not suffer in prison. It was a learning experience." Tranquilli continued her tax resistance as well as her work for peace and justice until her death in 1981.

> So long as my government acts immorally and illegally in my name, I will call it to account for those acts as I would any child of mine who has violated moral codes or legally constituted laws.

FOR MASON AND URIE it was the Second World War. For Baez, Bowman and Tranquilli it was the war in Vietnam. Today it is the US-backed war against Nicaragua that motivates many new war tax resisters. In 1987 in Brooklyn, New York, tax resister

Donna Mehle wrote an open letter to the IRS which was published in the local newspaper. She cited a religious basis for her tax resistance, protesting the war against Nicaragua.

> The decision to come into conflict with the laws of my country is very difficult, but it is a decision rooted in my Christian faith. As a Christian, I am called to affirm life and reject violence. . . . My commitment to tax resistance deepened in the past year when I travelled to Nicaragua. There I saw first hand the effect of my tax dollars ($100 million in Contra Aid 1986/87). I vowed to myself and to the Nicaraguan people I met that I would not be complicit in the U.S. backed Contra war, a war which targets innocent civilians and children.

Mehle informed the IRS that she intended to redirect the money she would have owed in taxes to an alternative fund "which supports life-affirming projects in New York City."

In the 1980s, some women in the United States proposed a specifically feminist perspective on war tax resistance. In New York City, the Women's Tax Resistance Assistance distributed a brochure which read in part:

> We can't keep working for disarmament, for women's rights, including an end to lesbian oppression, and for racial equality while paying for a male-dominated government which impoverishes and exploits us now and threatens to eliminate the world's future.

On tax day, April 15, 1985, this group performed street theater on the steps of Federal Hall. Some of the women dressed up as pieces of the federal budget "pie" while others, dressed as waitresses, explained the military menu to passersby and handed out leaflets.

IN CANADA IN 1982, sixty-eight-year-old Edith Adamson made headlines with her tax resistance. A lifelong pacifist and the coordinator of the Peace Tax Fund Committee of Canada, Adamson was one of approximately sixty Canadians who hoped to prevent the government from using their money to make war. Not that Adamson and the others wanted to keep the money for their own use: they wanted to redirect their dollars into a peace tax fund. With the adoption of the new Charter of Rights in the Canadian Constitution, there was a guarantee of freedom of conscience. "This means," Adamson explained for news reporters, "that the government should provide a legal alternative to war taxes for those who object to killing on religious or ethical grounds." Since the spring of 1982, Canadian war tax resisters— who call themselves "Peace Trusters" because they trust in peace, not war—have petitioned their government to develop a peace tax fund which would allow citizens the option of directing their money away from the military budget. They asked for a simple tax form which would allow taxpayers to check whether they want a portion of their taxes to go for warmaking or peacemaking.

In 1982, Edith Adamson explained her involvement:

> In a nuclear war, you wouldn't have a chance to be a conscientious objector. And, being an old lady, I wouldn't be drafted, so it seemed the peace tax fund idea was a sound way to get at the root of the problem.

> I not only want to exempt myself from the killing, but I want to try to influence the government to look at this problem— and other people as well to examine their consciences. A nuclear war would involve everybody and mean total destruction and I couldn't just hide under my little exemption and stay alive.

> This peace tax would be an extension of conscientious objector status for the military. It's more appropriate today because war now depends more on money than on personnel; it only took twelve men to drop the bomb over Hiroshima, but it took millions, perhaps billions of taxpayers' dollars in Canada, Britain and the United States to develop that bomb.

By 1987 there were approximately 440 Peace Trusters in Canada who were withholding a portion of their taxes and putting that money into a peace tax fund. They had agreed to waive the interest on this money in order to pay the court fees involved in taking on a test case to establish the legality of the peace tax fund. The claimant Jerilynn Prior, a physician and Quaker originally from the United States where she was also a tax resister, now lives in British Columbia. In a January 1987 press release, Prior said that paying for war violates her freedom of conscience and religion.

> This deep conviction rises from my commitment to work for peace. I try to live my life that way—as a mother, a physician, a teacher, a woman, a citizen of this world

community. It would be hypocrisy to voluntarily allow my tax contribution to be used for war or the military or pamphlets about bomb shelters. . . .

Each of us can work for peace in our own life, with our own resources, and in our own way. This tax appeal is the way I must work for peace.

Sources

Hubertine Auclert

Bidelman, Patrick Kay. *Pariahs Stand Up! The Founding of the Liberal Feminist Movement in France, 1858–1889*. Westport, CT: Greenwood Press, 1982.

Lucy Stone, Lydia Sayer Hasbrouck and Abby Kelly Foster

McHenry, Robert, ed. *Famous American Women: A Biographical Dictionary from Colonial Times to the Present*. New York: Dover, 1980.

Stone, Lucy. "Marriage of Lucy Stone Under Protest" from *Feminism: The Essential Historical Writings*, Miriam Schneir, ed. New York: Vintage Books/Random House, 1972.

Whitman, Alden, ed. *American Reformers: An H. W. Wilson Biographical Dictionary*. New York: H. W. Wilson, 1985.

Bacon, Margaret Hope. *I Speak for My Slave Sister: The Life of Abby Kelley Foster*. New York: Thomas Y. Crowell, 1974.

Kusunose Kita

Sievers, Sharon L. *Flowers In Salt: The Beginnings of Feminist Consciousness in Modern Japan*. Stanford, CA: Stanford University Press, 1983.

London Women's Tax Resistance League

Parkes, Margaret Kineton. *Why We Resist Our Taxes*. London: Women's Tax Resistance League, 1911.

Juanita Nelson, Eroseanna Robinson and Martha Tranquilli

Bromley, Ernest R. "Visit With Sis Robinson—'I Will Not Compromise.'" *The Peacemaker*, Feb. 1960.

Cole, Molly. "Ain't Gonna Pay for War No More." *Ms.*, Vol. 3, No. 6 (Dec. 1974).

Hedemann, Ed, ed. *War Resisters League Guide to War Tax Resistance*. New York: War Resisters League, 1983.

Nelson, Juanita. "A Matter of Freedom" from *Seeds of Liberation*. Paul Goodman, ed. New York: George Braziller, 1964.

"Too Much Trouble: Prison to Free Hunger Striker." *Beckley Post-Herald* (WV), May 20, 1960. Reprinted in *The Peacemaker*, June, 1960.

"We at the Gate to Alderson Prison Speak." *The Alderson Times* (WV), May 19, 1960. Reprinted in *The Peacemaker*, June 1960.

Edith Adamson and Jerilynn Prior

Adamson, Edith. *For Conscience Sake*. 2nd ed. Victoria, BC: Conscience Canada, 1985.

Conscientious Objection to Paying for War: Tax Court Appeal Denied to Dr. Jerilynn C. Prior (pamphlet). Burnaby, BC: Society for Charter Clarification, 1987.

Kelk, Doug. "Digging at the Root of the Nuclear Problem." *Times-Colonist*, Aug. 1–3, 1982.

Leddy, Mary Jo. "The Grandmother Is a Tax Resister." *Catholic New Times*, Feb. 27, 1983.

Stieren, Carl. "Peace Trusters Refuse Taxes for Arms." *Quaker Concern: Canadian Friends Service Committee*, Vol. 9, No. 3 (1983).

Other

Bowman, Meg. "Letter to the IRS" from *Reweaving the Web of Life: Feminism and Nonviolence*. Pam McAllister, ed. Philadelphia: New Society, 1982.

Handbook on Nonpayment of War Taxes: 1971 Edition. Cincinnati, OH: The Peacemaker, 1971.

Mehle, Donna. "Letter to the Editor." *The Phoenix* (Brooklyn, NY), May 7, 1987.

"National Tax Day Highlights." *National War Tax Resistance Coordinating Committee Newsletter*. East Patchogue, NY, April 8, 1985.

Sargent, Doris. "Letter to the Editor." *The Peacemaker*, vol. 19, no. 5 (April 2, 1966).

Women's Tax Resistance Assistance (brochure), 339 Lafayette, NY, NY 10012.

6
PAINT BRUSHES IN THE NIGHT

Graffiti: "A popular feminist sport."—Sona Osman,
Spare Rib

ONE MORNING IN 1980 the people of Belo Horizonte, Brazil awoke to find that the streets of their city had been transformed overnight. They opened their doors and stared in amazement. The whole city was blanketed with graffiti. Big block letters screamed from the flat surfaces—"HE WHO LOVES DOES NOT KILL!" "DOWN WITH THE FARCE OF HONOR!" "HOW MANY MORE CORPSES UNTIL WOMEN'S OPPRESSION IS ACKNOWLEDGED?"

Feminists in Brazil had had enough of the country's "defense of honor" plea that legally excused a man for killing his wife or girlfriend if he suspected her of infidelity. With this convenient legal loophole, men in Brazil were literally getting away with murder. Just the previous year, a wealthy playboy, Doca Street, had been acquitted of murdering Angela Diniz, his live-in companion, on the "defense of honor" plea. The graffiti campaign in Belo Horizonte, the capital of Brazil's most traditionally oriented state, sent shock waves through the nation and inspired Brazilian feminists in other states to rally against the legal system's handling of what are popularly called "crimes of passion." Women began counting: in 1980, feminists reported 772 cases of women murdered by their husbands or boyfriends in São Paulo alone. They took to the streets in massive demonstrations and sought public forums on the radio and television to denounce the *em defesa da honra* which exonerated killers and vilified victims.

The feminist campaign did have an effect and it seemed that some legal assumptions were reconsidered. On November 6, 1981, women celebrated when Doca Street's acquittal was reversed and he was finally convicted of murder. But changing ingrained assumptions is never that easy. Two years later in May 1983, feminists again demonstrated in Belo Horizonte, in protest of a man who'd been permitted to plead "defense of honor" after he'd killed his wife. The same week that this man was given a two-year suspended sentence, a woman in Brasilia was sentenced to fourteen years in prison for a similar crime.

> "If your back is up against the wall, turn around and write on it."—graffiti

GRAFFITI AS A TOOL for nonviolent protest and persuasion has been used effectively to promote a variety of concerns. While multinational corporations buy up the public billboard spaces to advertise their products and their way of life, graffiti is a way for those without access to power to have a say. Even people who do not own a newspaper, radio station or television network can carry a felt-tip marker.

London-based photographer Jill Posener has edited two books of political graffiti images gleaned from the British and Australian landscapes. In her introduction to *Louder Than Words*, she praised the work of the graffiti artists (graffitists) who are "redecorating and retaking the patriarchal streets." She wrote, "For me, all the paint, all the slogans, remind me that we are fighting back. . . . Many of us now carry our spray cans along with our front door keys and diaries."

Throughout the book, Posener has included quotes by the graffiti-activists themselves. One Melbourne graffitist quoted in Posener's book explained "The streets are public places. Graffiti is an expression of the experiences and ideas of people who live on those streets but don't own them or the houses or the businesses."

A photograph of one London billboard transformed by graffiti was widely reproduced in the feminist media. It was an advertisement for a Fiat. The original billboard depicted a compact car and giant block letters saying, "IF IT WERE A LADY, IT WOULD GET ITS BOTTOM PINCHED," beneath which two women had spray-painted, "IF THIS LADY WAS A CAR SHE'D RUN YOU DOWN." Posener found one of the witty women responsible and published her account in *Spray It Loud*.

> This ad was opposite my place of work. I had to stare at it
> out of the window. A colleague and I went out and added
> the graffiti. . . . It was a way of taking over the poster. You
> have to have a lot of money to afford billboards like that.
> We wanted to reclaim the open spaces that have been
> colonised by advertisers. By writing angry but humorous
> graffiti, we were also making the point that ad agencies
> don't have the monopoly on wit.

Graffiti has been used extensively to protest violence against
women. On the eve of International Women's Day, 1979, the
"Women Warriors" in the small city of Olympia, Washington
plastered the city's stop signs with stickers. The stickers bore the
word "RAPE" so that each traffic sign read "STOP RAPE!"

In Northampton, Massachusetts, feminists spray-painted giant
red X's and the words "A WOMAN WAS RAPED HERE" in eight
sites around the city. Then they sent an anonymous letter to the
Daily Hampshire Gazette explaining that they hoped the graffiti
would be "a daily reminder of how close rape is to all of us—it
happens on our street corners, in parking lots, in the center of
town, in schoolyards. . . . We urge other women to begin to take
action against rape and rapists: to speak of our experiences, to
confront and to name rapists. . . ."

When anti-pornography activist Dorchen Leidholdt was
arrested, handcuffed and booked in a New York City subway for
defacing a poster, she used her trial as an opportunity to make a
political statement about pornography and claimed that her
vandalism was an act of self-defense. When the judge asked her
how she pleaded, she said "Not guilty" and began to read her
statement in a loud voice:

> I did write "DEGRADES WOMEN AND PROMOTES RAPE" on
> a poster advertising *Penthouse* in a subway station. But I
> wrote this message not as an act of vandalism but to defend
> myself against the psychological and physical danger
> *Penthouse* poses to women.
>
> The posters advertising *Penthouse* depict women as
> sexual objects and targets. They carry sometimes
> subliminal, sometimes overt messages of violence. They
> frighten, intimidate, and humiliate women subway riders.
> By writing on the poster I was defending myself against
> sexual harassment.

> I was also defending myself against sexual violence.
> *Penthouse* actively promotes the abuse, rape, and murder
> of women. The issue advertised by the poster I wrote on
> contains a story celebrating the gang rape of a college
> woman in a fraternity house—frighteningly similar to real
> gang rapes that have been carried out in fraternity houses
> around the country. The issue also features a photo essay
> celebrating the bondage, rape, and death of a woman and
> a cartoon that pokes fun at the rape and murder of a
> woman.

> By using the subway system as a vehicle to promote
> *Penthouse* with its message of violence against women,
> the MTA is jeopardizing the psychological and physical
> safety of women. As a woman who is dependent on the
> subway system, I feel that I had no choice but to attempt
> to defend myself against *Penthouse*'s dangerous
> propaganda.

The judge declined to look at the issue of the magazine Leidholdt
offered and then dismissed the charges against her.

Graffitists often develop carefully orchestrated strategies for
executing their illegal actions. One eye-witness to such an action
described the strategy used by a group of women during the 1985
"Take Back the Night" march (a march protesting violence against
women) in Vancouver, British Columbia.

> Because I was acting as a safety woman on the march
> that night I had a sharp eye on the movement of the crowd.
> I spotted a group of women walking with the rhythm of the
> march then suddenly form themselves into a circle, link
> arms and stop. Half the women in the circle quickly turned
> to face the oncoming march. I could see them smiling
> broadly and speaking to approaching women. It was clear
> to those of us around that they had a little activity planned!
> Their voices and their faces alerted women to their
> presence, prevented women from being startled and
> stumbling, and encouraged women to veer slightly to the
> right and the left of them but to keep on the march. Several
> women were crouched on the pavement inside the circle
> and were stencilling furiously. They were protected from
> the view of the police and from the crowd stumbling over
> them by the women encircling them. As the end of the
> march came into view they seemed to all be standing,
> facing in the direction of the march and, completely in step

with the pace of the moving crowd of women, folded back
in among us.

Here and there along the march route the next day one could find
a little Day-Glo labyris (a two-edged sword, ancient symbol of
goddess worship) and the words "lesbians fight back!"

Women have used graffiti to counteract the well-financed anti-
choice campaigns of religious and secular institutions. Feminists
in Ireland spray-painted a papal cross in a Dublin park with the
words "IF MEN GOT PREGNANT, CONTRACEPTION AND
ABORTION WOULD BE SACRAMENTS."

And in *Louder Than Words,* Posener included a quote by a
graffitist from Melbourne, Australia who wrote:

> I started doing graffiti as an alternative to blowing things
> up. About a year ago I began to wonder what could be
> done about the Pregnancy Problem Action Centre, a Right
> to Life front, which tells young women terrifying lies about
> abortion. . . . Without their financial power and access to
> the media, graffiti seemed like an appropriate way to shriek
> defiance at them.

FEMINISTS IN MADISON, WISCONSIN got on the phone and
spoke in code. "We're having a decorating party. Can you come?"
"Sure. I'll be there!"

The "decorating parties" were well-organized clandestine
graffiti-actions coordinated by the Madison Billboard Brigade in
September and October 1979. The impromptu group of over 100
women and a handful of men had quickly formed to counteract a
$10,000 anti-abortion billboard blitz paid for by well-heeled
members of the Wisconsin Citizens Concerned for Life. Twenty-
five huge anti-choice billboards towered over motorists and
pedestrians along all the main streets and at each entrance to the
capital city where the state legislature was debating an anti-choice
amendment.

The Billboard Brigade didn't have $10,000, but it did have a
100-member graffiti force which quickly organized itself into
affinity groups (action teams) of four to five people each. Over
the course of five weeks, the Madison Billboard Brigade managed
to deface fifteen out of the twenty-five billboards at least once a
week. No sooner would the billboard company replace the signs

than another night-action would render them ruined. Eventually, it gave up replacing many of the signs altogether.

The actions took place on a different night and at different hours each week, but always in the wee hours of the morning when bars had closed and police were busy drinking coffee. The teams moved out silently into the night from a central meeting place and returned for coffee and cookies and to make future plans after each action.

Each affinity group was responsible for deciding how it would deface the billboard it was assigned and for bringing its own supplies. Through trial and error—experiments with paint rollers, balloons and baggies filled with paint—word soon spread that tempera paint in paper cups with lids worked best to deface the giant billboards.

In a grand finale, the Brigade sponsored a rally and open civil disobedience action. Three hundred local activists marched from the capitol building to a billboard near the University of Wisconsin where everyone who wanted to get in on the action was given a styrofoam cup filled with tempera paint and invited to throw it. No one was arrested.

As with the Madison Billboard Campaign, organized groups sometimes form specifically to use graffiti for the free exchange of ideas in the modern landscape of diminishing social space. Not surprisingly, the names of these groups are sometimes as original and witty as the graffiti they leave behind—BUGA UP (Billboard Utilising Graffitists Against Unhealthy Promotions), COUGH UP (Citizens' Organisation Using Graffiti to Halt Unhealthy Promotions), COUGH IN (Campaign On Use of Graffiti for Health in Neighborhoods) and FANG (Feminist Anti-Nuclear Graffiti).

Some graffiti activists concentrate on altering billboards which promote products that hurt people such as cigarettes and alcohol, or products that cause pain and death to other species such as fur coats.

Graffiti has also been used to protest war-making, though no one has yet taken up Yoko Ono on her suggestion that "If people want to make war they should make a color war and paint each other's cities up in the night in pinks and greens."

IN 1984, EIGHT WOMEN who had met and worked together in support of the Greenham Common peace camp decided something had to be done about London's Whitehall Theatre of War—

"Dedicated to the Fighting People of All Nations from World War Two." The theater marquee featured a tank breaking through a brick wall, life-sized figures of men with guns in a variety of military uniforms and a painted background sky filled with fighter planes. On the day of their action, the eight women walked along Whitehall carrying a long ladder. They propped it up against the theater and climbed onto the building.

> Originally the idea was to dismantle the display; we hadn't thought of painting the slogans. But when we climbed up, there was a pot of black gloss and a brush just lying there. Seemed a shame to waste it.

While several women began to pull the display apart, others wrote in large letters, "REMEMBER HIROSHIMA! DON'T GLORIFY WAR! NO MORE WAR."

> We threw ticker tape with women's symbols on it and shouted to let passersby know what we were doing and why. The painting really was an afterthought. Funny really. Lots of tourists smiled, especially Japanese. They were pleased to see our action.

The police arrived after only ten minutes and the women were arrested and later convicted of criminal damage. They were fined £290 each and given conditional discharges.

In Leeds, England, women from a Greenham support group "decorated" statues that glorified war, transforming them into anti–cruise missile tableaus. In West Germany, where graffitists write slogans like "MAKE LOVE, NOT WALLS," feminists have protested the lack of statues devoted to women by dressing male statues in women's clothes and draping them with signs that say "REMEMBER WOMEN."

AROUND THE WORLD, women have joined men in participating in a global graffiti campaign called the "International Shadow Project." The campaign has been conducted several times since it began in 1982 with anti-war activists participating in Brazil, Canada, Hungary, New Zealand, Nigeria, the United States and Western Europe. On the August anniversary of the Hiroshima bombing, people toting paint rollers slip silently into the night streets of their respective cities to stencil ghostly shapes of people and animals, leaving thousands and thousands of shadows splashed across the face of the earth. The milky white silhouettes are left on the streets and sidewalks in remembrance of those who were turned instantly to shadow in Hiroshima and Nagasaki and in warning to the living that all life could disappear in a modern nuclear war.

"This is our blood. Do not be afraid of it."

♀ IN ADDITION TO USING PAINT and ink, women have used blood to make necessary statements. In Seattle on June 13, 1978, BettyJohanna and Jane Meyerding entered the office of Save Our Moral Ethics (SOME), the group sponsoring an initiative which would have removed equal protection for lesbians and gay men from the Seattle civil rights ordinance. Betty and Jane disrupted the office by pouring blood (their own mixed with the blood of their friends) on SOME's petitions and financial records. "Our action was part of our ongoing experiment in integrating radical feminism and radical pacifism," Jane explained. "SOME's existence and purpose, we believe, were very much connected with other aspects of increasing repression against poor people, womyn, people of color, etc." At their trial, Betty and Jane submitted as their statement a copy of the "open letter to the staff, volunteers, and supporters of SOME" they had written to leave in the SOME office. That letter began:

WE CANNOT LIVE WITHOUT OUR LIVES

This is our blood. Do not be afraid of it, but know what it is. As the vital fluid of life, blood is symbolic of the precious human-ness we share with you and with all people. All of us desire to live our lives freely, to live securely, and to feel at home as contributing members of the human community. Throughout recorded history, the sharing or sacrificing of one's blood has been seen as the truest expression of human-ness.

We have brought our blood here to you today for three reasons:
—to share our lives, our human-ness, with you in the clearest, strongest way we can;
—to challenge your human-ness by showing you that the work you do here imperils our lives and our human-ness; and

> –to disrupt with our lives, with our blood and our human-
> ness, the anti-life Initiative 13 campaign
>
> We are lesbians. We are the people whose lives you want
> to take away and replace with lives which you have chosen
> for us. With our blood, we are telling you today that we
> cannot live without our lives. We want to be sure you know
> what *you* are doing here. You are trying to take our lives.

The statement ended with the words, "As long as you are working
against us. . . we must continue to work—not against *you* —but
against the work you do. We cannot live without our lives, and
we choose to live—WE CHOOSE TO LIVE OUR LIVES."

Through the hard work of Betty and Jane and many other people,
the initiative was soundly defeated. Betty and Jane were sent to
jail, but this only inspired in them new energy. Those eighteen
days behind bars, Jane wrote, "totally changed the next few years
of our lives because of our continuing involvements with the lives
and struggles of the other womyn we met there."

TO CALL THE HARTFORD, CONNECTICUT store Bare Facts a
"lingerie shop" seemed like bad fiction to some of the feminists
in town. Chains, whips, dildos tipped with metal spikes and
paperback books with titles like *Whippings for a Wicked Wife,
Incest Victims Ravaged by Parents* and *Trucker's Little Girl* were
more the stuff of torture (specifically, the torture of women and
girls) than lingerie.

A few nights before Valentine's Day, 1980, Linda Hand, Jane
Quinn and Shell Wildwomoon entered the store and emptied
containers of their own blood on the female mannequins, on the
store license, and on books and films inside the store's "Fantasy
Room." Outside the store, women supporting the action picketed
with signs which said, "THIS IS THE BLOOD OF RAPED AND
BATTERED WOMEN."

When the police arrived, the three women sat on the floor and
read a prepared statement explaining their action and stating their
demand that "the promotion of violence against women be stopped
immediately." Their protest was just beginning.

They were arrested and booked. When bail was set at $1500,
the three women refused to pay it. Instead, they issued a statement
about the class bias inherent in the bail system which discriminates

against poor people. They were subsequently sent to jail for eight days. Shell refused the vaginal exam which was required by the prison on the pretense of checking for venereal disease. She told the prison nurse that the penetration used in the exam, if it was done against a woman's will, was rape, and she further explained that venereal disease is virtually nonexistent among lesbians whose lovers don't have intercourse with men. Shell was carted off to segregation (solitary confinement). All three women went on a hunger strike during their imprisonment.

When they were again brought before the judge, they entered a plea of "self-defense for the lives of women and children," at which the judge threatened to lock them up again. They changed their plea to "not guilty" and chose to have a jury trial and to defend themselves. The judge assigned them stand-by counsel, but the women gave this lawyer orders to "remain silent in court and pretend that he no longer existed."

In the months before their trial, the women received letters of support from other women around the country who had done similar actions. Some of the letters contained helpful advice about organizing community support. The women also found law students and professors from the University of Connecticut Criminal Clinic who replaced the court appointed stand-by counsel and helped the women prepare for their trial.

Feminists in the late twentieth century have engaged in heated debate about pornography. While everyone is concerned with the very real issues of violence against women, not everyone is convinced of the role pornography plays in causing or perpetuating the climate of violence. And even the feminists who are convinced that pornography is a vital tool in the oppression of women are hesitant to do anything which would align them with proponents of censorship or sexual repression. Shell Wildwomoon later wrote an article in which she addressed some of these concerns. In it she said:

> The three of us have been committed to nonviolent actions against all forms of violence against life. Since we are womyn, we needed to act against the violence we face every day in a sexist society. We carefully chose to damage property rather than inflict violence on those that use the weapons. . . .

We would not use legal means for fighting back. The obscenity laws which apply to this case are routinely used against lesbians and gay men. . . . We do not seek to create or apply laws that censure any freedom of speech. We demand personal accountability for the end results of the products one makes, sells or profits from.

The act of pouring human blood, representing the blood of battered, raped and murdered womyn and children, was an attempt to make this statement: "This man's business leads to womyn and children bleeding. The blood was already there; we made it visible."

The women used every aspect of their court appearance to generate discussion about violence against women and about the part pornographic images might play in that violence. At the trial the women represented themselves. They asked the store owner, "Isn't it true that the only purpose of a metal-spiked dildo is to rip apart a woman's vagina?" to which he answered, "I have no idea."

Each woman also testified about the experiences that had led her to pour her blood on the store materials. Shell Wildwomoon used the opportunity to tell the jury about her experience of being raped. The rapist, she said, had used pornography during the rape. Linda Hand, a health care worker, talked about the rape survivors she had seen and spoke briefly about the tradition of nonviolent civil disobedience. Jane Quinn testified about her work with battered women in a Hartford shelter.

The women also called two outside witnesses to testify. Andrea Dworkin had documented cross-cultural varieties of violence against women (pornography, foot-binding, the mass murder of women as witches) in her first book, *Woman Hating* (New York: Dutton, 1974). She explained terms such as soft- and hard-core pornography and bondage. The other outside witness was a young woman who testified that her Yale-educated father had used bondage magazines as a guide to repeatedly rape her throughout her early childhood and adolescence.

When it was all said and done, the three women were acquitted, the town of Hartford had a new context in which to consider concerns about pornography, and Sidney Daffner, the owner of Bare Facts, stopped selling the whips and dildos.

BENEATH THE FULL MOON, in June 1981, seven rape survivors poured vials of their blood on the steps of the Santa Cruz Civic Auditorium to protest the Miss California Beauty Pageant. The women, all members of the Preying Mantis Women's Brigade—a group devoted to creating theatrical acts of civil disobedience—explained their action.

> The blood was poured as a reminder that a woman is raped every three minutes. It was poured to let Miss California promoters know that their use of women to sell products contributes to the rape of women and that selecting one representative of the female sex (as Miss California) is racist, ageist and sexist.

Several months later, at the Women's Pentagon Action where over 2000 women gathered to grieve, rage and symbolically disobey the huge war machine, three women smeared blood on the columns of the Pentagon and were charged with destruction of property.

That same year, in Armagh Jail in Northern Ireland, women prisoners demanding political recognition from the British government smeared menstrual blood on the walls of their cells in protest.

THE COLUMBUS, OHIO radical feminist group, Sisters of Justice, had been on the Moral Majority's mailing list for a year when they received a special invitation from Jerry Falwell. The computerized letter began, "Dear Mr. Justice." It was an invitation to Falwell's "closest friends and supporters" to attend a friendship and fundraising meeting on March 8, 1985. The Sisters wasted no time in responding. "Dear Jerry," they wrote, "I am looking forward to your visit to Columbus. Please send tickets to me and eighty-six of my closest friends. [Signed,] Mrs. Reverend Doctor Justice." The Falwell organization sent sixteen tickets and promised to send additional tickets to any specific names and addresses. The Sisters sent in their list, providing real addresses but playing a little with the names. The feminist bookstore Fan the Flames became "Ms. Fanny Flame," the gay and lesbian rights organization, the Stonewall Union, became "Mr. Stoney Wall" and the Columbus Communist Workers Party became "Connie Worker."

While other groups decided to picket Falwell's visit, the Sisters felt they owed their community something more colorful. "Columbus's press sees us as a theatrical, strident, outrageous bunch of witches. We try to live up to that image," they explained. They decided on something with a little blood—their own.

The night of the action, the Sisters walked past the feminists, progressives, lesbians and gay men who were picketing the event, handed over their tickets and were ushered inside the Columbus Baptist Temple. However, it soon became evident to the Sisters that any action in this highly charged closed space would be dangerous; they decided to go back outside. There they stood on the front lawn of the church beneath a huge neon cross. First they draped the cross with a banner reading "A WOMAN'S LIFE IS A HUMAN LIFE." Then they poured the blood into one woman's hands and she made handprints on the banner, some of the prints in the pattern of the international woman's symbol. When she was finished, she raised her blood-stained hands high over her head and sang a pledge, paraphrasing a 1945 song, "Beloved Comrade," originally written in honor of the International Brigades in Spain:

> To you, beloved sisters
> We make this solemn vow:
> The fight will go on,
> Your fight will still go on.
> To you, beloved sisters,
> We pledge our bodies now,
> The fight will go on.

The women had also come prepared with a press release. "The Sisters of Justice bring a message to Jerry Falwell and all those who seek to deny women the right to control our own bodies. WE PLEDGE WITH OUR BLOOD TO MAINTAIN OUR RIGHT TO SAFE, LEGAL ABORTION. DO NOT DOUBT OUR RESOLVE."

When the ceremony was over, five of the women decided to go back inside the church and display the now dramatically blood-stained banner. To their surprise, they were ushered in with no problem (though the banner was making a strange bulge in one woman's clothes). Clearly, the men standing at the door had no idea what had just transpired on their church lawn. The women made their way upstairs to a small balcony which was almost empty of the faithful. As they looked directly down on the pulpit, the women quickly draped the banner over the ledge and began chanting, "A WOMAN'S LIFE IS A HUMAN LIFE. A WOMAN'S LIFE IS A HUMAN LIFE." For a moment the famous Falwell grin faded clear away. The organist scrambled onto the organ bench to fill the astonished gape-mouthed silence with an emergency hymn while the Sisters of Justice were grabbed and pushed forcibly out of the church. The media loved it.

The Sisters counted this action a success because it clearly conveyed to the public that Jerry Falwell's views are opposed, and it sent a message to women that women's rights are worth fighting for. "We cannot afford to allow our enemies to hide behind religious façades," they explained. "The Sisters of Justice believe that if anything is sacred, it is women's lives."

Sources

Graffiti

Agnew, Bonnie. "Take Back the Night: Hints to Heloise." *off our backs*, vol. 16, no. 9 (Oct. 1986).
Allen, Terry Y. "The New Scarlet Letter." *Mother Jones*, Sept./Oct. 1978.
"A Sign of the Times." *off our backs*, vol. 9, no. 5 (May 1979).
Buchanan, Brenda, compiler. "Global Gayzette—West German Feminists Modify Statues." *Our Paper: A Voice for Lesbians and Gay Men in Maine*, vol. 4, no. 5 (Jan. 1987).
Gornick, Janet. "Anti-Porn: Vandalism as Self-Defense." *off our backs*, vol. 13, no. 9 (Oct. 1983).
Indiana, Gary. "Shadows of a Summer Night." *The Village Voice*, Aug. 20, 1985.
"The International Shadow Project." *The WREE [Women for Racial and Economic Equality] View of Women*, vol. 10, no. 2–3 (Spring 1985).
The Madison Billboard Brigade. "Billboard Blitz/Counter Blitz." *off our backs*, vol. 10, no. 1 (Jan. 1980).
Posener, Jill. *Louder Than Words*. London: Pandora Press, 1986.
————. *Spray It Loud*. London: Pandora Press, 1982.
Prado, Danda. "Brazil: A Fertile but Ambiguous Feminist Terrain" from *Sisterhood Is Global: The International Women's Movement Anthology*. Robin Morgan, ed. Garden City, NY: Anchor Press/Doubleday, 1984.
Wilson, Marie. "Irish Women's Eyes Aren't Smiling." *off our backs*, vol. 11, no. 1 (Jan. 1981).

Blood

Dejanikus, Tacie. "Judge Denies Motions." *off our backs*, vol. 10, no. 7 (July 1980).

———. "Hartford Women Acquitted." *off our backs*, vol. 10, no. 8 (Aug./Sept. 1980).

Khan, Billie. "Jerry Falwell Meets the Sisters of Justice." *off our backs*, vol. 16, no. 2 (Feb. 1986).

McCafferty, Nell. "Ireland(s): Coping with the Womb and the Border" from *Sisterhood Is Global: The International Women's Movement Anthology*. Robin Morgan, ed. Garden City, NY: Anchor Press/ Doubleday, 1984.

Meyerding, Jane. Private correspondence.

———. "Blood Poured on S.O.M.E. . . . So Many Lives Have Been Lost—On Open Letter to Our Friends." *Out and About: Seattle Lesbian/feminist Newsletter*, July 1978.

Mittler, Renee. "Hartford Women Fight Back—And Win!!" *Women Against Pornography Newsreport*, Dec. 1980.

Westerman, Kaila. "Preying Mantis Strikes Again." *New Women's Times*, vol. 8, no. 1 (Jan. 1982).

Wildwomoon, Shell. "We Will Not Be Silent Victims." *WIN Magazine*, vol. 16, no. 20 (Dec. 1, 1980).

"Women Mark Porn Display With Blood." *New Women's Times*, vol. 6, no. 7 (Mar./Apr. 1980).

"Women's Pentagon Action." *off our backs*, vol. 11, no. 11 (Dec. 1981).

7

SINGING FOR OUR LIVES

"Mother, I'm pregnant with a baby girl."
"What is she doing?"
"She is singing."
"Why is she singing?"
"Because she's unafraid."
　　　　　　　　　　—E. M. Broner, *Her Mothers*

ONE APRIL EVENING when I was eleven years old, I unlocked my little blue journal and wrote:

> Dear Diary,
> 　　Today at recess we sang the boys sick. This is the girls' secret method!

With preadolescent female ingenuity, my girlfriends and I had found a way to get revenge for all the hairpulling, pushing, bullying and name-calling which had been inflicted on us. "Singing the boys sick" also worked as a temporary measure to keep the boys at bay, nonviolently as it were.

Little did we know that we were not the first to "sing the boys sick." This tactic was used in the early 1900s by the great labor organizer Mary "Mother" Jones in Greensburg, Pennsylvania, just southeast of Pittsburgh. Well into her seventies, her motto was "Pray for the dead and fight like hell for the living," and when asked her address she would respond, "I abide where there is a fight against wrong." She was in Greensburg one summer to support a miners' strike, and, as she had done in other places, she mobilized an "army of women"—strikers' wives who brought their babies, brooms and mops to the picket line. This not only served to improve the morale of the strikers, but to confuse and lower the morale of the company men and strikebreakers. "Mother Jones is raising hell up in the mountains with a bunch of wild women," they'd say, and it would be true. The women let their hair loose and banged on pots and pans to frighten away the scabs (strikebreakers) and scare the mules out of the mines. Mother Jones told the women, "Whatever the fight, don't be ladylike!"

The brave women of Greensburg went to the picket line cradling their fussing little babies in their arms. When thirteen women were arrested and sentenced to thirty days in jail for disturbing the peace, they had no choice but to take their babies with them. The women sang as loud as they could all the way to the jail. This gave Mother Jones an idea. With a curious twinkle in her eyes, she advised the women to keep singing. As she told it:

> I sent them food and milk for the babies; and I said to the women, "You sing all night, sing all day if you want to, but sing all night and don't stop for anybody." And they didn't; they sang the whole night, and the people complained about the singing, and the women would not shut up, and the babies would not shut up, and nobody would shut up until they turned them all out.

Women sang to their babies all night long as a way of harassing their way out of prison again in 1962 in Zimbabwe (then Rhodesia). Two thousand women and their children had been arrested and sent to prison after a demonstration protesting the country's racial discrimination and the detention of political prisoners. The women refused to pay the fines which would have bought their early release. Instead, they did what they could to continue their protest in prison by staging sit-ins, destroying prison property and engaging other women prisoners in political dialogue. They also made a determined effort to disrupt the workings of the prison with loud singing until they were released.

♀ SINGING HAS BEEN USED extensively by women as a way to articulate political grievances and to ridicule and harass individual men whose actions have been deemed harmful or unjust. Singing was used in this way during the women's temperance movement in the United States in the late 1800s and early 1900s.

Today, while ultra-sophisticated party-goers alternate with fun-loving "simple guys" in wine and beer commercials, people flock to Alcoholics Anonymous meetings and rally behind Mothers

Against Drunk Driving. Our current associations with alcohol—whether we love it, hate it or fear it—exist on a vastly different plane than was experienced by our foremothers. To our modern ears, the women's efforts to combat the alcohol industry often sound obnoxious, pious and self-righteous. What confuses us, in part, is that the women's temperance movement, like most mass movements, encompassed a wide range of sometimes contradictory concerns. Women flocked to the temperance movement for a variety of reasons. These ranged from a prejudice against immigrant communities and an intention to convert the "heathens" to Christ, to the frustrated desire to be involved in political work in an age when women were expected to keep the home fires burning. Indeed, the movement proved to be a training ground for women who carried their new organizing skills into the suffrage and labor struggles.

But one interesting aspect of women's commitment to the temperance movement that is often overlooked, and one a modern feminist might most appreciate, was the women's desire to end the economic powerlessness and physical violence inflicted by abusive boyfriends and husbands. These were concerns about which many women in the ranks of the temperance movement knew from personal experience. These early activists blamed "demon rum" for the violence men brought into the home and the poverty families faced when the money for food, clothing and shelter was gone.

Mary Daly noted that the nineteenth-century women's temperance movement was more than a dreary obsession with the immorality of drink when she wrote:

> The crusaders against intemperance were not being prim and proper. They were fighting against the rape and battering of victims of all ages, against deprivation of needed food, drink, clothing, not to mention respect, kindness, health, independence.

This observation is backed up by some of the writing of that day. In an account titled *The History of the Women's Temperance Crusade* published in 1882, Annie Wittenmyer wrote about some of these impulses which led women to involvement in the movement.

> No pen can portray the utter hopelessness of the women into whose homes the drink curse had come. The men who

had sworn at the altar to protect and honor them had
become demons from whom they fled in fear. . . .

She also described the public reaction to women's protest and the
dismissal of their grievances by most institutions, initially
including the church. She noted that the women were subjected
to verbal harassment, accused of being "unwomanly" and "strong-
minded" and frequently told "go home, old woman, and mend
your husband's britches."

> . . . and the world joined in the laugh of scorn, and the
> church made no defence of the wronged and broken-
> hearted. And so the money that ought to have come to
> them to buy new clothing, went into the tills of the liquor-
> dealers, and they stayed at home till the home was gone,
> and mended garments till there were no garments to mend.

The specific concerns about male violence and the misuse of
money were also expressed many times in the words of popular
temperance songs written by both women and men. In "Dear
Mother, Cease Your Weeping," for example, a drinking father is
generously named "ungentle."

> I know that father is ungentle;
> I know he is not kind and true;
> But trust in God, my dearest Mother,
> And He will be a friend to you.

Another melodramatic song, "Mother is Dead," by Elisha
Hoffman, documented the vulnerability of children of that day.

> Home was so bright, so cheerful and glad,
> Till father drank, and made our hearts sad;
> Sorrow and pain came to us then,
> Ne'er could we smile or be happy again.

When Sarah Hagar witnessed a little girl crawl onto her father's
lap and ask, "Father, won't you stop your drinking?" she wrote
a temperance hymn which named both violence against the child's
mother and, in the verse quoted here, concern about money for
shelter and food as legitimate concerns of women in the temperance
movement.

> And your darling little Willie
> Often calls to us for bread

When the cupboard shelves are empty
And the hungry ones unfed.
Don't you love your darling Willie?
What if he should starve and die!
Won't you stop your drinking, father?
Dearest father, won't you try?

A New York woman who frequently wrote anonymously on the subject of temperance was accused by a friend of being melodramatic and obsessed with the issue, indeed of being "a maniac on the subject." In answer, the woman wrote another hymn:

Go, feel what I have felt;
Go, bear what I have borne,
Sink 'neath a blow a father dealt,
And the cold world's proud scorn;
Then suffer on from year to year,
Thy sole relief the scorching tear.

The anonymous author concluded her poem with the assurance that anyone who had felt the father's blow and the world's scorn as she had would "renounce the cup . . . the bitter, bitter cup."

Not only were temperance songs outlets for women's grievances about male violence, singing was used in the movement as a way of harassing and publicly shaming individual men into more responsible behavior. Women in small towns and in cities across the United States organized bands and choruses which invaded the pharmacies and bars where liquor was being sold. Once inside, they sang Christian hymns and temperance songs and prayed that the men would be guided back to the ways of Jesus and to a gentler impulse.

Sometimes women visited prisons where men were jailed for drink-related crimes. They would invite the men to sing the old, familiar hymns with them. To their credit, the women were often compassionate and generous toward the men and boys who were jailed, considering them to be the first victims of "demon rum." They consistently directed their criticism at men who actually made money from the liquor business. One Newark, Ohio woman wrote of her jail-visiting experience,

Going to one after another of these cages, unfit for animals, and pressing my face against the iron bars, I could see that the rooms were about 7 x 4 or 5 feet. More than half of the prisoners were under age. Where were the saloonkeepers who sold them liquor in violation of the law? Why were they not behind these bars instead of these boys? Perhaps about that hour they were hobnobbing with some politician as to how they would carry the next election and break down the crusade and all law.

In the tiny railroad village of New Vienna, Ohio, a barkeeper by the name of John Calvin Van Pelt boasted of his reputation as "the wickedest man in Ohio." His saloon, the Dead Fall, was the last in the area to "surrender." The first day women came singing into his saloon, he pulled himself up to his full and considerable height and bellowed that if they ever dared visit his saloon again he would personally "hang, draw and quarter them, every one!"

The women couldn't resist such a dramatic challenge, and the very next day fifty of them marched to the Dead Fall. Van Pelt was ready with some theatrics of his own. He had prepared a special window display for the women—an ax smeared with blood. He played the part of a drunken madman as though the women had handed him the script. The women began to sing and pray in front of the bar, and a crowd soon gathered around them. They prayed in loud, earnest voices for Van Pelt himself, so obviously in need of a little "amazing grace." They asked especially that he be baptized with the holy spirit. Suddenly, Van Pelt opened the window shouting, "I'll baptize you!" and dashed several buckets of cold, dirty water on the women. Though the women pleaded on his behalf, Van Pelt was arrested and spent several days in jail, emerging more bitter than ever.

The next time the women visited the Dead Fall, Van Pelt invited them inside for a prayer-meeting on the condition that he be allowed to make every other prayer. Somewhat mystified, the women agreed. They got an earful that afternoon. When it was his turn, Van Pelt thanked the Lord for making the first wine and promised to follow the Lord's example by helping make this gift even more widely available.

The story of John Calvin Van Pelt and the singing temperance women, like hundreds of similar ones recorded by activists in the temperance movement, takes a sudden turn at this point. It is said that one week after the prayer-duel, boys were sent running through the streets of New Vienna, ringing hand-bells and crying out, "Everybody meet at Van Pelt's saloon at two o'clock and hear his decision. Van Pelt's at two!" Stores closed for the afternoon and the whole town turned out for the event. There, in front of the Dead Fall, stood Van Pelt. He was a changed man. He bowed his head and, in trembling voice, said, "I do not yield to law or force, but to the women who have labored in love." He then rolled out his entire stock, took up his ax and smashed the casks until the gutters overflowed with liquor. "Ladies," he said, "I now promise to never sell or drink another drop of whiskey as long as I live and also promise to work with you in the cause with as much zeal as I have worked against you."

The women rushed to congratulate Van Pelt and shake his hand as the crowd cheered and burst into several rousing choruses of the doxology, "Praise God from whom all blessings flow!" All the bells of the town were rung that afternoon in Van Pelt's honor, and that night he was the featured speaker at a mass temperance meeting where he confessed that he had often taken the last 10¢ from a man who had a wife and starving children at home. "Every man who sells whiskey does this," he said before he again promised to quit the business forever.

♀ LIGHT-YEARS AWAY from nineteenth-century Ohio, Nigerian women used song in 1929 to ridicule, protest and pressure a man and, by extension, the system he represented.

In November of that year, women streamed into Oloko, Nigeria from throughout Owerri Province. Word had been sent via the Ibo (Igbo) women's network that it was time to "sit on" Okugo, the arrogant warrant chief of the Oloko Native Court. "Sitting on a man" was the figurative expression given a traditional process of punishment during which women gathered in front of a man's home to sing songs which outlined the women's grievances or insulted the offender. The women would dance and sing all day and all night, and sometimes, for the most serious and unrepentant offenders, give added impetus to their words by dismantling the roof of the hut until the man promised to cooperate.

On this November day, the women prepared as their mothers and grandmothers before them had prepared for the traditional settling of grievances: they bound their heads with ferns, smeared their faces with ashes, and put on the short loincloths tradition ordained. Each woman picked up a sacred stick wreathed with young palm fronds. These sacred sticks were necessary for invoking the spirit and power of their female ancestors. Thus attired, they massed on the district office to "sit on" Okugo until he got the message.

Of course the situation wasn't all Okugo's fault, but the Ibo women had to start somewhere. Thirty years before, Southern Nigeria had been declared a British protectorate and the women's decision-making powers and authority had increasingly been undermined. Before colonization, the people west of the Niger River had always made decisions by consensus, reasoning that the justice of any decision should be clear to everyone involved. They were aided in this process by an *obi* (male) who looked after the happiness and well-being of the men and by an *omu* (female) who, assisted by a council of women, saw to the happiness and well-being of the women. Oral tradition recalled the *omu* who'd led a boycott in which the women had refused to cook for their husbands until the men grasped the urgency of the women's concerns.

But when the British came, they incorporated only the *obi* into their new system, giving him a monthly paycheck, while the *omu* was left unrecognized, stripped of her power and voice.

Likewise, the women living east of the Niger had experienced great loss of power under British rule. Under the British, Igboland was divided into "Native Court Areas" which lumped together previously unrelated villages, and warrant chiefs were chosen to represent whole villages and to see that the people obeyed the rules of the colonial power. This new system of representation left out the many voices of the people and left women particularly powerless.

Before, there had been a balance of male and female power and shared responsibility, and the women had participated in a system of daily self-rule. They had gathered in village-wide meetings called *mikiri*, forums where complaints about mistreatment by husbands could be aired, disputes between women settled, and decisions made about the market, crops and livestock or about rituals of protection, fruitfulness and healing. Occasionally the men would fail to cooperate on a matter of deep concern to the women, and the women would then go on strike, refusing to cook, care for the children or have sexual relations. In more extreme cases and only very rarely, the women would decide to "sit on" the male offender, punishing him with song and ridicule.

On the November afternoon in 1929, the women were preparing to "sit on" Warrant Chief Okugo and, by extension, the whole

British system. Just days before, the women had met in the market to discuss the new taxation rumors. They remembered that four years earlier, after promises to the contrary, the British had taken a census and begun collecting taxes from the men. The women were worried that taxes would soon be imposed upon them as well, especially since a district officer had ordered a new census in which they and their property would be counted. At the marketplace meeting the women had agreed to spread the alarm and act if any of them were approached for information.

And could anyone doubt their cause for alarm now? Just that morning Warrant Chief Okugo had approached Nwanyeruwa, a married woman. He had asked to count her goats and sheep. She had spat back an insult, "Was your mother counted?" In anger, Okugo had attacked Nwanyeruwa who had immediately set in motion the women's network. Now the women were ready to act. Nwanyeruwa's name became the watchword, Nwanyeruwa herself the catalyst.

Carrying their sacred sticks high, thousands of women marched on the district office. They danced. They sang songs of ridicule and protest, they chanted, and they demanded Okugo's cap of office, taking from his head the symbol of his authority over them. A British officer who witnessed the event claimed that the cap, tossed into the crowd of women, "met the same fate as a fox's carcass thrown to a pack of hounds."

After several days of such protest, the women secured written assurances that they were not to be taxed. They also succeeded in having Okugo arrested, tried, and convicted of physical assault and of unnecessarily worrying the population.

When the news of this victory spread through the women's networks, thousands of other women throughout the region organized to "sit on" their local warrant chiefs. The protest spread to Aba, a major trading center along the railway. The women in Aba, like those in Oloko, dressed in their traditional ferns, ashes and loincloths and carrying the sacred sticks to invoke the mothers, gathered to dance, sing and demand the cap of the warrant chief.

The protest spread to neighboring areas with thousands of women in the region making their demands known in angry songs and chants according to custom. In some places their demands included that "all white men should go to their own country," or, failing that, that women should be appointed to serve on the Native Courts as well as men and should not be subject to taxation.

Although they singled out individual government representatives, the women injured no one. There were, however, reports of widespread destruction of property in some areas of the region. In several villages, women broke open prison doors and released the prisoners, looted European stores, and in sixteen villages, actually took apart the Native Courts. These reports prompted a telegram from the women of Oloko who had started the women's war: "Please inform our women friends there stop such they are doing thats not our objects the tax matter is settled to our satisfaction nothing like houses destroying at Oloko where tax matter first started."

The women's action spread throughout the Calabar and Owerri provinces that cover the southeast and southwest quarters of Igboland—approximately 6000 square miles. Observing the rules of the ritual, the women had no intention of hurting or killing anyone. They believed they were safe from harm because of their sacred sticks. But they were wrong.

The British, blinded by both a racist and sexist Victorian perspective and knowing nothing of the Ibo women's custom of "sitting on a man," saw only "frenzied mobs" consumed by "savage passions." They called out the police, the soldiers and even the Boy Scouts to crush the women's rebellion. In mid-December, the troops fired at the women, killing more than fifty and wounding another fifty. The women were stunned. Though here and there protests continued into 1930, most of the rebellion ended abruptly in the face of such barbarity.

The British as victors wrote the history of the 1929 action. While the Ibo people called the action *Ogu Umunwanyi*, the "Women's War," the British called it the "Aba Riots," falsely conveying the image of irrational and violent action with the word "riots" and erasing women from the picture altogether. But British rule was destined to be shortlived, perhaps partly due to acts of resistance such as the Women's War.

♀ SOMETIMES SONG HAS BEEN USED to pass on secret information. For Harriet Tubman, as for most African-American conductors on the Underground Railroad, songs were used as coded messages to alert people that she was in the area and ready to move. In the woods behind the slave shacks, a husky voice would sing in the night, "Steal away, steal away, steal away to

Jesus. Steal away, steal away home. I ain't got long to stay here."
A voice in one of the shacks would take up another coded song,
"Oh, Sinner, you'd better get ready." From another hut a voice
would answer, "Dark and thorny is the pathway where the pilgrim
makes his way, But beyond this vale of sorrow lie the fields of
endless days."

Some songs were used to relay crucial plans pertaining to the
escape. One song gave instructions to "follow the drinking gourd."
The "drinking gourd" was a code for the Little Dipper, the
constellation which contains the North Star. The song meant
literally, go north—north to Canada and freedom. Word got
around while the white master drifted off to sleep.

> When the sun comes up and the first quail calls,
> Follow the drinking gourd.
> For the old man is a waiting for to carry you to freedom
> Follow the drinking gourd.
>
> The river bank will make a mighty good road,
> The dead trees will show you the way,
> Left foot, peg foot, travelling on,
> Follow the drinking gourd.
>
> The river ends between two hills,
> Follow the drinking gourd,
> There's another river on the other side,
> Follow the drinking gourd.

IN NAMIBIA IN 1973, women passed crucial information to their
imprisoned husbands by singing to them. The men, political
prisoners in Oshikango Prison, were frequently denied food, water
or contact with anyone from the outside. While some of the women
alerted the United Nations and successfully called world attention
to the prison conditions, others walked back and forth past the
prison walls, singing at the top of their lungs songs filled with
pertinent news and messages of encouragement.

♀ SINCE ANCIENT TIMES women have used songs to wail
about, protest and grieve the injustices they faced—from brutal
husbands to brutal factory bosses. Sometimes they sang alone. In
England in 1729, sad wives sang a song which began, "O that I
had never married," and ended with, "Here I labour out of measure,

Woman's work is never done." In colonial America too the women
sang:

> Oh hard is the fortune of all womankind,
> They're always controlled, they're always confined,
> Controlled by their fathers until they are wives,
> Then slaves to their husbands the rest of their lives.

In some parts of the world, women are jailed for singing their
grievances. Albertina Sisulu, a South African nurse and midwife
whose courageous involvement in the resistance to apartheid
resulted in years of banning and house arrest, was again arrested
in 1984 at the age of sixty-eight. This time she was sentenced to
four years' imprisonment for her support of the African National
Congress and for the crime of singing freedom songs at the funerals
of South African activists.

Miriam Makeba, on the other hand, was not jailed in South
Africa but forced into exile for singing the truth and celebrating
her African heritage. Makeba incurred the wrath of the white
minority government after she appeared as the female lead in a
semidocumentary movie, *Come Back Africa*. The movie, which
had been shot in secrecy and released to great acclaim outside
South Africa in 1959, exposed the evils of apartheid. Living in
exile first in the United States and then in Guinea, Makeba is
sometimes called the Empress of African Song. Whether she is
singing the "Click Song" in her native Xhosa language, or
folksongs in Zulu, Swazi, French or Yiddish, Makeba uses her
music as a tool for liberation. One interviewer in 1982 wrote,
"There is a quality in Makeba's music that speaks to a primal part
of our Black experience; she brings back that part of our culture
and heritage that almost drowned in the wake of slave ships plying
the Atlantic."

♀   SONGS HAVE FREQUENTLY BEEN USED to heighten the
solidarity of those resisting oppression. Songs were used by the
striking textile mill workers in 1912 in Lawrence, Massachusetts
to express defiance and lift the spirits of the women. One witness
of the strike observed:

> It is the first strike I ever saw which sang. I shall not soon
> forget the curious lift, the strange sudden fire of the mingled
> nationalities at the strike meetings when they broke into

the universal language of song. And not only at the
meetings did they sing, but in the soup houses and in the
streets. I saw one group of women strikers who were
peeling potatoes at a relief station suddenly break into the
swing of the "Internationale." They have a whole book of
songs fitted to familiar tunes—"The Eight Hour Day," "The
Banner of Labor," "Workers, Shall the Master Rule Us?"
But the favorite of all was the "Internationale."

DURING THE SUMMER OF 1962 in the United States, many
people were moved to action by the songs of the civil rights
movement. Fannie Lou Hamer, a poor black sharecropper,
attended a meeting in a church that summer in Ruleville,
Mississippi that changed her life. "I had never heard the freedom
songs before," she said later. She was amazed to hear people
talking about voter registration for the black community. "They
really wanted to change the world I knew—they wanted blacks
to register to vote!" Ten years later, the League of Black Women
called Hamer the "First Lady of Civil Rights" in recognition of
her work on voter registration.

THE SUMMER OF 1962 was also central to the life of Bernice
Reagon. She had attended one year at Albany State College in her
home town of Albany, Georgia, and her participation in campus
civil rights actions had resulted in her suspension from the college.
In 1962 she became the leader of the Student Non-Violent
Coordinating Committee (SNCC) Freedom Singers and began
touring the country singing and talking about the movement.

I witnessed and participated in the wedding of music with
political struggle; where songs served to bind segments of
the Black community together in jails and on the marches,
where songs provided the necessary strength to help
demonstrators endure abuse and continue, where songs
articulated for the masses of people what their struggle
was all about. I made a lifetime commitment to always be
a *freedom singer*.

Today, in addition to being a cultural historian and director of the
Black American Culture Program at the Smithsonian Institute, Dr.
Reagon is a singer, major songwriter and founding member of
Sweet Honey in the Rock, an ensemble of black women who sing

traditional and contemporary black American songs. "I have to talk about being a *Black woman,*" she says. "I was born female, the strongest people in my life were women. They were the ones who taught us to sing the old songs."

IN 1971, A DECADE AFTER Bernice Reagon began touring with the Freedom Singers, a young white singer, Holly Near, found a way to integrate art and politics when she joined Jane Fonda and Donald Sutherland in the "Free the Army" (FTA) tour in the Pacific. The tour supported the GIs who were resisting the war in Vietnam from the inside. Holly was strongly influenced by the women she met in the Pacific who were organizers and activists along with the women on the FTA show and the women in the military. Later she became familiar with feminists back home, including musicians like Maxine Feldman, Alix Dobkin and Meg Christian who were taking risks with their artistic lives, experimenting with women-only concert spaces and singing songs which reflected the new feminist sensibility, songs which celebrated women's strength, history, spiritual connections, women's love for one another, women's grief and rage and compassion for the planet.

As the women's movement became increasingly effective, Holly was compelled to investigate the possibilities of women's culture. By the mid-seventies, she broadened her peace and justice focus to include feminist and lesbian concerns and briefly experimented with women-only concerts, singing the stories of women's lives in songs that both articulated an oppression and the intent of women to challenge that oppression. In a 1977 interview with *Art for Humanity,* Holly explained the ways in which women's concerts and women's music had become tools of liberation within the feminist movement.

> My experience with women's music has been over the last few years. What I have seen from it is that it's fulfilling a need women have had—to be able to hear songs about our lives, so we can weep openly and celebrate freely. It gives women a chance to look around and see other women sharing our problems, our struggles, sharing our joys and giving us courage that we are not alone. . . . Women's music has served to bring some women together in one place.

> I get a lot of letters from women whose lives have been changed at one of my concerts. To some degree it has to do with the songs. But to a great extent it is the whole event including who they were sitting next to, how loud the person behind them laughed and sang, how safe the environment was. It is the whole experience that affected their lives. Most of all, they were ready to change, they just needed space and permission.

In the 1980s, Holly continued to broaden the range of concerns addressed in her concerts, reaching ever wider audiences in cross-cultural events, articulating with her cultural work and her music the truth that everything is connected.

> You can't possess music. You can't possess that which has gone before us. It just goes out into the world and it becomes part of whatever's happening next—and we're gonna watch women's music disperse. . . . You can't hold onto it. . . . It affected a huge number of women's lives, and men's lives. I think that music was one of the things, in fact, that altered a lot of men so that it's possible to work in coalition with them now.

"I care about every part of this world," Holly said in a 1986 magazine interview. "I refuse to simplify that to 'I support' or 'I don't support.' I care about the survival of all races and cultures and people on this planet. . . . I try to do a variety of things with the music—entertain, educate, challenge people and also heal."

In the hindsight of the late 1980s Holly can look back and see how her own lack of experience with cultural diversity at times may have made her insensitive to the perspectives of women from other cultures.

> The dominant presence of white middle class women in the women's movement didn't make our work bad, it just made it dangerously incomplete. My work with people of color, working-class people, disabled people and internationalists has profoundly affected my ability to think and sing clearly. . . .Sometimes this inclusive perspective threatens white lesbians because they fear I'm betraying lesbianism. On the contrary, I'm acknowledging that there are lesbians in Nicaragua and they cannot be free to openly investigate lesbian culture until they are assured the survival of Nicaraguan culture, that means that there must

be peace. And that is the connection for me between the peace movement and my feminism.

♀ WOMEN HAVE FOUND many ways to use singing as an act of resistance. Liz Lagrua learned that singing can function to sustain a revolution, as it has in Ireland's Armagh Prison among the women political prisoners. An Englishwoman and member of Women Against Imperialism, Liz was arrested on International Women's Day, 1979 in a solidarity protest outside of Armagh Prison. She opted for imprisonment so she could see for herself what was happening inside and presented herself at a Belfast police station in May 1980.

> The night before I went in was agonising. I had heard that the women held concerts every night in the prison and that I would be expected to sing a song. I spent my last few hours of freedom trying to memorise tunes and lyrics. When I was finally deposited in Armagh I knew by heart what I thought would be a collection that would appeal to the women as Provos and myself as a Republican feminist; I had learned to sing the H Block song, newly issued, which the women wouldn't have heard, "Sean South" about the death of an IRA volunteer in the Fifties, and "The Women's Army is Marching." I didn't want them to think I was a real drag on my first night in prison.

Liz was herself buoyed by song when sister members of Women Against Imperialism stood outside the police barracks singing "Oh sister don't you weep, don't you moan. . ." as she presented herself for her two-month sentence. That evening in the prison after the women had said the rosary together ("Prayers can be political if you look at them in the right way," Liz noted), she found that her preparations had been worth the effort.

> I was nervous as hell. I heard all these Northern accents lilting away, shouting welcomes to Margaret and me, and it steadily got round to our turn. We started off awkwardly at first, but they began to join in and a few songs later I was belting along like an old lag and they were banging their mugs on the walls, keeping the beat with us. They wanted the Women's Army song again and again. Even if they hadn't liked it, it was new after the months of silence, no word coming in from the outside world. We sang along until midnight and then the O.C. [the woman elected by

other prisoners as an "Officer Commanding"] announced it was time to go to sleep. They're very disciplined like that. Everybody has to act together in solidarity, keep moving along in a body. Otherwise you fall off, by yourself, cracking up. So we learned to do many things together.

♀ IN HER NARRATIVE POEM "Songs That Cannot Be Silenced," Vietnamese poet Hien Luong described the use of song as a nonviolent action of solidarity and defiance. In 1969 she was among a group of women taken as political prisoners to Con Son Island. (The following year, this US-backed prison island was made notorious when a congressional committee found "tiger cages" there. Prisoners were kept in such tight confinement in the cages that, if they lived, they were sometimes left paralyzed for life.) Hien Luong and the other women prisoners defied their jailers by singing liberation songs in their cells. The rebellious singing always brought the guards who demanded to know which women were singing. Then the women, from the youngest teenager to the oldest grandmother, would stand in defiant silence. The guards beat them into bloody unconsciousness. When the women regained consciousness, they smiled at each other and began to sing again with even stronger voices and sweeter harmony, defying the guards with every note. They knew nothing could hold back their songs of liberation.

Even so, Hien Luong marveled at their courage. "Such power in such frail bodies," she wrote. "Does it come from magic?"

Sources

Singing as nonviolent action (general)

Abernathey, Diane. "Holly Near Singing for Freedom." *Art for Humanity*, No. 4 (1977).

Hien Luong, "Songs That Cannot Be Silenced" from *The Other Voice: Twentieth-Century Women's Poetry in Translation*. Bankier, Cosman, Earnshaw, Keefe, Lashgari, Weaver, eds. New York: W. W. Norton, 1976.

Bernice Johnson Reagon (pamphlet). Washington, DC: Roadwork.

Boccafola, Joan, Andrea Piccolo, and Marcia Steel. "Making Room for the Optimum—An Interview with Holly Near." *The Feminist Renaissance*, vol. 1, no. 1 (Dec. 1982).

Diachishin, Diane, and Leah Warnick. "Music as Cultural Work: The Power to Change." *New Women's Times*, Oct. 1979.

Foner, Philip S. *Women and the American Labor Movement: From Colonial Times to the Eve of World War I*. New York: Free Press/ Macmillan, 1979.

————, ed. *Mother Jones Speaks: Collected Writings and Speeches*. New York: Monad Press, 1983.

Gayle, Stephen. "Makeba at 50." *Essence*, July 1982.

IDAF Research, Information and Publications Department. *To Honour Women's Day: Profiles of Leading Women in the South African and Namibian Liberation Struggles*. London: International Defence and Aid Fund for Southern Africa in cooperation with the United Nations Centre Against Apartheid, 1981.

Kling, Susan. "Fannie Lou Hamer: Baptism by Fire" from *Reweaving the Web of Life: Feminism and Nonviolence*. Pam McAllister, ed. Philadelphia: New Society, 1982.

Long, Priscilla. *Mother Jones, Woman Organizer*. Boston: Beacon Press, 1984.

McCafferty, Nell. *The Armagh Women*. Dublin: Co-op Books, 1981.

McHenry, Susan. "An Interview with Bernice Johnson Reagon: Stepping Across the Line, Voter Registration Then and Now." *Ms.*, Nov. 1984.

Meyer, Denise. "Civil Rights, Music Combine in Career." *The Oregonian*, July 31, 1980.

Morgan, Robin, ed. *Sisterhood Is Global: The International Women's Movement Anthology*. Garden City, NY: Anchor Press/ Doubleday, 1984.

Richardson, Derk. "Holly Near's Current Tour Aims to Disarm." *In These Times*, Nov. 10–16, 1982.

Silverman, Jerry. *The Liberated Woman's Songbook*. New York: Macmillan, 1971.

Smith, Eleanor. "And Black Women Made Music." *Heresies: A Feminist Publication on Art & Politics—Third World Women: The Politics of Being Other*, vol. 2, no. 4 (1979).

Wallach, Van. "Interview: Holly Near." *Whole Life*, Apr. 1986.

"We're Not the First and We're Not the Last: An Informal History." Holly Near, Ronnie Gilbert promotional literature. 1983.

Wertheimer, Barbara Mayer. *We Were There: The Story of Working Women in America*. New York: Pantheon Books, 1977.

Women's temperance movement

Daly, Mary. *Pure Lust: Elemental Feminist Philosophy*. Boston: Beacon Press, 1984.

Tenney, J. H., and E. A. Hoffman. *Temperance Jewels for Temperance and Reform Meetings*. Boston: Oliver Ditson, 1879.

Wittenmyer, Annie. *The History of the Woman's Temperance Crusade*. Boston: James H. Earle, 1882.

Ibo women's war

Leith-Ross, Sylvia. *African Women: A Study of the Ibo of Nigeria.* London: Routledge & Kegan Paul, 1939/1978.

Okonjo, Kamene. "The Dual-Sex Political System in Operation: Igbo Women and Community Politics in Midwestern Nigeria" from *Women in Africa.* Hafkin and Bay.

Van Allen, Judith. "'Aba Riots' or Igbo 'Women's War'? Ideology, Stratification, and the Invisibility of Women" from *Women in Africa: Studies in Social and Economic Change.* Nancy J. Hakfin and Edna G. Bay, eds. Stanford, CA: Stanford University Press, 1976.

8
EXTEND THIS SAFE CIRCLE

STORIES OF WOMEN'S RESISTANCE to male violence are as old as the Mayan tale of Ix Chel. In the very beginning of time there were two great lights of equal brilliance in the sky. One was Ix Chel, the moon goddess and the first woman in the world. It was Ix Chel who cleansed the earth with the great flood and ruled women's menstrual cycles. Ix Chel could ease the pain of childbirth, comfort and heal the sick. Eagles were her messengers, spiders her special friends.

The other great light was the sun. He was so fascinated by Ix Chel's radiance that he devised a clever scheme and took great risks to visit her. The Mayans told many stories about how Ix Chel met the sun, how she fell in love with him and agreed to fly off with him into the sky, how they had many adventures—including her death and resurrection—and how eventually they got married and lived side by side in the heavens.

And it is at this point that the stories begin to sound familiar to anyone who has worked in the battered-women's movement of the late twentieth century. According to the Mayan legend, soon after they were married trouble began. The sun grew hot with jealousy, especially whenever his brother, Venus, would visit, for Venus could often be seen at the moon's side. After such visits, the sun would scream at the moon, accusing her of being unfaithful. Finally the day came when the sun was in such a rage that he threw the moon out of the sky.

Hurt by false accusations and exhausted by the strain of living under the sun's constant threats, Ix Chel was, understandably, none too eager to return home. For awhile she rested in the love and shelter offered by the King of the Vultures. But on the day that the repentant sun finally appeared, begging for forgiveness and promising never to hurt her again, Ix Chel took pity on her poor husband. She returned with him to the sky, thinking, perhaps, that this time would be different, that the sun had truly changed as he said he had.

No sooner was she home but the accusations began again. The sun's insane jealously was even worse than before. He ranted and raved and accused her of cheating on him. Finally, he began to beat Ix Chel, scarring her face so that no one else would desire her. At first confused, worn out and wanting to be faithful, Ix Chel tried to endure the blows, but soon she grew weak. Her radiance dimmed. When finally she understood that it was unlikely the sun would ever change, Ix Chel used her last ounce of strength to fly off into the night sky.

The Mayan people told this story to explain why the moon deliberately left the sky whenever the sun appeared, and why she wandered off sometimes, deep in thought, and disappeared for several nights at a time. And it is Ix Chel we hear whispering in the moonlight, telling us that it is indeed better to be able to come and go as one pleases, free from harm or the threat of it, than to stay with a violent man. Escape!

Stories of women's resistance to male violence are also as old as the story of Latona told in ancient Rome (Leto in Greek mythology). After a sexual liaison with the supreme deity Jupiter, Latona gave birth to twins, Apollo and Artemis. Juno, the queen of heaven, found out about her husband's infidelity and drove Latona from the land in a rage.

Latona, who was still nursing her babies, ran for a long time until she could run no more. She was unbearably thirsty, and her arms ached from carrying the twins. Just then Latona saw some men gathering willows beside a pond which glistened in the sunlight with clear, cool water. Eagerly she approached the pond and laid the babies down on the grassy bank. She knelt and cupped her hands, but just before her fingers touched the water the men shouted at her to stop.

"Get out of here," one of the men yelled at her. The others smirked and scuffed their feet. "Yeah," they called out. "Get your babies and go."

"But why?" asked the thirsty woman. "No one owns the sunlight, the air, the water. These are common blessings free to all of us. I ask only to stay for a moment to drink. I promise I have no intention of bathing in the water."

But the men were feeling mean that day. Even the sight of the two babies did nothing to soften their hearts or change their minds. They began jeering at Latona out of pure spite. The jeers soon changed to curses and the curses to threats.

Seeing that Latona was still not frightened off, the men jumped into the pond and stirred up the mud with their feet.

"Very well," cried Latona, shocked into rage, "may you never leave this pond!"

In an instant the men were turned into frogs. It is said that even today one can hear their harsh, bass voices still croaking in the slimy, muddy waters where they once made the mistake of harassing a bone-tired woman.

> we stand in a circle
> we face out into the dark
> we face danger
> we're not afraid
> we are so many
> we reclaim the night
>
> we make this vow
> to ourselves and each other
> to our daughters
> we will extend this safe circle
> until its boundaries dissolve
> and its power is everywhere
> and we are safe everywhere
> all women safe everywhere

—Ritual, Portland, 1978
Women's Night Watch Second Annual
Flashlight March to Stop Violence
Against Women and Children

The goddesses of ancient mythology had to contend with male harassment and violence, but this was merely a reflection of the struggle faced by mortal women. Today, movements such as those for rape survivors and battered women are global in scope. Women around the world are naming the violence in their lives and learning from each other strategies to counter it, so that the safe circle may be extended until all women are safe everywhere.

These movements are not consciously nonviolent, though nonviolent tactics are their backbone. Women fighting male violence have provided sanctuary for each other, marched through the streets, blanketed cities with graffiti, committed civil disobedience. They have sponsored speak-outs, forums and international tribunals on crimes against women. They have used guerrilla theater, obstruction, letter-writing campaigns and consumer boycotts. Instead of taking up guns against their batterers or castrating their rapists, survivors of male violence have found increasingly effective and creative ways of collectively fighting back. Keeping a steady focus on each other rather than giving more energy to their male antagonists, women fighting male violence have transformed fear and powerlessness into rage, and rage into healing powers with the dexterity of a Rumpelstiltskin spinning straw into gold.

Movements of women fighting male violence are laboratories for experimentation with nonviolent strategies. In this chapter we will consider women's creative, collective responses to three traditions believed to promote gender-linked violence or to foster assumptions and attitudes that are harmful or unfair to women. These are beauty pageants, dowry marriages in India, and the official or unofficial curfews that restrict the movement of women in public spaces.

♀ IT HAS BEEN SUGGESTED that the beginning of the late twentieth century women's movement dates from September 7, 1968. On this day, 200 women descended on Atlantic City, New Jersey for an all-day protest of the Miss America Pageant. The protest, organized by members of New York Radical Women, included such media grabbers as the crowning of a live sheep as Miss America, a mock-auction of a Miss America dummy, and a Freedom Trash Can into which the demonstrators threw their steno pads, dishcloths, curlers, false eyelashes, girdles and bras. Seeing the discarded underwear, news reporters nicknamed the trash-can action "bra-burning." Though no bras were ever burned, the image stuck, and bra-burning became synonymous in the popular imagination with women's liberation.

That evening, twenty protesters infiltrated the official pageant which, at that time, was still being broadcast live. The women sat tensely in the audience. Suddenly the balcony erupted with the shout, "Freedom for Women!" Faster than you can say "boys will be boys," the women unfurled a huge banner with the words

"WOMEN'S LIBERATION" and flung it over the balcony. Veteran Miss America emcee Bert Parks, ordinarily the smoothest of the smooth, entirely lost his place on the cue cards. The show screeched to a halt for ten minutes until order could be restored, but not before the seed of discontent was planted in the imaginations of many female viewers.

Since this historic protest, women in other cities have dared to openly condemn the seemingly innocuous beauty pageants. They recognize that wherever they take place, they serve to sanction public scrutiny and ranking of female bodies and thus legitimize the objectification of women. This objectification, the protesters claim, feeds the climate of violence against women.

In the United States, West Coast women have targeted the Miss California Pageant each year since 1974 with creative if somewhat disruptive protest actions. They articulate their concern that beauty pageant contestants are used to sell American products and to promote one ideal of beauty (white, thin, able-bodied, young and rich).

Over the years, pageant protesters have infiltrated the official pageant parade with unofficial "Myth California" floats, and have splattered the blood of rape survivors on the steps of the auditorium where the competitions are held. One year, activist and artist Nikki Craft, a guiding spirit at the protests, entered the auditorium and raced up the aisle to throw raw meat on the pageant stage. In the streets outside the auditorium, feminists have found the pageant an easy mark for verbal puns. They chant, "Mold jello not women" and wear banners with the inscriptions, "MISS-INFORMED," "MI$$-USED," "MISS-FORTUNE," "MISS-OGYNE," and "MISS ANNA-REXIA." Some demonstrators wear necklaces made of diet soda cans and drag bathroom scales chained to their bodies. One year, a Chicana donned a blonde wig and carried a sign which read "AM I WHITE ENOUGH FOR YOU?" Another year Ann Simonton, a daring protester, wore a twenty-five-pound "meat dress" of bologna and salami with a collar of hotdogs to satirize the "meat-for-sale" mentality of the beauty pageants.

IN APRIL 1970 in the Philippines, the first mass action of MAKIBAKA (the Liberation Movement of New Women) made front-page headlines with an all-women picket at a national beauty contest. The women, outraged at the decadence of beauty pageants

in their poverty-stricken country, protested the commercialization
of sex and the degradation of women as playthings or objects of
pleasure. Two years later, the MAKIBAKA picket was back, this
time with three ex-beauty queens leading the action.

HALF A WORLD AWAY, in Zimbabwe in 1982, Teurai Ropa
Nhongo, the Minister of Community Development and Women's
Affairs, and Dr. Naomi Nhiwatiwa, the deputy minister, had a
suggestion for their new government: "If there is a future 'Miss
Zimbabwe' she should be someone who has rendered distinguished
service to the nation." Both women petitioned the government to
withdraw all support of beauty contests, claiming that it was
contradictory to the idea of establishing a socialist state and an
insult to the women who had died fighting for Zimbabwe's
independence. Despite their dissent, Zimbabwe participated in the
Miss World contest that year.

WHILE WOMEN IN ZIMBABWE repudiated the Miss World
contest, women in Lima, Peru that year protested the Miss
Universe pageant. One Indian woman from Cuzco, in Lima the
day of the contest to attend a farm workers' union meeting, was
interviewed by television reporters.

> As women, as farm workers, we're angry because we don't
> go along with the idea that people should be bought and
> sold for their beauty. . . .
>
> What I'd like to say is that, really, the government is using
> these women, spending the people's money on women
> who sell themselves, who show themselves off. We've
> seen how they're taken from one place to another, sleeping
> and eating in the best hotels, all made up and dressed in
> fancy clothes, each one with a policeman at her side to
> protect her, while there are so many of us sick and poor—
> we give birth right on the ground, without any help. There
> are so many children without food, and the government
> spends our money on things like this! . . . .
>
> Almost all of us here [in the women's meeting] are mothers.
> We have daughters who don't have shoes, sons who don't
> have a single decent pair of pants. We can't even buy a
> notebook to send to school with our children and have to
> put pieces of paper together from here and there to make

one. . . . We women, now that we're organized, we're going to protest.

The farmwoman's eloquent testimony was never broadcast. Consequently, many people in Lima were probably confused and annoyed by the actions taken by the Peruvian feminists who vigorously disrupted the beauty pageant. The protesters shouted, "Women do not want beauty contests," and carried signs that read, "BEAUTY CONTESTS DON'T HIDE POVERTY!" and "WHETHER SHE IS UGLY OR BEAUTIFUL, A WOMAN IS NOT AN OBJECT." Some protesters leafletted the crowds watching the pageant parade. In the text of the leaflets, the feminists explained why they found beauty pageants debasing to women, benefiting only the multinational corporations which used the pageants to advertise their products. The women presented a list of demands—a new civil code, adequate medical services, jobs with equal pay and access to birth control.

The protesters paid heavily for their actions. The police surrounded the women and began beating them with clubs and dispersing the crowd with tear gas. Over twenty women were arrested and many more were hurt. (Not everyone protesting the pageant was committed to nonviolence. On the night of the Miss Universe Pageant, someone threw several bombs at the entrance of the coliseum.)

♀ IN 1982, NEWSPAPERS IN INDIA reported the case of a prominent businessman who'd had three wives in seven years. Each wife had been burned to death.

The year before in the city of Delhi alone, more than 500 newly married women had burned to death in their homes. A few of the grisly deaths were assumed to be genuinely accidental, but in most cases, what looked like the result of kitchen accidents were actually "dowry murders." The women had been set on fire by their husbands or in-laws. In other cases, the women had left suicide notes and had immolated themselves with kitchen stove paraffin or kerosene. The crime is known in India as "bride-burning."

One Indian feminist, quoted in a news article and sounding a refrain familiar to women who work against domestic violence in other countries, explained, "Mostly, bride burning is ignored as something very normal. Whenever I try to discuss it, people tell me it's a domestic problem and I mustn't interfere. The assumption is that a husband has a right to do with his wife whatever he thinks proper."

The Hindu marriage practice of transferring wealth from the bride's father to the groom and his family has been protested by reformers for over a century. Gandhi once expressed the opinion that "any man who makes dowry a condition for marriage discredits his education and his country and dishonors womanhood." Indeed, the custom was officially declared illegal in India with the 1961 Prohibition of Dowry Act. Nevertheless, it has continued to flourish under the guise of gift-giving. Today, though the custom varies widely depending on geographical region and class, the family of a young man who is fair-skinned and "foreign-educated" (a graduate of a British or US university) can demand a dowry of as much as $45,000 (US) in cash and a car or a video recorder. The family of a dark-skinned, uneducated man might negotiate for $2000 and a sewing machine or bicycle.

After the humiliation of the bargaining, buying, selling and competing involved in the marriage arrangement, the new bride might be physically threatened, harmed or harassed by her husband and in-laws. The excuse often used to justify the violence is that a dowry "gift" has been insufficient. The dowry becomes a form of blackmail or extortion and a convenient excuse for wife harassment. Some families, burdened with daughters, are pushed into financial hardship or ruin and cannot keep their dowry agreements. Dowry murders clear the way for a new marriage arrangement for the groom and a fresh source of "gifts" for the groom's family.

Bride-burning, a relatively new aspect of the old dowry tradition, is, some say, a result of the increasingly Westernized consumer-orientation of modern India. But feminists there suspect it has less to do with greed and more to do with violence against women, even when the violence is inflicted by other women such as the mother-in-law or sister-in-law, pawns of the male-dominant system. In a radical feminist analysis of dowry, Indian feminist Madhu Kishwar wrote:

> ... dowry demands are as little or as much related to greed
> as rape is to sexual satisfaction. Both are essentially forms
> of violence whose primary purpose is to degrade and

victimize a woman so that she retains a desperate fear of disobeying the powerful.

As Indian women in the 1980s began to protest dowry marriages with marches, sit-ins and petitions, an editorial entitled "Beginning With Our Own Lives" appeared in the fifth issue of India's feminist journal, *Manushi*. It called on women to publicly pledge to boycott dowry marriages in the following ways:

1. Refuse to attend or participate in a marriage ceremony where a dowry is given or taken in however veiled a form, even if the marriage is that of a relative or close friend. Make the reasons for this action known.
2. Protest whenever a dowry is involved, whether the focus be an extravagant marriage or a dowry murder.
3. Refuse to attend a marriage ceremony in which the woman has had no active choice in deciding whether to get married at all or in choosing the man to whom she is to be married.

Manushi published commitments made by individual women and invited other women to make such commitments. In the seventh issue the editors explained why public statements were important:

We feel that such pledges need to be publicly taken, not just to ensure our accountability to each other as sisters in struggle but to inspire one another with the assurance that we are moving towards a collective and open boycott of dowry weddings rather than making purely personal, private decisions.

The editors also asked that, if anyone who'd made the commitment ever changed her mind, she make a statement publicly explaining her position.

Manushi printed statements from women who were willing to sign their names to the pledge to boycott dowry marriages.

Dear Sisters,
You are absolutely correct in saying that until we boycott the marriage of even our own brother or sister, if lavish dowry is given, we have no moral right to shout slogans. . . .
—Madhavi Sharma

. . . I hereby swear in the name of all that is good not to attend any dowry marriages. . . .

—Gayatri Saberwal

. . . After much discussion and thought, today on International Women's Day, 1981, I solemnly vow that I will not accept dowry when I get married. I am a middle class girl and a native of UP [Uttar Pradesh] where the devilish custom of dowry is widely prevalent. If I cannot marry without dowry I will stay unmarried.

—Vimla Ram

I am opposed to the giving and taking of dowry because I have in my own life seen and experienced how many women are driven to suicide because their parents could not give them enough dowry.

—Dolly Nath

I will not accept dowry when my sons get married.

—Leela Bai

I will refuse dowry at my marriage and will try to spread consciousness against dowry, because I do not want to take my parents' property at the cost of my own degradation.

—Jacinta Kinho

♀ IN 1905, TEN YEARS BEFORE the publication of Charlotte Perkins Gilman's *Herland* in the United States, Bengali Muslim Rokeya Sakhawat Hossein (1880–1932) wrote a feminist, utopian short story titled, "Sultana's Dream." The story, published in English in a Calcutta magazine, described a reversal of *purdah* (the practice of using a curtain or veil to seclude women): men were kept in the seclusion of a harem while women walked free, and the world—run by women—was at peace.

The idea that men, who are a source of danger to women, should be restricted and women be allowed to walk free once occurred to Israeli Prime Minister Golda Meir during a cabinet meeting. One item on the meeting's agenda was the troubling increase in nighttime assaults on women. When one minister suggested that a curfew be imposed on women so that they would stay safely at home after dark, Golda was quick to retort, "But it's the men who are attacking the women! If there's to be a curfew, let the men stay at home, not the women."

This anecdote has inspired feminists in a number of North American and European cities. On December 12, 1979, following a speak-out on rape, men at Rochester Institute of Technology in New York were alarmed at the sight of official-looking "curfew notices" posted on campus. The notices declared in bold print:

ATTENTION R.I.T. MEN—11 PM CURFEW—IN LIGHT OF RECENT RAPES ON CAMPUS, AND TO INSURE THE SAFETY OF WOMEN FROM ANY FURTHER SEXUAL VIOLENCE, ALL MEN—STUDENTS, FACULTY AND STAFF—ARE HEREBY ORDERED TO BE IN THEIR DORMS OR OFF CAMPUS BY 11 PM—VIOLATORS WILL BE SUBJECT TO PROMPT DISCIPLINARY ACTIONS, INCLUDING CRIMINAL PROSECUTION. THERE ARE *NO* EXCEPTIONS. IN THE EVENT OF EMERGENCY, CONTACT PROTECTIVE SERVICES AT [*phone number*].

Many men, believing the notices were official, flooded the switchboard with irate calls. Some of the women allegedly responsible for posting the notices were apprehended by campus security, forcibly removed from campus and told never to return. While this may seem like an unhappy ending, the action was a success in inspiring similar actions in other cities, notably in Leeds, England where 800 women marched through the streets chanting "curfew on men" and "men off the streets," and in Toronto, Canada where the action was code-named "Operation Golda."

IN RHODE ISLAND in March 1983, many early morning rush hour traffickers were alarmed to see the city of Providence plastered with notices proclaiming a curfew on all males over the age of fourteen. The notices listed the mayor's office phone number for those with questions. At the bottom of the very authentic-looking document in extremely small lettering was a disclaimer stating that this was *not* an official proclamation. While the disclaimer worked as a legal safety net for the women activists, it did nothing at all for the frantic men who failed to notice it and flooded the mayor's office with calls.

Meanwhile, the action organizers provided the press with a temporary phone number at which an unnamed woman was available to answer questions. She explained that this was a consciousness-raising exercise designed to help men understand what it feels like to have one's freedom curtailed. Many women, she explained, live with the lifetime inconvenience of an unofficial curfew, locking themselves in at night in fear of male violence.

Television reporters on the Providence evening news programs gave the action a fair amount of coverage, generally treating the curfew notices as a clever and effective if not humorous consciousness-raising exercise on a serious issue. Against this good-natured response, the mayor's reported outrage looked silly and inappropriate, the perfect ending to a splendid media event.

In Peru and India and in Rhode Island the women say: "We stand in a circle. . . . we are not afraid. . . . we are so many. . . we reclaim the night." On pageant stages, at weddings, on college campuses and in city streets, women dare to confront the seemingly innocuous traditions that foster the climate of gender-linked violence they must deal with daily wherever they are. The women stand in a world-embracing circle. They make a vow: "We will extend this safe circle until its boundaries dissolve and its power is everywhere and we are safe everywhere—all women safe everywhere."

Sources

Mythology

Bulfinch, Thomas. *Bulfinch's Mythology: The Age of Fable, The Age of Chivalry, Legends of Charlemagne.* New York: Thomas Y. Crowell, 1970.

Stone, Merlin. *Ancient Mirrors of Womanhood: Our Goddess and Heroine Heritage, Volume I.* New York: New Sibylline Books, 1979.

Ritual

Griffin, Susan. *Rape: The Power of Consciousness.* San Francisco: Harper & Row, 1979.

Beauty pageant protests

Andreas, Carol. *When Women Rebel: The Rise of Popular Feminism in Peru.* Westport, CT: Lawrence Hill, 1985.

Hayes, Loie. "More Actions Against Violence and Porn." *off our backs*, Aug./Sept. 1981.

"Miss California—Shattering the Myth." *off our backs*, Oct. 1983.

Morgan, Robin. *Going Too Far: The Personal Chronicle of a Feminist*. New York: Vintage Books/Random House, 1978.

"Myth California Contested." *Win*, Sept. 1, 1982.

"Peru: Demonstration Attacked." *off our backs*, Aug./Sept. 1982.

"Zimbabwe Women Protest Beauty Contest." *off our backs*, Apr. 1982.

Boycotts

Brata, Sasthi. *India: Labyrinths in the Lotus Land*. New York: William Morrow, 1985.

Fishlock, Trevor. *Gandhi's Children*. New York: Universe Books, 1983.

Frankl, Vera. "Indian Women Fight Apathy Over Bride Burnings." *The Globe and Mail* [Toronto], Jan. 25, 1986.

"Indian Women Speak Out Against Dowry." *Manushi: A Journal About Women and Society*. Reprinted in *Third World—Second Sex: Women's Struggles and National Liberation, Third World Women Speak Out*. Compiled by Miranda Davies. London: Zed Books, 1983.

Kishwar, Madhu. "Dowry—To Ensure Her Happiness or to Disinherit Her?" *Manushi: A Journal About Women and Society*, no. 34 (1986).

"Letters That Came In Response to Our Call for Boycotting Dowry Marriages." *Manushi*, no. 7 (1981).

"Pledges in Response to Manushi's Call for Boycotting Dowry Marriages." *Manushi*, no. 8 (1981).

Women post curfew notices

Hossein, Rokeya Sakhawat. *Sultana's Dream and Selections from "The Secluded Ones."* Roushan Jahan and Hanna Papanek, eds. Translated by Roushan Jahan. New York: Feminist Press, 1987.

Medea, Andra, and Kathleen Thompson. *Against Rape: A Survival Manual for Women*. New York: Farrar, Straus and Giroux, 1974.

Snowden, Rosie, and Al Garthwaite. "Fear Into Anger Into Action." *off our backs*, July 1981.

"Women Impose 'Curfew' On Men." *New Women's Times*. Jan. 4–17, 1980.

9

WE CANNOT LIVE WITHOUT OUR LIVES

"I CANNOT LIVE WITHOUT MY LIFE," cried Heathcliff, dashing his head in anguish against the trunk of an old ash tree. These words, spoken by a fictional male character, were written by a woman, Emily Brontë, author of *Wuthering Heights*. In the essay "Two Perspectives on Women's Struggle," Barbara Deming urged readers "to enter in imagination that storm center, and listen for Heathcliff's cry—in something written by a woman, or something said by her; or you may be a woman saying it to yourself, not quite audibly yet: 'I cannot live without my life!' A lot of women still feel uneasy about uttering that cry aloud." But, Barbara promised, "that is what women now are going to keep on crying: 'I cannot live without my life! I cannot live without my soul!'"

It is this cry we hear in our imaginations as we consider some of the struggles women have waged—struggles with demands as basic as the right to live fully on this planet with black skin or white, to enjoy intellectual integrity whether female or male, to love fully in this lifetime partners of the same or the opposite sex. The demands are as basic as the right to live as though planet earth were truly home to each one of us, as though each life were entitled to its wholeness. We cannot live without our lives.

These particular struggles are often the ones waged against custom and attitude, against the unwritten rules, the rules made by closed and frightened minds and vigorously enforced by tradition, unwritten rules that crush lives or shape them to fit narrow, coffin-like boxes.

In 1902, Carrie Chapman Catt wrote:

> There are two kinds of restrictions upon human liberty—the restraint of law and that of custom. No written law has ever been more binding than unwritten custom supported by popular opinion.

It is a sad fact of the planet that custom has often decreed division, separation, brokenness. In most of North America, for example, custom has usually decreed that people of color be kept separate and less privileged than white people; that females be kept separate and less privileged than males; that people who love others of the same sex be kept hidden, or, if acknowledged at all, be shunned and deprived of basic rights; and that the earth, the animals, the fish, the birds be conceptualized as separate from humans and devoid of rights, existing only to be used. Customs decreeing such separation are found with little variation the world over.

As we will see in this chapter, women sometimes have challenged those customs that reinforce negative attitudes about skin color, gender and sexual orientation. Women have broken unwritten rules, defied old social patterns and have introduced new attitudes, new behaviors. They have turned the world upside down with simple gestures—walking arm-in-arm with a person of another race, forming a women-only club, wearing a Gay Pride T-shirt to school. With each gesture they have said in essence, "We cannot live without our lives."

♀ IN THE YEARS PRECEDING the US Civil War, some brave women were breaking all the rules—both written and unwritten. To their bewildered neighbors there must have seemed no end to the outrages committed by these women who dared defy tradition, traditions so deeply entrenched they seemed as basic as breathing. Bad enough that they had started speaking against slavery before "promiscuous" audiences—mixed audiences of women and men—a practice that alarmed even the most liberal abolitionist men and not a few women. Now they were insisting on making a point of mixing the races as well.

How this had all begun no one could say. Perhaps the women had taken their cue from the black family in Randolph, Massachusetts which had purchased a pew in an otherwise "white" Baptist church in the early 1830s. One Sunday, upon arriving for worship, the family had found their pew removed from the sanctuary. After a few trembling moments, they had quietly seated themselves on the floor. The next Sunday, even the floorboards in that spot had been removed. White supremacists seemed ready to dismantle their own world rather than open its doors to embrace racial diversity, and anti-slavery folks wondered if that dismantling was necessarily a bad thing. Black and white abolitionists began to follow the Randolph family's lead.

Sarah Douglass and her mother, two black women attending Quaker meetings in Philadelphia, were made to sit separately on the "colored" bench. Two white abolitionist sisters, Sarah and Angelina Grimké, were shocked. If Quakers were about "finding that of God in everyone," as they claimed, how could they justify this racist sorting of black from white? From then on, in protest, the four Quaker women, two black, two white, began sitting together each week. They became lifelong friends and co-conspirators in exposing instances of racism readily supplied by Sarah Douglass.

BUT WOMEN'S RACIAL MIXING was not to be confined to churches; it spilled out into the streets. In a nation of slaves and slaveholders, it was the matter of safety that first inspired black women and white to link arms and walk together after their meetings. Maria Weston Chapman, who often chaired the meetings of the Boston Female Anti-Slavery Society, realized that the black women in attendance were in danger of being isolated and attacked by the white mobs who lay in wait for them outside. She insisted that the white women link arms with their black sisters and accompany them past the mobs after each meeting.

It was in Philadelphia in May 1838 that this tactic was really put to the test. Women had gathered from all over the Northeast to attend the second Anti-Slavery Convention of American Women. On May 14 they joined in the dedication ceremony for brand-new Pennsylvania Hall, a building well worth celebrating. It had been built by well-to-do abolitionists and reformers in response to the increasing denial of public building space for their anti-slavery meetings. From the outside, the new hall looked like a Greek temple, and inside was an auditorium, offices, galleries, and a "free produce" store (for the sale of goods not linked to slave trade). All of this was decorated in blue and white with lovely blue plush chairs. John Greenleaf Whittier wrote a special poem for the dedication ceremony, and everyone marveled at this building which was specifically intended for the anti-slavery cause.

The very next day, the women held their convention in the new hall. They got down to business immediately and resolved to call for the boycott of all slave produce and to start a campaign to end slavery in the District of Columbia. In one area, however, they could not agree—and that was the delicate matter of the propriety of delivering anti-slavery speeches to mixed (female and male) audiences. They decided to hold a special meeting Wednesday evening, May 16, for all those who wanted to debate the issue in depth. Meanwhile, they agreed to move on to less controversial matters.

Outside the convention, hostility was growing. It deeply irritated pro-slavery Philadelphians to see this grand hall open for the business of anti-slavery agitating. But what really irked them was seeing black women walking and talking with white women during the course of the convention. Where would this end? Just that week two white abolitionists, Angelina Grimké and Theodore Weld, had gotten married and had invited both black and white guests to attend their wedding. Those damned "amalgamators!"

By the time the women met for their special session on Wednesday evening, the angry, jeering mob could no longer be ignored. William Lloyd Garrison stood outside the hall to reason with the crowd. He was followed by the newly married veteran speaker Angelina Grimké Weld, and then the young newcomer Abby Kelly stood up. Abby spoke passionately from the heart and discovered, in that moment of fearlessness, her true calling to the anti-slavery lecture circuit. Finally, Lucretia Mott stepped up to speak to the over-heated mob. Lucretia's magic was in her calm, sensible, down-to-earth openness and trust. The mob listened to her. For the time-being, those brimming with fear and hatred were soothed and went home.

During the night, however, some diehards posted notices all over the city urging the pro-slavery faction to "interfere, forcefully if you must" with the women's convention.

Thursday, the mob outside the hall was ready for action. A delegation from the hall visited the mayor to ask for protection, but the mayor just shook his head. Any trouble, he said, was the women's own fault. They should have known better than to hold such a convention in the first place. He would do nothing. He did have a suggestion, however—tell the black women to stop attending the meetings.

Lucretia Mott returned to the convention with the mayor's suggestion, saying she didn't agree with it and hoped no one else there would either. On this occasion the women stood strong, black and white very solidly together. Their only concern was the safety of the black women. That evening they bravely left the convention in pairs, black women linking arms with white women.

Even after the women had safely exited the building, thousands of white, pro-slavery citizens waited in front of Pennsylvania Hall, their numbers and their restless rage growing by the minute. Too late, the mayor appeared and nervously appealed for peace. Then he went home. The mob, of course, did not. It broke down the doors of the beautiful new building, ransacked the offices and, not satisfied, made a bonfire of the anti-slavery literature, burning Pennsylvania Hall to the ground.

Inspired by their acts of destruction, the mob went on to attack Mother Bethel Church and the Shelter for Colored Orphans. They would have attacked the Mott's home if an alert friend hadn't shouted, "On to the Mott's!" and waved the stupid crowd in the wrong direction.

With Pennsylvania Hall in ashes, the final session of the Anti-Slavery Convention of American Women was held in a little schoolhouse at the invitation of Quaker schoolteacher Sarah Pugh. Far from being intimidated by the terrorism they had encountered, the women pledged to strengthen their bonds with each other and expand their social relations.

The white women in attendance adopted a resolution proposed by Sarah Grimké which affirmed in part:

> It is . . . the duty of abolitionists to identify themselves with these oppressed Americans, by sitting with them in places of worship, by appearing with them in our streets, by giving them our countenance in steamboats and stages, by visiting with them at their homes and encouraging them to visit us, receiving them as we do our white fellow citizens.

Black women and white resolved they would meet again the following year.

In addition to holding such conventions, women continued to use the abolitionist tactic of interracial "walk-alongs." They took to heart the admonition of black anti-racism leader Frederick Douglass that the way for people to combat the ignorance of racial prejudice was "to act as though it didn't exist, and to associate with their fellow creatures irrespective of all complexional differences."

In 1858 in a Newport, Rhode Island Baptist church, a white parishioner invited a young black girl to sit with her during the worship service. Though both were members of the congregation, the fact that they dared sit together so outraged the white church-goers that church officials refused to renew the lease on the pew of the white woman. Undaunted, she returned the next Sunday with a camp stool and sat in the aisle beside the pew which had formerly been hers. And the fight against racial separation continued.

♀ IT IS NO EASY TASK to establish new social patterns, and groundbreakers are always ridiculed, at the very least. Nor is the way to healing and wholeness always a straight line. In 1838 Philadelphia, black and white women sought to heal the wounds of racial hatred by walking together arm-in-arm. But in the following story, women deprived of access to the male domain looked elsewhere and created another, separate place for themselves. In healing the brokenness of their lives, they also set a social precedent.

The New York literary world was buzzing with anticipation. Charles Dickens was arriving in the States and the New York Press Club had announced a reception for him and a dinner where he was to speak. Surely this was the place to be.

But when the Press Club announced that tickets for the evening were reserved for men only, women journalists and writers were outraged, none more so than Jane Croly. A successful and hard-working journalist and advocate of equal rights for women, Croly had established a popular syndicated newspaper column which she signed with her pen name, "Jennie June."

Shut out of the men's Press Club, Croly decided it was time women had a club of their own. In this spirit, Sorosis, the pioneer of the white women's club movement, was founded in 1868. Mainly for writers and journalists but open to other creative and professional women, the club's purpose was to promote "agreeable and useful relations among women of literary, artistic and scientific tastes."

The men found the idea of a women's club quite amusing and jeered that it couldn't last a year. Nevertheless, being "good sports" the men invited the members of Sorosis to a "Breakfast." The women accepted the invitation only to discover that they were not allowed to speak at the Press Club but were only to sit, eat and listen. Good sports, indeed!

In what became a game of tit-for-tat, the women then invited the men to a "Tea" and, in retaliation for their humiliation at the Press Club, allowed those men who condescended to attend the Tea no chance to speak, not even to respond to a toast.

Having tasted their own bitter medicine, the men called a truce. Both clubs jointly sponsored a "Dinner" for the newly empowered women and the newly enlightened men. As stipulated, the women and men who attended the dinner each paid her/his own way and all shared equally in the responsibilities as well as the honors of the evening.

After she became president of Sorosis in 1870, Croly published a satirical letter to a hypothetical man who had applied for membership in the women's club. She graciously explained why membership had to be denied him.

> Reputation and position are alike unexceptionable; but the unfortunate fact of your being a man outweighs these and all other claims to membership. We willingly admit, of course, that the accident of your sex is on your part a misfortune, and not a fault. Nor do we wish to arrogate anything to ourselves because we had the good fortune to be born women. We sympathize most truly and heartily with you and the entire male creation, in their present and prospective desolation and unhappiness; but this is all we can do.

♀ SINCE THE BLOOD-RED DAWN of patriarchy, many women who have sought to live without aligning themselves with a male partner have in some way defied unwritten rules. In her essay "Compulsory Heterosexuality and Lesbian Existence," Adrienne Rich suggests that it is useful, when examining the historical presence of lesbians, to consider the notion of a "lesbian continuum," by which she means:

> a range—through each woman's life and throughout history—of woman-identified experience; not simply the fact that a woman has had or consciously desired genital sexual experience with another woman. If we expand it to embrace many more forms of primary intensity between

> and among women, including the sharing of a rich inner
> life, the bonding against male tyranny, the giving and
> receiving of practical and political support . . . —we begin
> to grasp breadths of female history and psychology which
> have lain out of reach as a consequence of limited, mostly
> clinical, definitions of "lesbianism."

Keeping in mind the "lesbian continuum," Rich invites us to reconsider such diverse lives as the Beguines of the twelfth and fifteenth centuries who formed women-only ascetic and philanthropic communities throughout Europe, and women in Chinese silk mills who formed marriage resistance sisterhoods. Though we have ample evidence of women who have made great contributions to the world while living on the lesbian continuum, Rich points out that "women's choice of women as passionate comrades, life partners, co-workers, lovers, tribe, has been crushed, invalidated, forced into hiding and disguise." This virtual neglect of lesbian existence, she says, continues even in the work of feminist scholars today. It has been the work of lesbians in the twentieth century to make their lives visible, to resist disappearance and to unearth the history of which they have been deprived.

An essential first step in challenging negative attitudes about homosexuality in society at large is claiming for oneself a positive identity. This is the work of confronting internalized oppression, of "coming out," of accepting the truth—"I cannot live without my life." In an interview for *Feminary: A Feminist Journal for the South,* Barbara Deming talked about this process.

> Back in my twenties (which was in the 1930s) I was keeping
> a journal, and I wrote in the journal, "I am a lesbian; I must
> face this truth." Then, re-reading my journal a few days
> later, I thought, "Gosh, I shouldn't have that down here in
> black and white. Someone might read it." So I took my
> scissors and cut out that sentence and tossed it in the
> wastepaper basket. Perhaps half an hour later, as I was
> moving around the room, I glanced down and there, glaring
> up at me most conspicuously from the wastepaper basket,
> was this cut-out sentence. And I remember that it hit me:
> you can't throw truths away. If you try to throw them away,
> you get into worse trouble than the trouble you were trying
> to escape.

Simply by daring to become visible, lesbians and their allies (often heterosexual friends and relatives) have confronted the world's homophobia (the irrational fear of homosexuality)—in the classroom, the church, the office, at the family dinner table, in government chambers, on the streets. With their visibility they proclaim, "We cannot live without our lives."

IN THE 1970S IN A SMALL US TOWN, two students, Mitzi and Jackie, endured the daily taunts of their high school classmates who called them "lezzies" and "queers." After seeking the help of some supportive heterosexual friends, Mitzi and Jackie decided they'd had enough of tears and denials. They began a campaign to be both visible and thoughtfully provocative in school in order to counteract some of the assumptions and knee-jerk reactions of the students who harassed them.

On the first day of her senior year, Mitzi wore a Gay Pride T-shirt to school.

Mitzi and Jackie asked the public library as well as the school library to purchase positive books about lesbian identity such as *Sappho Was a Right-On Woman* by Sidney Abbott and Barbara Love.

In government class, when students were asked to write a bill or amendment to be debated and voted on in a mock senate, Mitzi and Jackie introduced an amendment that would grant equal rights for homosexuals. A heated debate followed during which some students argued that the Bible condemned homosexuality and therefore the law should not protect the rights of homosexuals. On the basis of this argument, the amendment was defeated. The next day, Mitzi and Jackie came to class with a mischievous gleam in their eyes and another provocative proposal—this time to legalize slavery. As the other students gasped in amazement, Mitzi and Jackie defended their proposal by pointing out that in some passages the Bible not only permitted but even condoned slavery. The shocked students were speechless. The point had been made. Later, Mitzi wrote:

> I realize these are small victories, but it's a start. If we can raise the consciousness at the high school level, then a foundation is established to build on in the future. The day

of equality for all human beings is coming—I dream of it;
I feel it; I believe in it.

IN NEW ZEALAND, early in 1972, Maori feminist Nghula
Volkering applied for a United States Student Leadership Grant.
She was vice-president of the Auckland University Students'
Association and stated in her application that she intended to study
the Native American and gay liberation movements in the United
States. When the US Immigration Service refused her application,
she sought the support of lesbians and gay men in Auckland in
protesting the US action. This was the beginning of New Zealand's
first gay liberation group, and within three months groups had
formed in two other cities to fight government repression such as
the banning of fourteen books by lesbians.

IN THE UNITED STATES AT THE JUNE 1981 National Women's
Studies Association annual convention, there were enough women
qualified to join in a "Fired Lesbians Caucus." Almost none of
them had been fired outright for being lesbians: they had been
"dismissed" due to budget cuts, expired contracts or some other
technicality that could not be fought directly. But the women in
the caucus understood that they had been fired because they had
challenged heterosexist assumptions. In writing about the caucus,
one of the fired lesbians, feminist activist and author Judith
McDaniel, explained:

> We were fired for what we are, for what we say, for the
> work that we insist on doing, for the vision we hold of
> ourselves as political women. . . .
>
> What we must remember in order to survive is that we
> cannot change our dress, or speech, or the focus of our
> academic interests in order to become acceptable. Hiding
> our anger will not save us. If we cannot be who we are and
> be acceptable, that is a political reality we must recognize
> and consider in every act of our day-to-day existence.

MANY LESBIANS HAVE JOINED FEMINISTS and anti-patriarchal
men in challenging the homophobia of religious institutions. Some
have joined churches that exist specifically to serve the lesbian
and gay community such as the Universal Fellowship of

Metropolitan Community Churches. Others seek to work within mainstream denominations for acceptance and appreciation of a lesbian or gay sensibility. In the early 1960s, when Nancy Krody was accepted into Crosier Seminary in Minnesota, she was the only woman in the three-year bachelor of divinity program. Her first year she received an award for the highest grades and was well accepted by both students and faculty. But in April of her second year, her seminary "career" came to an end when she publicly identified herself as a lesbian. She was allowed to complete that year, but was told not to reapply for the third year.

Though Krody had never met another lesbian nor read any literature by lesbians, she felt instinctively the importance of being honest about herself. Only after the advent of the gay liberation movement did she find support. She began to help establish new attitudes about homosexuality by lecturing as a lesbian Christian.

> The church is the "home" in which I was nurtured, where I learned what love and justice and liberation are about, where I learned what affirmation and dignity and wholeness mean. I have learned through the church that my sexuality is God-given and is good and necessary for me to be a full human being. . . .
>
> I will not be heard if I leave the church. Only if I remain inside will my words have any effect on those who disagree. Only as they see my life as a responsible person who glories in her lesbianism and celebrates her covenant with her spouse will they come to understand and eventually to accept same-sex love. . . .
>
> May we all know liberation from our fears and pain and learn to love and affirm one another in our differences.

WOMEN HAVE WORKED to change attitudes about same-sex love from the point of view of daughters, sisters, lesbian mothers and mothers of lesbians. One mother, Constance Shepard Jolly, wrote an article for the Wellesley alumnae magazine describing her experience of publicly supporting her daughter's choice to be a lesbian.

> Last June 26, my husband and I received a standing ovation from a cheering crowd of a quarter of a million. Men and women ran out from the sidelines to embrace us and to thank us for being there. The air was full of balloons,

> marching band music, exuberant joy and overwhelming love, much of it directed toward . . . Bob and me! . . .
>
> The June 26 extravaganza was, in fact, a celebration of our pride in Margaret, as Bob and I walked in the San Francisco Lesbian and Gay Freedom Day Parade along with ten other middle-aged men and women under a banner that read "Parents and Friends of Lesbians and Gays." . . . I was deeply moved that parents publicly demonstrating their love for their homosexual children was, to the gay men and lesbians in that vast crowd, a cause for cheering, clapping, and often tearful gratitude.

She ended her article with a recognition of the work that must continue to be done to change the harmful attitudes in society.

> . . . There is still a long way to go until discrimination in jobs, housing and child custody is a thing of the past. There is a long way to go until the parents of homosexual children are free to love them completely without fear or shame. There is a long way to go before gay men and lesbians no longer think it's a big deal when ten parents march the length of Market Street the way we did in the Freedom Day Parade.

SEVERAL YEARS EARLIER and half a world away from the San Francisco Parents and Friends of Lesbians and Gays, in the southeast Asian nation of Indonesia, parents and friends celebrated the "holy union" of Jossie and Bonnie. Before 100 guests, the two young women exchanged vows, and publicly proclaimed their love for each other and their commitment to be life partners.

Part of what made this celebration of a lesbian union so brave was that, just a week before, the newspapers had been filled with the details of two other young women, Aty and Nona, also from the island of Java, who had been arrested and found guilty of "committing indecent acts with each other." They had been sentenced to eight months imprisonment and twenty months probation and a doctor had been sought to surgically cure Aty of her "male hormonal imbalance." These two women had run away from home together, first to Malang and then further east to the island of Bali, where they were found by their parents. "Until I die," Nona told her parents, "I have chosen Aty as my partner for life."

Do you hear the unspoken cry, "I cannot live without my life"?

> I don't remember the exact moment that I understood that
> Nazi Germany had destroyed hundreds of thousands of
> homosexuals solely on the basis of their Gayness. But I
> know that the fact will haunt me all my life, for I can never
> trust my citizenship, never take for granted that my
> neighbors will not stand idly by while I am killed for my way
> of life. The Holocaust will be with us forever.
> —Judy Grahn, *Another Mother*
> *Tongue: Gay Words, Gay Worlds*

IN 1982 IN THE NETHERLANDS, Evelien Eshuis was elected to
parliament. Every day in parliament she made it a point to wear
a pink triangle badge on her lapel as a public sign of her lesbian
identity. She did this, she said, "for all those women who can't—
who can then at least know that there are lesbians in political
circles." The pink triangle is a sign of homosexual identity,
reclaimed, lest it be forgotten, from the time of the Nazis. Tens
of thousands of gay men and some lesbians were forced to wear
pink triangles on their coats and were sent to concentration camps
where they were killed for the crime of being gay.

Before the Third Reich came into power in 1933, Germany was
a haven for lesbian and gay culture with an estimated community
of over 50,000 living in Berlin alone. A lesbian newspaper, *The
Girlfriend: Weekly for the Ideal Friendship Between Women*,
could be found on Berlin newsstands from 1923 to 1932. Fifty
years later, when Evelien Eshuis wore her pink triangle to
parliament, she was saying in effect, "We cannot live without our
lives. Remember what happened to us. Remember this."

A THOUSAND KISSES! On January 23, 1987, Spanish women
held a "kiss-in" on the streets of Madrid to protest the harassment
of two women who had been arrested earlier that week for kissing
in public. They had been held in a high-security cell for forty-eight
hours. After their release, they had reported mistreatment at the
hands of the police and had mobilized the Madrid lesbian
community. Hundreds of women gathered on the site of the arrest
for a peaceful protest, chanting slogans and kissing each other to
show that love between women is not a crime.

Do you hear the unspoken cry, "We cannot live without our lives"?

Sources

Barbara Deming

Deming, Barbara. "Two Perspectives on Women's Struggle" from *We Are All Part of One Another: A Barbara Deming Reader.* Jane Meyerding, ed. Philadelphia: New Society, 1984.

Segrest, Mab. "Feminism and Disobedience: Conversations with Barbara Deming." *Feminary: A Feminist Journal for the South,* vol. 11, nos. 1 & 2 (1980).

Women's anti-slavery efforts

Bacon, Margaret Hope. *Valiant Friend: The Life of Lucretia Mott.* New York: Walker, 1980.

Davis, Angela Y. *Women, Race & Class.* New York: Random House, 1981.

Lerner, Gerda. *The Majority Finds Its Past: Placing Women in History.* New York: Oxford University Press, 1979/1981.

McHenry, Robert, ed., *Famous American Women: A Biographical Dictionary From Colonial Times to the Present.* New York: Dover, 1980.

Sharp, Gene. *The Politics of Nonviolent Action: Part Two—The Methods of Nonviolent Action.* Boston: Porter Sargent, 1973.

Sorosis tea party

Boulding, Elise. *The Underside of History: A View of Women Through Time.* Boulder, CO: Westview Press, 1976.

Croly, Jane Cunningham. *Sorosis: Its Origin and History.* New York: J. J. Little, 1886.

Papachristou, Judith. *Women Together: A History in Documents of the Women's Movement in the United States.* "A Ms. Book." New York: Alfred A. Knopf, 1976.

Lesbians seek recognition

Grahn, Judy. *Another Mother Tongue: Gay Words, Gay Worlds.* Boston: Beacon Press, 1984.

Jolly, Constance Shepard. "Purple Balloons on Market Street: A Story of Love." *Wellesley Alumnae Magazine,* Summer 1984.

Krody, Nancy E. "On Being a Lesbian Christian" from *The Lesbian Path: 37 Lesbian Writers Share Their Personal Experiences, Viewpoints, Traumas and Joy.* Margaret Cruikshank, ed. Monterey, CA.: Angel Press, 1980.

McDaniel, Judith. "We Were Fired: Lesbian Experiences in Academe." *Sinister Wisdom,* no. 20 (1982).

"New Zealand: An Island of Many Cultures." *Connexions: An International Women's Quarterly—Global Lesbianism,* no. 3 (Winter, 1982).

Rich, Adrienne. *Compulsory Heterosexuality and Lesbian Existence.* Denver, CO: Antelope, 1980.

Simmons, Mitzi. "The Days of Guilt and Shame Are Gone" from *Our Right to Love: A Lesbian Resource Book*. Ginny Vida, ed. Englewood Cliffs, NJ: Prentice-Hall, 1978.

"Spain: A Kiss Is Just a Kiss." *off our backs*, May 1987.

"Trial and a Marriage." *Connexions: An International Women s Quarterly—Global Lesbianism*, no. 3 (Winter, 1982)

10
STOPPING THE CANNONS, BLOCKING THE TANKS

WOMEN KNOW ABOUT WALLS and barriers. They have been
hidden behind veils, forbidden to enter the marketplace, universities,
voting booths, courtrooms. They have been denied access to
positions of power, to professions, to orgasms, to money and
movement, to books and libraries. Sometimes they've been locked
into gilded cages and told it is their nature to be weak, to think
small, to want nothing. Other times they've been locked out of the
gilded cages and sent to labor in fields or factories and been told
to think small and want nothing. Women know about walls and
barriers.

For the most part, women have despaired of the barriers in their
lives. On rare occasions, however, women have been moved to
sing a different song. "It isn't nice to block the doorways," wrote
folksinger Malvina Reynolds in the sixties, and the women joined
in the chorus, "but if that's freedom's price we don't mind." Turning
their knowledge of barriers to good use, women have collectively
made walls, putting their bodies in front of cannons and between
troops to make the fighting stop; putting themselves or some object
in the way of business as usual when that business meant harm to
the earth, their families, their lives.

Women have employed the tactic of nonviolent obstruction to
thwart those who would curtail their rights as workers. In
Johannesburg, South Africa in 1943, three women chained
themselves to the railings outside the OK Bazaar where they were
employed. They had been picketing the store in an effort to win
union recognition, and had gotten out the chains only after they
were driven away from the storefront by the police. Largely as a
consequence of the women's dramatic action, a number of the major

stores in Johannesburg granted recognition to the National Union of Distributive Workers.

In Poland, women joined the "underground" and acted in support of Solidarity, a free trade union. In the northern city of Gdańsk in 1980, over 3000 women handed out flowers and Solidarity bulletins while they bravely stared down tanks preparing to crush the shipyard gates. In the southern city of Katowice, women suffered broken bones when they formed a blockade with their bodies, but they were successful in preventing the police from entering a worker-occupied steel mill.

Women have acted from love of their country, their homeland and their people with the use of nonviolent obstruction. In Zambia in the 1920s, women working in solidarity with the nationalist movement for independence cut down trees to block the roads used by government soldiers who were searching for saboteurs. And in the 1950s, Zambian women blocked a road leading to the Ndola Airport to prevent a car carrying the British Colonial Secretary from passing. This was but one of many nonviolent actions taken by women in Zambia.

♀ EARLY IN THE PINK MORNING of March 18, 1871, the housewives of Paris set out on their usual errands to buy bread and milk. Little did they know that they were about to step into the pages of history.

Their winter had been long and bitter. Prussian troops had invaded France, but Paris had not accepted defeat easily though Emperor Napoleon III had been captured in September. One of those who resisted the invasion was Louise Michel, nicknamed the "Red Virgin," a poet and revolutionary who would soon be captured, tried and sentenced to exile in a prison colony for almost ten years. But during that winter, Michel was both a participant in and witness to the Parisian uprising. In her *Memoirs* she wrote about the women revolutionaries in Paris at that time:

> Heroic women were found in all social positions. . . . They would have preferred to die rather than surrender, and dispensed their efforts the best way they could, while demanding ceaselessly that Paris continue to resist the Prussian siege. . . They didn't become like those harpies the following May who dug out the eyes of our fallen comrades with the tips of their parasols. . . .

> I salute all those brave women of the vanguard. . . . The
> old world ought to fear the day when those women finally
> decide they have had enough. Those women will not slack
> off. Strength finds refuge in them. Beware of them! . . .
> Beware of the women when they are sickened by all that is
> around them and rise up against the old world. On that day
> the new world will begin.

But for all this courage, the city was forced to surrender in
Jaunary 1871. The young soldiers of the National Guard (the
Parisian popular militia) sank into mud up to their ankles and were
slaughtered by Prussian forces. Michel wrote:

> Hundreds stayed behind, lying quietly in death; these men
> of the National Guard—men of the people, artists, young
> persons—died with no regret for their lost lives. The earth
> drank the blood of this first Parisian carnage; soon it would
> drink more.

The bitterness remained even when the conquering Prussians
allowed the French to elect a national government housed in
Versailles, just outside of Paris.

The Versailles government was nervous about the Parisians'
inability to accept defeat, so in March, when the Parisian popular
militia (the National Guard) began reclaiming their lost cannons
in a show of bravado, Versailles reacted. The government ordered
its troops back into the city to put an end to this foolishness and
force Paris to comply with the invaders' will. After all, the war
was supposed to be over.

Silently, the Versailles troops crept into the sleeping city to
seize the cannons. At dawn on March 18, the women of Paris
opened their doors to find that soldiers from Versailles had
occupied Paris during the night. Word spread quickly as more and
more women came out of their houses. Soon a crowd of over 1000
stood gaping at the young soldiers.

Meanwhile, the men of the National Guard were slumped in
defeat and humiliation, but when the Vigilance Committee got
wind of the women's presence on the streets, it sent orders to the
National Guard to retake the city's beloved hilltop, Montmartre.
Suddenly the city was at war again, and the streets were filled
with French soldiers, those from Versailles fighting in the spirit
of the invading Prussians, those of the Parisian National Guard
ready to fight for their hilltop, if not for their city and their nation.

No one knows how it happened that the women found themselves speaking with one voice that day. As though they had strategized for just such circumstances, they began approaching the soldiers from Versailles, asking them, "Will you fire on us? Will you fire on your brother Parisians? On our husbands? Our children?" The women surrounded the soldiers of the Eighty-eighth Battalion and formed a barrier between them and the local men of the National Guard.

And so it happened that, when General Lecomte got nervous and ordered his soldiers of the Eighty-eighth to fire, the soldiers turned around and arrested their own general. And several streets over on rue Houdon, General Susbielle encountered similar amazing difficulties. He too was nervous and ordered his cavalry to "charge," but to his chagrin, instead of charging, the men on their horses retreated. The women cheered.

Louise Michel was there. Later, she remembered March 18:

> The Butte of Montmartre was bathed in the first light of day through which things were glimpsed as if they were hidden behind a thin veil of water. Gradually the crowd increased. . . . The women of Paris covered the cannon with their bodies. When their officers ordered the soldiers to fire, the men refused. . . . When we had won our victory, I looked around and noticed my poor mother who had followed me to the Butte of Montmartre, believing that I was going to die. . . . On this day, the eighteenth of March, the people wakened.

All over the city, women stopped horses, cut their harnesses and urged the soldiers from Versailles to join their brothers in the National Guard. Finally, in the evening of that remarkable day, the troops were ordered to withdraw and the women went home, most, presumably, to fix dinner for their families.

It was just the beginning of the actions women would take in the difficult days of death and defeat which lay ahead for the people of Paris, including, most notably, the march to Versailles by 800 women carrying the red flag of the Paris Commune, women set on demanding an end to the bloodshed. But that story is for another time. . . .

♀ IF THIS STORY SOUNDS FAMILIAR—of ordinary citizens courageously putting their bodies between troops and urging soldiers to greet each other as friends, not enemies—it may be because history once again repeated itself, not long ago, in the Philippine Revolution of 1986.

The majority of Filipino people had suffered severely under twenty years of the corrupt and ruthless dictatorial rule of President Ferdinand Marcos, especially after he imposed martial law in 1972. While the president wined and dined the heads of US-based multinational corporations and made laws by personal decree, his wife, Imelda, bought shoes, supervised extensive renovation of their home, the Malacanang Palace, and devoted her life to supporting her husband's regime.

Outside the palace walls, in a nation of 55 million people and over 7 thousand islands, children in the countryside were starving to death while their parents worked lush, green land that belonged to absentee landlords and rich corporations. Just outside the cities many children spent their days climbing mountains of garbage looking for anything salvageable to sell or food scraps to eat. Over 70 percent of the people lived below the poverty line.

And there was fear. When tenant farmers of one rural area organized to discuss their anger at having to buy high-priced seeds from a multinational corporation, Marcos' soldiers murdered the group's leaders and displayed the mutilated bodies in the barrio centers so that people would be afraid to speak out again. Such terror was inflicted daily in myriad ways. The people were to be kept in line while the president and an elite few danced.

People were filled with fear, but they were also determined to fight for their freedom, and their resistance took many forms. In the early 1970s, women in the cities founded MAKIBAKA (the Liberation Movement of New Women), the first organization to equate women's liberation with the national struggle. MAKIBAKA brought together women students, workers and professionals for rallies and demonstrations, and, though the organization disbanded after martial law was declared in 1972, it had a major impact on women in the Philippines. Many women went underground at that point and joined in secret revolutionary work. Some women and men joined the New People's Army (NPA), carrying guns while they organized for land reform and literacy programs and an end to the Marcos regime. Still others began to organize in their churches and religious communities. Hundreds of Basic Christian Communities were formed which maintained that Christians were obligated by their faith to work to build a just society. This contention put believers at odds with the Marcos regime and in the early 1980s church centers were raided, church publications were censored or prohibited and the lay people, nuns, priests and ministers involved in organizing the poor were arrested and jailed.

While many people risked their lives every day to empower the people to overthrow the dictator, most of the millions of Filipinos just tried to survive, taking care to stay out of the way of Marcos' soldiers. And then something happened that changed that and gave momentum to the long struggle to overthrow the dictator Marcos.

On August 21, 1983, the popular opposition leader Benigno (Ninoy) Aquino was assassinated as he got off the plane returning him to the Philippines from his eleven-year exile in the United States. Before he could take even one step on Philippine ground, he was assassinated in broad daylight and in full view of the international press. Ten days later, 2 million people took to the streets and mourned with the widow, Corazon Aquino, on an eleven-hour march to Ninoy's grave in Paranaque. And the next month, thousands of people came into the streets for a "National Day of Sorrow" mourning Ninoy's death. They looked at each other in amazement. Something had changed.

Their amazement with each other continued to grow as more and more people dared to come out of the shadows. Suddenly they were signing petitions asking Cory Aquino to run for president, and everywhere, everyone and everything was draped in yellow, the official color of the Aquino crusade. Yellow confetti from shredded telephone books fell from high-rise buildings, even from the business offices which had always been the territory of Marcos supporters. People began flashing the L-sign for *laban*, which means "fight." It had been the name of Ninoy Aquino's party and was now the code for the new spirit in the very air.

Throughout 1984, people who had never dared raise their voices suddenly found themselves mobilizing for action. By March, a mammoth umbrella organization linking women activists from over fifty organizations had formed—GABRIELA (General Assembly Binding Women for Reforms, Integrity, Equality, Leadership and Action). The name also honored an eighteenth-century woman who had led a revolt against the repressive force of another age—Spain. Women were reclaiming their history of resistance.

Many women had been sent to prison, tortured, killed or made to "disappear" during the Marcos regime, and with thousands of people openly organizing, the imprisonment and torture continued. Mila Aguilar, a Filipina poet, teacher and journalist who had been widely published in the US feminist media, was imprisoned in August 1984 by the Marcos military under a decree that allowed Marcos to hold prisoners for one year without filing charges against them. Still, the women continued to organize, coming together around an endless variety of common interests and concerns— Alliance of Women Towards Action and Reconciliation (AWARE), the Women Workers Movement (KMK), and Samahan ng Mga Kababaihang Nagkakaisa (SAMAKANA), the organization of urban poor women.

Also in 1984, the Little Sisters of Jesus in Manila and other communities of nuns worked together to bring to the Philippines Hildegard and Jean Goss-Mayr, the vice presidents of the International Fellowship of Reconciliation. Acknowledging that the Church had been an accomplice for too long in perpetuating the Marcos regime, Hildegard argued, "We Christians should be the first to open our eyes to injustice, and to speak out and bring the power of nonviolence into the revolution." To do this, the church communities invited Hildegard and Jean to offer seminars in preparation for nonviolent revolution. Hildegard described the process used in the seminars:

> In each seminar, we would first analyze the situation of violence together and discover how we were part of it, for the violence is in the structures, of course, and the dictator, but isn't it also in ourselves? It is easy to say that Marcos is the evil, but unless we tear the dictator out of our own heart, nothing will change. Another group will come into power and will act like those whom they replaced.

The people who attended the seminars did not always trust each other at first. At some meetings the political leaders of the opposition and the peasant leaders would not speak to each other. After one such meeting, Hildegard saw the act of communion work to heal the wounds of the community.

> Then one evening we celebrated the Eucharist together. After the consecration, Fr. Jose Blanco distributed the host to each person. Then he said, "Now let us take this bread and give it to those with whom we have not yet spoken." We saw the peasants bring the host to the politicians, and the politicians bring their host to the peasants. . . . These seminars are more than just training people in

methodology. The goal is for each one of us to undergo a deep change, a conversion.

In July 1984, AKKAPKA was formed. *Akkapka* is the Tagalog word for "I embrace you," as well as an acronym for Action for Peace and Justice. From its base in Manila, AKKAPKA began to organize three-day seminars throughout the country, preparing people to take nonviolent action. "Base groups" were formed from each seminar—small gatherings of people who agreed to work together in on-going projects and who met regularly to support each other and pray.

Indeed, for many people prayer became a part of their resistance, a tool for revolution. Hildegard Goss-Mayr explained:

> We cannot emphasize enough the importance of deep spirituality. It is this which gives people the strength to stand in front of tanks when the time comes. In the Philippines, people developed the discipline of praying every day, prayed for all who suffered in the process of trying to change the society, prayed for the military, and prayed for Marcos—prayed that he would find strength not to use his huge arsenal against the people. Such prayer makes a great difference. In a revolutionary process, people are highly emotional. It makes a difference whether you promote hatred and revenge or you help the people stand firmly for justice without becoming like the oppressor. You want to love your enemy, to liberate rather than destroy.

On December 15, 1985, Cory Aquino agreed to run for president against Marcos and began a nationwide campaign. She spoke to the masses of supporters who dared attend the rallies, "They say I have no experience. It is true: I have no experience in lying, cheating, stealing and killing." Marcos didn't take her too seriously. "What qualifications does she have," he quipped, "except that her husband was killed?"

Marcos was proclaimed president after an election marred by terrorism and fraud committed by his supporters, but on February 16, 1986 2 million people turned out at a rally to repudiate the election fraud and proclaim the victory of the people over Marcos. That day, the people began a massive program of civil disobedience and nonviolent protest.

Then, on Saturday, February 22, the Minister of Defense Enrile and Vice Chief of Staff Ramos held a press conference to announce the withdrawal of their support from Marcos and to declare the rightful president to be Corazon Aquino. They called on the armed forces to join them in siding with the people. The tide was definitely turning but this was the point of gravest danger. No one knew what would happen next and everyone was afraid.

That night, the Archbishop of Manila, Jaime Cardinal Sin, made an appeal to the nation over the radio. He knew that the people would be listening, depending on Radio Veritas (Latin for "truth"), the Catholic station, as they had for the last few months to find out what was really happening in their country. They listened too for words of encouragement and ideas about nonviolence, about building a just society, about standing together. The broadcasters read passages from Martin Luther King, Gandhi, Jesus' "Sermon on the Mount." The station brought into people's homes the words of the Philippine nonviolent movement for peace and justice as well as messages to the soldiers—"Refuse to shoot at the people on whose side you should stand. Refuse unjust orders." That Saturday night, the whole country seemed to be tuned in as Archbishop Sin aired a radio message calling on all peace-loving Filipinos to stand together—to come out of their homes, to bring food to the soldiers and keep vigil with them. Radio Veritas played this message over and over throughout the night until it was abruptly stopped: at 5:25 Sunday morning, forty Marcos-loyalists broke into the station and smashed the radio equipment. The radio was quiet but the message had gotten through to the people.

Suddenly the streets were filled with men, women and children using what they called "People Power." They created barricades in the streets and passed out flowers, food and cigarettes to the soldiers in an effort to win the hearts of the very men who were so feared. One woman, Yolanda Lacuesta, remembered:

> I used to hate the military and the police, but on Sunday I found myself preparing sandwiches for them. I heard over Radio Veritas that they needed food. I had to squeeze through the crowd just to bring food to the soldiers. I remembered all the times when I cursed them during rallies and was amazed that now I walked so far and worked so hard for them.

Everywhere, people carried with them their statues of the Virgin Mary, the beloved patron saint of the Philippines. According to their beliefs, Mary had always been the advocate for the least powerful, appearing not to kings, but to poor peasant children at Lourdes and Fatima. Surely her love would shelter and inspire them now.

At times it felt like one huge picnic. All day vendors sold yellow ribbons, yellow T-shirts, fans, umbrellas and pennants. But in fact, it was not a picnic. The people were looking death straight in the eye. The soldiers were confused, afraid to wind up on the wrong side of the fight, and they were very used to killing people with little provocation. They were used to following orders. When Enrile and Ramos asked the soldiers to defect, only 200 of the 200,000-member armed forces were willing to risk opposing Marcos. And so there were times in the next three days when it felt like a picnic—in hell. And whenever it felt like a picnic in hell, it seemed the women stepped forward to take their places on the front lines. Many of the women who did this were nuns.

> I was at Ortigas when the tanks tried to attack on Sunday afternoon. There were a lot of people, but the real heroes were the nuns. They were the frontliners. When the tanks started to move, the nuns did not budge. Other people began to retreat, but the nuns clutched their rosaries and did not move.

> They had a very good strategy. The nuns were cool. They instructed us to stay behind them while they talked to the soldiers. They said that nothing could be settled by arguing. "Let's talk to them. Offer them water or cigarettes," they said. They pacified those who were hot-tempered.

> The nuns were our leaders.

> —Carlos G. Guiyab, Jr.

That Sunday, the marines headed into the conflict with tanks and armored personnel carriers but they were stopped by a human barricade of tens of thousands of people. The commander announced his intention to shoot, but no one moved. They prayed and asked the soldiers to join the rebellion. The tanks were forced to withdraw.

> People prayed the Rosary in front of tanks and stopped them simply by staying put and continuing in prayer. It was as if Our Lady herself, heeding the prayers, worked directly on the officers directing the tanks.

One father of three daughters related how, on Sunday evening, he chanced on all three of his daughters, all in their teens. Quite unexpectedly he saw them there, sitting on the road directly behind a small group of nuns and seminarians, praying the Rosary, two tanks only inches away from the head of the group. They just sat there and prayed the Rosary.

And they finished another Rosary and another and another. In spite of the tough talk of the fidgety and impatient commander of the lead tank: "Let's finish this," the two tanks later quietly withdrew into the dark.
—George Winternitz

I heard about Mrs. Monzon, the owner of Arellano University. She is 81 years old and bedridden. She has to use a wheelchair to go anywhere.

She had herself brought to EDSA [Epifanio de los Santos Avenue] and there she met the tanks. With a crucifix in her hand, she said to the soldiers: "Stop. I am an old woman. You can kill me, but you shouldn't kill your fellow Filipinos." The soldiers came down and embraced her: "I cannot kill you. You are just like my mother." Mrs. Monzon stayed there on EDSA all night—in her wheelchair.
—Jaime Cardinal Sin

But the people needed Radio Veritas back. The station had become the lifeline of the revolution and without it they were lost. Shortly after midnight, as Sunday turned into Monday, to the great relief of the people, a clandestine station called Radio Bandido began to broadcast from a secret location. As people tuned in, they heard the familiar voice of the announcer June Keithley. Everyone knew her as the host of a popular children's television program. Now she was risking her life in support of Radio Veritas/ Radio Bandido. Hidden in a makeshift studio on the twelfth floor of a city building and with only the help of several frightened teenagers, June began to broadcast. She started with the theme song of Radio Veritas, "Bayan Ko" ("My Homeland"). It includes these words:

Birds that fly freely
Weep when caged.
How can my land so fair
Not long to be free?
My cherished Philippines,

Home of my sorrow and tears,
I vow to see you truly free.

If we come together
This will come true.
Our country will be free,
And we will savor justice.
Evil will not rule
If we do not let it.
Let us all be one,
Let us do battle
With the reigning darkness.

June broadcast for twelve hours straight, sending out vital information she received from a network of people located all over the city as well as from General Ramos himself. She broadcast information on how to set up a more effective barricade, how to handle tear gas. During a period when the people on the streets were being tear-gassed, June played "Bayan Ko" to give them courage. Over and over she sent out the message to the people, "Get out there to help. This is the time to stand up and be counted."

The worst time was when I heard the cries of the people being teargassed and when I learned that the helicopters were coming. . . .

I began to pray on the air: "Lord, . . . you know what we are going through right now. . . . Please take care of all who are out there. . . . There are children out there, young girls and boys, parents, brothers and sisters, husbands and wives. Who knows what they may have to face this morning? . . . Lord, I am not very good at this but I just ask you please, in Jesus' name, please save our people."

The sun came up at 6:08 that morning. I know the precise time because I was waiting for it and I was wondering: "What is taking the sun so long?"
—June Keithley

June was terrified that soldiers would burst through the door and open fire with their machine guns. So was everyone else. When Monina Mercado, the mother of two of the teenaged boys who were helping June, discovered where the radio station was hidden, she ran to the building to be with her sons. What was there to stop the soldiers from simply storming the room where they were working? she wondered. When she got to the building, she found that the elevator did not go to the twelfth floor, but only to the eighth. When the elevator doors opened, she found, to her amazement, wall-to-wall nuns quietly saying the rosary. Just as the people on the streets were using their bodies to form walls, the nuns had blocked the entrance to the precious radio station, filling every inch of the corridor and sitting on the stairs leading to the upper floors. Monina's boys were safe. Marcos' soldiers never found the radio station, though they searched mightily, nor would they have had an easy time getting past the nuns if they had found it.

Out in the streets, people were teargassed that morning, but when seven helicopter gunships were sent to destroy the rebel camps, the pilots refused and defected to the rebel side. That afternoon the government-owned television station was taken over by reformist soldiers. By evening, the majority of the 200,000 soldiers had defected to stand with the people against Marcos. And that night, everyone simply ignored a curfew imposed by Marcos. The next day Corazon Aquino took her oath of office.

People Power had not transformed the country into a paradise of peace and justice. The Philippine people, like people everywhere, went back to their homes knowing they faced years of work, struggle and confusion to bring about true change. But the People Power revolution in the Philippines had dramatically succeeded in showing the world how a nonviolent revolution would look and what could be done when the people themselves stare down the tanks and simply refuse to obey a dictator's commands.

Sources

Paris Commune women's obstruction

Lowry, Bullitt, and Elizabeth Ellington Gunter, editors and translators. *The Red Virgin: Memoirs of Louise Michel.* Tuscaloosa: University of Alabama Press, 1981.

Thomas, Edith. *The Women Incendiares.* Translated by James and Starr Atkinson. New York: George Brazillier, 1966.

Philippine revolution

Clines, Francis X. "Putting It Together: How Corazon Aquino is Tackling the Host of Problems She Inherited in the Philippines." *The New York Times Magazine*, Apr. 27, 1986.

Conason, Joe. "Letter from Manila: The Snap Revolution." *The Village Voice*, Mar. 11, 1986.

Forest, Jim and Nancy. *Four Days In February: The Story of the Nonviolent Overthrow of the Marcos Regime*. Hauts, UK: Marshall Morgan and Scott, 1987.

Kashiwahara, Ken. "Aquino's Final Journey." *The New York Times Magazine*, Oct. 16, 1983.

Lohr, Steve. "Inside the Philippine Insurgency." *The New York Times Magazine*, Nov. 3, 1985.

Goss-Mayr, Hildegard. "When Prayer and Revolution Became People Power." *Fellowship*, Mar. 1987.

Karl, Marilee. "Double Oppression: The New Women's Movement in the Philippines." *off our backs*, Nov. 1983.

Mercado, Monina Allarey, ed. *People Power: An Eyewitness History: The Philippine Revolution of 1986*. Philadelphia: New Society, 1987.

"Philippines: Women's Activism." *off our backs*, Apr. 1986.

Rosca, Ninotchka. "Between the Gun and the Crucifix: Cory Aquino and the Women of the Philippines." *Ms.*, Oct. 1986.

West, Lois. "Women's Int'l Solidarity in the Philippines." *off our backs*, May 1987.

Women's International Resource Exchange. *Philippine Women: From Assembly Line to Firing Line*. New York: WIRE, Summer 1987.

Other actions

Morgan, Robin, ed. *Sisterhood Is Global: The International Women's Movement Anthology*. Garden City, NY: Anchor Press/Doubleday, 1984.

Lapchick, Richard E., and Stephanie Urdang. *Oppression and Resistance: The Struggle of Women in Southern Africa*. Westport, CT: Greenwood Press in cooperation with the United Nations, 1982.

11
LAUGHING IN THE FACE
OF IT ALL

There is nothing like the sound of women really laughing. The roaring laughter of women is like the roaring of the eternal sea.
—Mary Daly

"I'D RATHER BE IRONING!" That's the motto of the Ladies Against Women. According to "founderettes" Mrs. T. Bill and Mrs. Chester Cholesterol, the group is dedicated to bringing America back—"As far back as possible."

Sporting pillbox hats, beads and white gloves, seventy-five Ladies upstaged anti-women's-rights activist Phyllis Schlafly in Cleveland in 1982 with their demands—"PROTECT THE UNCONCEIVED!" "SUFFERING NOT SUFFRAGE!" "BAN THE POOR!" They chanted, "What do we want? *Nothing!* When do we want it? *Now!*" "Sperm are people too!" "Fifty-nine cents is too-oo-oo much!" and "Push us back! Push us back, Push us waaaay back!" The Ladies' rally was co-sponsored by a range of groups including Another Mother for World Domination, League to Protect Separate Bathrooms, Future Fetuses of America, Students for an Apathetic America, Americans Against Civil Liberties and Unions, and the National Association for the Advancement of Rich White Straight Men.

The Ladies nodded and gasped appreciably throughout Schlafly's speech entitled "Do We Want a Gender-Free Society?" They stand in staunch (but ladylike) opposition to gender-free society. "We can't just hand out genders free to anyone who wants them," one spokes-lady explained, adding, "The only thing that should be free in America is the market."

Actually, Ladies Against Women began in 1980 as the all-women faction of the mixed (male/female) California-based political performance group Plutonium Players during their "Reagan for Shah" campaign. The Ladies in stage performances inspired other "ladies" in a number of cities to do street performances. The concept is so popular that there is now a Men's Auxiliary of Ladies Against Women.

The Ladies have had some strange experiences, especially when they've played to people whose ideology they mimic. While progressives tend to catch and appreciate the humor immediately, right-leaners do double- and triple-takes and sometimes still don't quite know what to make of these seemingly kindrid spirits. It is, the Ladies have found, difficult to parody something that is already absurd. This was a problem, for example, at the Republican Convention in Dallas. In an interview in the feminist newspaper *off our backs*, the Ladies explained:

> The problem was, that everyone looked so absurd. People were wearing weird hats and buttons that said "My Country tis of thee." We couldn't come up with something sillier than that. . . The slogans looked a little weird to them, but they couldn't tell for sure. They thought we might be renegade Republicans—moderates. For instance, our bake sale for the deficit. Of course there are lots of Republicans who very much want to get rid of the deficit, and they'd say very funny, we agree with you. They'd come closer and see the budgetary pie with "REAGAN'S FOREIGN POLICY: WHITE SUGAR, WHITE FLOUR, WHITE POWER" written on it in day-glo frosting. Then they'd start to realize they were being offended.

Be forewarned: next time you see a group of well-dressed, polyester-clad "ladies" chanting "Keep our nation on the track! One step forward, three steps back!"—somebody's probably pulling your leg. Smile.

> *Man:* Do you know the women's movement has no sense of humor?
> *Woman:* No, but if you hum a few bars I can fake it.

Women have long been accused of having no sense of humor except that evidenced by the inane, self-deprecating, school-girlish giggle expected in response to comments about women's own foolishness. Trouble is, when women laugh at something other than their own foolishness, men stop laughing. Around a woman's laugh, like an aura, one can almost see the faint tinge of rage and pain. Indeed, women's humor has sometimes been a political tool, a vehicle for making a statement about a world that is no laughing matter, more often taking the form of wit, sarcasm and satire than belly-laugh.

♀ MARY ASTELL (1666–1731), the English feminist whose brilliant writings preceded Mary Wollstonecraft's 1792 *Vindication of the Rights of Woman* by almost 100 years, wrote with a witty, sharp-tongued pen which brought a sly smile to the women who had access to her work. In three sentences she could deflate the ego of the male-dominant system while sustaining the awe-struck tone expected of women. "Have not all the great actions that have been performed in the world been done by men? Have they not founded empires and overturned them? Do they not make laws and continually repeal them?"

On the title page of her best-known work, *A Serious Proposal to the Ladies* (1694), Astell boldly identified herself as "a Lover of her Sex." In the book, written when she was twenty-eight and living alone in Chelsea, Astell argued for the establishment of a women's college and urged unmarried women to pool their resources in order to create all-women retreats where they could live safely and happily without men. She longed for women to take themselves and each other seriously and to take men's opinions far less seriously. In a straightforward, lively style, she answered a common objection to educating women: "If any object against a learned education that it will make women vain and assuming, and instead of correcting increase their pride, I grant that a smattering of learning may, for it has this effect on the men." Little wonder her then outrageous quips and tart observations were popular with women readers of her day. Biographer Ruth Perry claims that Astell had an enormous impact on a number of women who were inspired to take up their pens with a similarly spirited and witty style in defense of women as an oppressed class of people.

A SIMILAR IRONIC TONE was employed by American writer Alice Duer Miller in the early 1900s when, lamenting that women still did not have the vote, she wrote:

Why We Oppose Votes for Men

1. Because man's place is in the armory.
2. Because no really manly man wants to settle any question otherwise than by fighting about it.
3. Because if men should adopt peaceable methods, women will no longer look up to them.
4. Because men will lose their charm if they step out of their natural sphere and interest themselves in other matters than feats of arms, uniforms and drums.
5. Because men are too emotional to vote. Their conduct at baseball games and political conventions shows this, while their innate tendency to appeal to force renders them peculiarly unfit for the task of government.

Those who do not know how to weep with their whole heart don't know how to laugh either.

—Golda Meir

♀ WHEN THE MEMBERS of Spinsters Opposed to Nuclear Genocide (SONG) heard about plans by the US military to displace hundreds of Central Americans and practice war in the Big Pine III Maneuvers, they decided to practice their own maneuvers. At noon on February 20, 1985, while forty protesters chanted, leafletted and waved banners, six women entered the New Haven, Connecticut Armed Forces Recruiting Station. With a Jane Fonda workout tape blaring in the background, the women did their "peace exercises," first taking care to reassure the recruiters that this would be a nonviolent action. The "good maneuver fairies" set a good example for the US government by distributing symbols of medical supplies, food, schooling materials and clothing—the sorts of things SONG members would like to see distributed in Central America instead of bombs. They passed out miniature loaves of bread with the baked-in message "NO BOMBS" etched on the tops and kneaded bread dough on the desks. While one woman sprayed pine scent into the four offices to reassert the integrity of the pine, others managed to add anti-intervention posters to the walls of the recruiting station. A leaflet drop was successfully executed, blanketing the offices with thousands of tiny pieces of paper declaring "BREAD NOT BOMBS." The bewildered recruiters got a taste of what it feels like to be invaded, and they didn't like it. A young marine resorted to chair-throwing while the army and navy recruiters tried grabbing the women. They were evidently not impressed with the women's statement of purpose:

> All branches of the U.S. Armed Forces will be participating in the Big Pine III Maneuvers. In the process, these U.S. troops will be displacing hundreds of civilians from their homes and land, damaging crops and foliage, and leaving behind all kinds of military equipment, thus indirectly aiding the Contras. To demonstrate the kinds of disruption these maneuvers have in the lives of Central Americans and to voice our protest, we are today practicing our own maneuvers at the Armed Forces Recruiting Offices.

When the police arrived, the women could barely contain their amusement as each of the four recruiters competed against the others to represent their branch of the armed forces in describing what the women had done. The women were detained briefly before being allowed to join the other protesters still singing and waving banners outside the station.

> Our humor turns our anger into a fine art.
> —Mary Kay Blakely

♀ THEY CALLED HER DOLLE MINA (Mad Mina)—labeling it madness that a woman should have such untiring and enthusiastic devotion to women's rights. Clearly, the Netherlands of the late nineteenth century wasn't ready for Wilhelmina (Mina) Elisabeth Drucker. Born out of wedlock in 1848 to a poor family, Mina was drawn to socialism and feminism early in life. In 1889 she founded the Association of Free Women, later editing the group's newsletter, *Evolution*.

Eighty-one years after the founding of the association, Dutch feminists, still not sure the world was ready for them, took for themselves the name Dolle Mina. Theirs was the work of confronting the little acts of humiliation and discrimination faced by women every day, creating consciousness-raising events with more than a little humor. To dramatize the miserable lack of women's public toilet facilities, they closed the men's public lavatories by encircling them with yards of pink ribbon. They distributed free birth control materials to teenaged girls at some of Amsterdam's schools and began a campaign of whistling back at men who ogled women on the streets. Media attention became so extensive that any woman connected with feminism in the Netherlands is still sometimes called a "Dolle Mina" the way women in the United States are sometimes called "bra-burners."

> When you know to laugh and when to look upon things as too absurd to take seriously, the other person is ashamed to carry through even if he was serious about it.
> —Eleanor Roosevelt

♀ IT IS A SAFE BET that not many women have actually laughed in the face of patriarchal oppression very often, but some feminists in West Germany have been experimenting with laughter as a nonviolent direct action. They got the idea from Mary Daly, author of *Beyond God the Father, Gyn/Ecology* and *Pure Lust*, who has encouraged "wonderlusty" women to laugh out loud at the "perils precipitated and perpetuated by patriarchal penocrats."

In the fall of 1986, some West German women, inspired by Daly's call, signed up for a tour of an atomic energy plant at Stade, West Germany. The laughter started when the tour guide said "Hello, Ladies . . ." It continued as the guide ran through his routine rap about the benefits of nuclear energy and technology. The women burst into raucous laughter which echoed through the halls. Finally the guide asked, "What do you people want here anyway?" to which the women replied, "We want a shutdown. Where's the switch?" Seeing that this particular group would never appreciate the benefits of nuclear energy, the guide called for assistance in escorting the women out.

Suddenly, one woman asked, "Where's Renate? Have you seen her?" Hearing this, the other women in the group picked up the question, asking with mock concern, "But she was just here a minute ago. Have we lost her?" They continued to ask this loudly even as the gates were locked behind them. Several hours later, the guide received a phone call that asked if Renate was still there, to please give her the message to come home. According to one West German woman, "Rumor has it that puzzled power plant personnel are still looking for Renate today." There was truth in the women's laughter, and the exercise itself functioned to mildly disrupt business as usual at the power plant for at least one afternoon.

♀ FARTHER TO EUROPE'S NORTH and several months later, on Father's Day 1987, forty Finnish women waving brooms and cleaning rags danced past the guard at the Olkiluoto nuclear power plant shouting "We have come to sweep away the nuclear plant!" Inside the gates, the women knelt to write anti-nuclear slogans on the pavement and sang songs about the hazards of nuclear energy.

The women were arrested and detained for several hours but their day's work was not done. After they were released, the women toured the near-by village of Eurajoki, delivering little black bags labeled "PLUTONIUM" and "CESIUM" to the mayor and other public officials. The women told the town fathers that they should put the bags under their beds if they really believed radioactive materials were safe. To close their day of action on a positive note, the women went to the homes of four people who had taken public stands against nuclear power and presented them with red roses.

> *Man (wearing suit and tie) to woman Guru:*
> Oh Guru, Ancient Mother of the World, we men have been crippled. We have never learned how to feel; we don't know how to cry. Oh my wise guru, can you teach me to cry?
> *Guru:*
> Sure. No problem. Tomorrow I'll start you at a dead-end job . . .
>
> —cartoon by Nicole Hollander

♀ IN FEBRUARY 1970, fifteen women at Yale Law School launched "Operation Hassle." Led by the relentless "Lady Teazle," the women began to harass male passers-by with the annoying comments women get every day, interrupting the men's conversations and private musings as they walked across campus the way women's conversations and musings are frequently interrupted. The men didn't like it, but a number of women at

Yale thought Operation Hassle a delightful and effective consciousness-raising exercise and enthusiastically joined in the action.

> O, we have a desperate need of laughter!
> —Beatrice Llewellyn-Thomas

♀ IT WAS REALLY AN OLD IDEA, one that had been bounced around quite a bit during the Vietnam War when anti-war posters proclaimed, "IT WILL BE A GREAT DAY WHEN THE MILITARY HAS TO HOLD A BAKE SALE TO BUY A BOMB." In the summer of 1981, some feminists in Boston decided the "great day" had come.

Calling themselves the Future Moms for the MX Missile, the women set up their bake sale table on Boston Common and delighted the lunch-hour crowd with Plutonium Fudge, Trilateral Treats, Bombshell Brownies, Agent Orange Cake and Apocalypse Muffins (which everyone agreed were out of this world). Along with the tasty home-baked goods, people were given literature with information about the MX, such as its $300 billion cost and its power to "destroy Hiroshima 50,000 times." As the women leafletted, chanted and sang, passersby signed a no-joke petition prepared by the Council for a Nuclear Weapons Freeze of Cambridge.

The Moms' list of sponsors included such well-known groups as the Peace Resisters League, Mobilization for Extermination, Union of Concerned Capitalists and the National Association for the Advancement of Rich People.

Sources

Ladies Against Women

"Gazette." *Ms.*, vol. 10, no. 10 (Apr. 1982).

"Interview: Ladies Against Women." *off our backs*, vol. 16, no. 6 (June 1986).

Van Kleef, Deborah. "Further Antics of Ladies Against Women." *Ms.*, vol. 11, nos. 1 & 2 (July/Aug. 1982).

———. "I'd Rather Be Ironing: Ladies Against Women in Ohio." *off our backs*, vol. 12, no. 4 (Apr. 1982).

Early feminist humor

Kaufman, Gloria. "Feminist Humor." *Women: A Journal of Liberation—Humor and Fantasy*, vol. 5, no. 1 (1976).

Perry, Ruth. *The Celebrated Mary Astell: An Early English Feminist*. Chicago: University of Chicago Press, 1986.

Spender, Dale. *Women of Ideas (And What Men Have Done to Them)*. Boston: Routledge & Kegan Paul, 1982/1983.

Spinsters Opposed to Nuclear Genocide

"Peace Maneuvers in New Haven." *Womanews*, vol. 6, no. 5 (May 1985).

Dolle Mina

"We Are Not Alone." *Women: A Journal of Liberation—Women In Revolution*, vol. 1, no. 4 (Summer 1970).

Oudijk, Corrine. "The Netherlands: In the Unions, the Parties, the Streets, and the Bedrooms" from *Sisterhood Is Global: The International Women's Movement Anthology*. Robin Morgan, ed. Garden City, NY: Anchor Press/Doubleday, 1984.

West German women laughing

"Chicken Lady—letter from Lilian Friedberg." *off our backs*, vol. 16, no. 11 (Dec. 1986).

Finnish anti-nuclear action

Moore, LeRoy. "Grassroots Report: Finnish Women for Peace 'Sweep Back' Nuclear Power." *Resist Newsletter*, Dec. 1987.

Yale—Operation Hassle

"Operation Hassle." *Women: A Journal of Liberation—Women in Revolution*, vol. 1, no. 4 (Summer 1970).

Boston bake sale

"Moms for the MX Missile." *New Women's Times*, vol. 7, no. 10 (Nov. 1981).

Divider quotes

Daly, Mary. *Gyn/Ecology: The Metaethics of Radical Feminism*. Boston: Beacon Press, 1978.

Hollander, Nicole. *Ma, Can I Be a Feminist and Still Like Men? Lyrics from Life*. New York: St. Martin's Press, 1980.

The Quotable Woman: 1800–On. Elaine Partnow, ed. Garden City, NY: Anchor Press/Doubleday, 1978.

RECOMMENDED READING: SOME BOOKS FOR THOSE WITH NO TIME TO READ THEM

It may seem a strange thing to begin a book with:—This Book is not for any one who has time to read it—but the meaning of it is: this reading is good only as a preparation for work. If it is not to inspire life and work, it is bad.

—Florence Nightingale
Notes on Nursing, 1859

I HAVE A BAD HABIT . . . well several, actually, when it comes to books. When friends come to visit, I tend to offer them a book before a cup of tea. In bookstores and libraries I sometimes whisper "hello" to a familiar title. I've been known to spend a quarter at a sidewalk sale to rescue a musty, dusty book if the copy looks cold and lonely, even if I've already read it. I also write in books. A lot. In college I had a friend—a linguistics genius and a scholar—who would not write his name in a book because he believed it violated the book's soul. He had the shock of his life one day when he opened one of my books. Not only had I put my name in it, but various passages were high-lighted in different fluorescent colors, and in the margins were comments and questions—"Right!" "Is this true?" "You've got to be kidding!" "Baloney!"

Books have been central to my development as a feminist advocate of nonviolence, not to mention central to my spiritual, political and social development. Except for that done for fun and relaxation, reading is not a passive or self-indulgent activity for me, but an active one. I have been dependent on books to expand my thoughts and range of experience my whole life—from my childhood days in isolated, rural America to my adult life in New York City where, in some of my more vulnerable moments, fears sometimes keep me from venturing beyond my front stoop for days. Books can be tools of liberation, and the reading (not to mention the writing) of some books is in itself an act of resistance to oppression.

In reviewing those books that have most touched and moved me these past few years, I've found a number, published in the 1980s, in which readers who have found something of value in *You Can't Kill the Spirit* may be especially interested.

Women's History

At the end of the dystopian novel *Fahrenheit 451* by Ray Bradbury, the agents of total mind control are burning books in the streets. Reading is a criminal activity. But some reading rebels have escaped to a remote woods. There they wander day after day, each reciting the words of a book they've committed to memory so that the book will not die though its pages be burned.

I fantasize . . . the days of total censorship and repression are upon us. Books about feminism, nonviolence, women's history and the histories of oppressed peoples are being forcibly removed from our homes, schools and libraries and burned in the streets. Readers are being jailed. I escape, find the rebels' woods and begin to live out the rest of my days as the embodiment of Dale Spender's book *Women of Ideas,* repeating over and over the words I have memorized. . . . "Page thirteen: The simple answer to my question—why didn't I know about all the women of the past who have protested about male power—is that patriarchy doesn't like it. These women and their ideas constitute a political threat and they are censored." A year later, still wandering, I am reciting page 696: "From Aphra Behn to Adrienne Rich it has been suggested that among the most subversive and powerful activities women can engage in are the activities of constructing women's visible and forceful traditions, of making *real* our *positive* existence, of celebrating our lives and of resisting disappearance in the process."

I hope I will never have to memorize all 800 pages of this book, but I feel it is crucial that Dale Spender's work not disappear. We have all heard the repeated claim that women's history has been buried. In *Women of Ideas (And What Men Have Done to Them): From Aphra Behn to Adrienne Rich* (London: ARK Paperbacks, Routledge & Kegan Paul, 1982/1983), Spender shows us exactly *how* women's history has been buried and *who* buried it. With unfaltering attention to detail, she documents the deliberate suppression of works by women who have challenged the patriarchal point of view—women who were harassed, trashed, carted off to mental institutions, locked up, married off, denied access to education, ridiculed, censored or in some other way deliberately banished from history. Here is women's lost intellectual and political heritage found, invisible creative women made visible again. Best of all, Spender is as readable as she is prolific.

Most Dangerous Women: Feminist Peace Campaigners of the Great War (London: Pandora Press, 1985) by Anne Wiltsher tells the story of the British suffragists who, unlike Emmeline Pankhurst and her militant band, opposed the First World War, made connections with the international feminist peace movement of that day and effectively combined their suffrage and anti-war work. Like Spender, Wiltsher writes in a style which makes the women and their struggles come alive.

When and Where I Enter: The Impact of Black Women on Race and Sex in America (New York: Bantam Books, 1985) by Paula Giddings fills in many of the gaps in our history books with carefully documented accounts of black women's activism in the club movement, the anti-lynching campaigns, the movements encompassing labor issues, women's suffrage and civil rights. Giddings' pen brings to life our black foremothers—Ida B. Wells, Mary McLeod Bethune, Fannie Lou Hamer, Mary Ann Shadd Cary and many others. Another book that effectively fills in a lot of gaps in our history books is Judy Grahn's *Another Mother Tongue: Gay Words, Gay Worlds* (Boston: Beacon Press, 1984). Weaving her own personal experiences into the text, Grahn presents details of lesbian and gay history, mythology, culture and etymology.

Female Revolt: Women's Movements in World and Historical Perspective (Totowa, NJ: Rowman & Allanheld, 1986) is by Janet Saltzman Chafetz and Anthony Gary Dworkin. This book will be of use to fewer readers, however, it is worth mentioning as a reference tool. The book includes summaries of forty-eight different women's movements as they manifested in a range of countries, movements as diverse as those addressing suffrage, temperance, witchcraft, religious heresy. *Feminism and Nationalism in the Third World* (London: Zed Books, 1986) by Sri Lankan feminist Kumari Jayawardena, like *Female Revolt* briefly describes women's political struggles, though this book focuses exclusively on women in Asia and the Middle East. Both books are also alike, sadly, in their minimal discussion of women in Africa.

Feminism and Nonviolence

Since the publication of the 440-page anthology, *Reweaving the Web of Life: Feminism and Nonviolence* (Philadelphia: New Society, 1982) which I was privileged to edit, a number of books have been published addressing the interconnection of feminism and nonviolence. *We Are All Part of One Another: A Barbara Deming Reader* (Philadelphia: New Society, 1984) edited by Jane Meyerding, is a collection of Deming's essays, speeches, letters, stories and poems spanning the years from 1959 to 1981, an outline of the journey she made toward truth. Black feminist Barbara Smith wrote the foreword to this collection of precious words, essential reading for feminists and advocates of nonviolence.

In 1964, Barbara Deming wrote *Prison Notes,* diary writings about her experience of being jailed in Albany, Georgia during the civil rights movement. Almost twenty years later she wrote about being jailed in Waterloo, New York after her arrest with other women from the Seneca Peace Encampment. These writings, along with two corresponding photo essays edited by JEB (Joan E. Byron), have been published under one cover in *Prisons That Could Not Hold: Prison Notes 1964–Seneca 1984* with an introduction by Grace Paley (San Francisco: Spinsters Ink, 1985). (An aside—the cover of this book is my hands-down favorite of all the books I own.) *Prison Notes* is the book that most influenced my own journey into experimenting with truth as an advocate of nonviolence, and it is a true gift to have it back in print.

Piecing It Together: Feminism and Nonviolence (Devon, England: 1983) is a slim but effective volume by the Feminism and Nonviolence Study Group. In it, British feminists argue that there is a profound relationship between the fact that individual women are commonly attacked and that a nuclear war threatens the entire world.

In *Reclaim the Earth: Women Speak Out for Life on Earth* (London: Women's Press, 1983) edited by Leonie Caldecott and Stephanie Leland, feminists from the United States, India, the United Kingdom, Canada, Japan, Kenya, Italy and New Zealand address the various interconnecting threats to life on earth—racism, militarism, nuclear power, poverty, the exploitation of Third World women, pollution, animal abuse. The writers also address the ways women around the globe are becoming empowered to act.

A number of books have come out of the women's peace camp movement, many of them very good, or at least very readable. My favorite of these books so far is one of the earliest—*Greenham Women Everywhere: Dreams, Ideas and Actions From the Women's Peace Movement* (Boston: South End Press, 1983) by Alice Cook and Gwyn Kirk. The authors address such substantial topics as nonviolence, direct action, women-only campaigns and peace camp coverage in the media. Woven throughout the text are bold-print passages from women's diaries and interviews relating women's experiences, lessons learned, sacrifices made.

Two booklets worth noting here are *Empowerment of People for Peace* (Women Against Military Madness, 3255 Hennepin Ave. South, Minneapolis, MN 55408, 1984) by Mary S. White and Dorothy Van Soest, and *Peace & Power: A Handbook of Feminist Process* (Buffalo, NY: Margaretdaughters, 1984) by Charlene Eldridge Wheeler and Peggy L. Chinn. The first booklet reviews a process developed by Women Against Military Madness by which people can discover their capacity—as individuals or members of small groups—to make change in the world. The process encompasses making personal connections with issues, grieving, overcoming barriers to action, beginning to act. The booklet includes a chapter on how to organize a small empowerment group. The second booklet describes a feminist process for group work for those who know that Robert's Rules of Order leave a lot to be desired but don't know what else to try. This booklet offers both the rationale for and suggestions for using consensus decision-making, criticism/self-criticism, a check-in process and rotating chair. Examples of situations and solutions are given from the authors' experiences in women's groups.

There are two books I'll slip into this section, though they do not specifically advocate or address nonviolence, because they are books by feminists who are doing the work of making connections. *Yours In Struggle: Three Feminist Perspectives on Anti-Semitism and Racism* (Brooklyn, NY: Long Haul Press, 1984) by Elly Bulkin, Minnie Bruce Pratt and Barbara Smith, offers an essay by each of the authors—one a white Christian-raised Southerner, one an Afro-American and one an Ashkenazic Jew. *Passionate Politics* (New York: St. Martin's Press, 1987) is by clear-headed lesbian-feminist theorist and activist Charlotte Bunch. This book is a collection of her essays and includes some of her more recent insights on "global feminism."

I would also recommend two books that will challenge any readers who identify themselves as feminist advocates of nonviolence. The first is a forty-four-page booklet, *Breaching the Peace: A Collection of Radical Feminist Papers* (London: ONLYWOMEN Press, 1983). Here, British feminists express their concern that the women's peace movement will detract from other vital feminist work such as the work to combat rape and battery, that anti-war work is draining women's energies, and that it threatens to return women to the role of mother and nurturer. The second book is *Valiant Women In War and Exile: Thirty-eight True Stories* (San Francisco: City Lights Books, 1987) edited by Sally Hayton-Keeva. The book includes interviews with a nun who works with refugees on the Mexico-Guatemala border, a mother of a conscientious objector to the Vietnam War, a woman who helped draft resisters and deserters during the Vietnam War, a Japanese woman who survived the US bombs and is now one of the well-known "Hiroshima Maidens," a Jewish woman who survived Auschwitz, and a nurse who is fasting to protest US government policy in Central America. But many of the stories in this book are about women who are participating in war—one woman who worked with the French Resistance during World War II, another who became the youngest sniper in the Soviet army, a US nurse who volunteered in the fight against fascism in Spain in 1936, and a guerrilla who lives in the mountains near San Salvador.

Nonviolence

One of the most provocative arguments for nonviolence in the context of liberation struggles is Walter Wink's little book *Violence and Nonviolence in South Africa: Jesus' Third Way* (Philadelphia: New Society, 1987—published in cooperation with the Fellowship of Reconciliation). Wink, a white theology professor in the United States, addresses his words primarily to white clergy of South Africa, but his arguments provide an exciting defense of both liberation theology and radical nonviolent resistance.

Another general book about nonviolence I recommend is *The Power of the People: Active Nonviolence in the United States* edited and produced by Robert Cooney and Helen Michalowski. It was first published in 1977 and was updated and republished in 1987 by New Society Publishers. It is a pictorial encyclopedia with over 300 photographs documenting how nonviolence has been used by people working for peace and social justice. The information is arranged by struggle—abolition, women's rights, labor, civil rights, anti-war. An empowering resource, this book includes portraits of peace activists and organizations.

In the novel *Stranger Than Love* by Graeme Woolaston (London: GMP, 1985), Eddie, a gay pacifist, comes face-to-face with Rick, a self-proclaimed "queerbasher." The Scottish-born author uses the gay-straight confrontation as the vehicle with which to explore a defense of religion-based nonviolence. This is provocative reading for gay or gay-aware advocates of nonviolence despite the total absence of female characters in the story.

Analysis of the War Machine

In *Fathering the Unthinkable: Masculinity, Scientists and the Nuclear Arms Race* (London: Pluto Press, 1983) Brian Easlea argues that the arms race is the inevitable outcome of science based on male creativity which wages war against "feminine" values, women and nature. Heavily documented and detailed, Chapter Three, "Alamogordo, Hiroshima and Nagasaki," highlights perhaps the most terrifying and fascinating material. Here, Easlea analyzes examples of aggressive sexual and birth metaphors scientists have used in their communications with each other. For example, the Los Alamos physicists named the bomb dropped on Hiroshima "Little Boy." One scientist received word about the 1945 Trinity test of the bomb detonation in a telegram worded, "The baby is expected . . ." Two days after the test, President Truman's Secretary of War, Henry Stimson, received a cable from Washington which read:

> Doctor has just returned most enthusiastic and confident
> that the little boy is as husky as his big brother. The light

in his eyes discernible from here to Highhold and I could
have heard his screams from here to my farm.

In Britain, Winston Churchill was told about the news when a
paper bearing three words was placed in front of him, "Babies
satisfactorily born." Physicists received telegrams saying,
"Congratulations to the parents. Can hardly wait to see the new
arrival." And that year J. Robert Oppenheimer, the "father of the
atomic bomb," was made Father of the Year by the National Baby
Institution.

In *Ain't No Where We Can Run: A Handbook for Women on
the Nuclear Mentality* (Norwich, VT: WAND, 1980), Susan Koen
and Nina Swaim, like Easlea, identify an imbalance in male and
female energy and the resulting overload of male-defined power
as the primary cause of the nuclear mentality. They detail
arguments to use in order to defeat pro-nuclear reasoning and
provide short portraits of women who have been in the forefront
of the anti-nuclear movement including Helen Caldicott, Holly
Near, Grace Paley and Karen Silkwood. In her book *Sexism and
the War System* (New York: Columbia University, Teachers
College Press, 1985, foreword by Patricia Schroeder), Betty A.
Reardon calls for the integration of feminist scholarship with peace
research in determining the integral relationship between sexism
and militarism.

Does Khaki Become You? The Militarization of Women's Lives
(Boston: South End Press, 1983) by British feminist Cynthia
Enloe, shows how our lives as women are touched by various
aspects of the military. She addresses sexual harassment of women
in the armed forces throughout the world, military homophobia,
women in liberation armies, and the use of women as prostitutes,
factory workers, nurses and military wives.

Women's varied but ageless roles in time of war are dramatized
in Karen Malpede's play *The End of War,* written in 1977 and
included in the collection of Malpede's plays *A Monster Has Stolen
the Sun* (Marlboro, VT: The Marlboro Press, 1987). Galina, the
young mother, embroiders a shirt with a scene of triumph while
she waits for the return of her hero husband, but her fingers are
stiff "with centuries of inexpressible grief." Elena, the brave
comrade and intellectual, praises the memory of Rosa Luxemburg
who, she tells the peasants, "died bravely in service to ideals not
unlike ours." The Old Mother has seen everything and is resigned

to the inevitability of war and the suffering it brings. The Raped Woman confesses, "I have witnessed many things. Many foul, unclean deeds have I seen. I could not stop them, but neither could I turn my eyes away from them." At the play's end, Elena, battlescarred and disillusioned with violent revolution, warns that human life on earth will cease "unless the whole pattern is reversed and in each head a wakening occurs and in each heart a way to love what we most fear is found." Galina, too, has changed. She has decided no longer to follow her hero husband but to end her own complicity in perpetuating war. As she gives birth, we sense that more is promised than new hope, but a new vision, a new cycle which will mean the end of war.

Chaos of the Night: Women's Poetry & Verse of the Second World War (London: Virago Press, 1984) edited and introduced by Catherine W. Reilly, includes poems by eighty-seven women who recorded their reactions to the Second World War. In these poems, the women describe the air attacks, Nazi persecution, their children's nightmares and their own, as well as their hopes for peace.

Letters from Nicaragua by Rebecca Gordon, foreword by Barbara Smith (San Francisco: Spinsters/Aunt Lute, 1986), is the testimony of a Jewish, lesbian-feminist from the United States who witnessed daily life from the Nicaraguan war-zone. Culled from her six months with Witness for Peace, these observations were written with a poet's eye and an activist's heart.

Women Taking Action

The most well-worn books in my personal library are usually the autobiographies, diaries, letters—stories of challenge and change told in first-person accounts. The process of getting from point *A* to point *B*, the trials of body and soul, the fears overcome, the dreams, the hard work, the little insights and the things that nurture and keep a person going—these are the things that sustain me on my own journey and they generally make great reading to boot.

Author and activist Judith McDaniel has written *Sanctuary: A Journey* (Ithaca, NY: Firebrand Books, 1987). It is a collection of essays, poems and recollections about taking risks—physical risks, risks of the heart, risks of class security or race security—and about seeking sanctuary, a safe place in an unsafe world. Central to her writing in this book is her experience as a member of the

Witness for Peace delegation which was captured by the contras
in Nicaragua and held in the jungle for twenty-nine hours in 1985.
This collection also includes Judith's writing about spending a
night in a New York City shelter for homeless women, learning
from the Native Americans at Big Mountain, visiting radical writer
Margaret Randall in Albuquerque, New Mexico, and encountering
the fear and loathing of people angered by the Seneca Women's
Encampment for a Future of Peace with Justice. Judith is walking
through this life with her heart open and her pen ready.

A most exciting book published recently is *Revolutionary
Forgiveness: Feminist Reflections on Nicaragua,* written by the
Amanecida Collective and edited by Carter Heyward and Anne
Gilson (Maryknoll, NY: Orbis Books, 1987). The Amanecida
Collective is made up of thirteen white US citizens, twelve women
and one man, most of whom are seminary-based educators and
students. In fresh, personal accounts, the thirteen relate their
experiences and ponderings during their five recent trips to
Nicaragua where they confronted their own identities,
assumptions, confusions, privileges and responsibilities. Though
nonviolence tends to be misunderstood in these dialogues, the
questions the Collective members ask are useful and their insights
about being Christian and North American are profound.

Keeping the Peace: A Women's Peace Handbook (London:
Women's Press, 1983), edited by Lynne Jones, is a compact
volume of personal accounts by women involved in peace
actions—in West Germany, the Netherlands, England, the United
States and Japan, with specific organizing suggestions and
graphics throughout. Very neatly done, from its cover photo of
women blockading an entrance at Greenham Common to its
resource list at the back of the book.

In *Her Wits About Her: Self-Defense Success Stories by Women*
(New York: Harper & Row, 1987) edited by Denise Caignon and
Gail Groves, women tell about being attacked and fighting back
with their voices, their brains, their fists and feet, and occasionally
with objects turned weapon. An empowering book, the stories are
about women's strength and spirit and about addressing the
violence in our lives in order to make this planet a safe home for
each of us. Read a few of these and you're bound to remember
your own stories of survival. We must tell our stories.

Heart Politics (Philadelphia: New Society, 1986) is by Fran
Peavey, a white, North American woman who writes "as one

four-billionth of the human species." And what a precious and
unrepeatable one four-billionth she is. She writes here about the
many people whose lives have somehow intertwined with hers.
My favorite chapter is the one in which she tells about
implementing her idea of sitting in a public place with a cloth sign
that reads "AMERICAN WILLING TO LISTEN." She tells about
feeling silly, maybe even ridiculous, but curious and hopeful. And
it works. She has sat in listening mode while other people have
talked to her, sometimes in languages she doesn't understand, in
Japan, Thailand, India, England, Scotland, East Germany, the
United States, Israel, Palestine and Sweden. "Listening to people,"
she writes, "I began to learn how each individual puzzled out large
issues from her or his own vantage point." And of her own
perspective she writes:

> I'm continually thinking of the people I've met around the
> world. That couple on the Punjab Mail: Is their
> granddaughter growing up healthy and strong? How are
> the street people in Kamagasaki doing? Have the squatters
> near the One Baht School successfully resisted eviction?
> In August I think about the monsoons in India. I can see
> the waters of the Ganges rising.

> My listening project is a kind of tuning-up of my heart to
> the affairs of the world. I hear the news in a very different
> way now, and I act with a larger context in mind.
> Conspicuous consumption has become more difficult now
> that I have met poor people around the world. I hold myself
> accountable to the people whose lives I have seen. And I
> work to keep nuclear war from happening to us all.

Alternative values and future visions

Our imaginations can be jogged by others' future visions. I was
privileged to write an introductory essay for the republication of
a book first published in 1893, *A Sex Revolution* by Lois
Waisbrooker (Philadelphia: New Society, 1985). In
Waisbrooker's novel, mothers rise up en masse to govern the
world in order to establish peace on earth for their children.
Another early feminist utopian vision has recently been
republished—*Sultana's Dream and Selections from The Secluded
Ones*—written by Bengali Muslim feminist Rokeya Sakhawat
Hossein in 1905 (New York: Feminist Press, 1987). It is a story

about the reversal of *purdah* (the practice of secluding women from public view) in a world where women have taken to the public sphere and the men are confined.

Daring to Dream: Utopian Stories by United States Women: 1836–1919 compiled, edited and introduced by Carol Farley Kessler (Boston: Pandora Press, 1984), is a collection of excerpts from early feminist utopian visions. *How Peace Came to the World* (Cambridge, MA: MIT Press, 1986) edited by Earl Foell and Richard Nenneman, is a collection of essays chosen from a "Peace 2010"contest sponsored by the *Christian Science Monitor*. In the year 2010, the world is at peace and the threat of nuclear devastation has vanished. In the forty essays published here, the writers tell how peace came to the world. It is an interesting experiment which would have been even more interesting with more contributions by women, nonacademics and people of color.

Women's utopian visions have not only been limited to the printed page. Some women have actually tried to live out their visions. *Women In Search of Utopia: Mavericks and Mythmakers* (New York: Schocken Books, 1984), edited and with introductions by Ruby Rohrlich and Elaine Hoffman Baruch, is a cross-cultural anthology describing a range of utopian experiments—from the matriarchy of ancient Crete to women's experiences at Findhorn, Scotland and Twin Oaks in the United States. This book also includes fictional visions, an essay on "Lesbian Visions of Utopia," and works by Marge Piercy, Sally Miller Gearhart, Audre Lorde, June Jordan, Tucker Farley, Ntozake Shange, Eve Merriam, Batya Weinbaum and many others. *This Way Daybreak Comes: Women's Values and the Future* (Philadelphia: New Society, 1986) is by two "futurists," Annie Cheatham and Mary Clare Powell, who traveled 30,000 miles to document the lives and visions of 1000 North American women who are transforming the world. Some are healers, some are artists, others are activists, and still others are experimenting with new definitions of family, community and friendship.

Women's Spirituality

Each issue of the quarterly periodical *Women of Power: A Magazine of Feminism, Spirituality, and Politics* (Woman of Power, Inc., P.O. Box 827, Cambridge, MA 02238) is not only beautifully produced but gives voice to a full, rich range of current feminist visions and concerns. Two anthologies that hold hours of empowering stories are *The Stories We Hold Secret: Tales of Women's Spiritual Development* (Greenfield Center, NY: Greenfield Review Press, 1986), edited by Carol Bruchac, Linda Hogan and Judith McDaniel, and *Hear the Silence: Stories by Women of Myth, Magic & Renewal* (Trumansburg, NY: The Crossing Press, 1986), edited by Irene Zahava.

In *Motherpeace: A Way to the Goddess through Myth, Art, and Tarot* (New York: Harper & Row, 1983) by Vicki Noble, visionary art, political consciousness and a grounding in Goddess mythology are filtered through the tradition of the tarot. Noble calls us to allow the Goddess to awaken in us and reclaim our right to a life without war. In *Dreaming the Dark: Magic, Sex & Politics* (Boston: Beacon Press, 1982), author Starhawk fuses spiritual vision and politics and shares her own increasing involvement in direct action politics, passionately addressing her/our despair at the threat of nuclear war and the persistence of racism. She includes here some empowering rituals women have created. German feminist, peace activist and Christian theologian Dorothee Solle provides another challenging read in *Of War and Love* (Maryknoll, NY: Orbis Books, 1983). She focuses her concerns on liberation struggles in Central and South America and peace activists' work against the threat of nuclear annihilation. She urges her readers to "become as militant, as nonviolent, and as illegal in our actions as Jesus and his friends were."

Resource Tools

There are several resource books on my desktop that fill in some of the gaps between *Bulfinch's Mythology* and *Roget's Thesaurus*. *Sisterhood Is Global: The International Women's Movement Anthology*, edited by Robin Morgan (Garden City, NY: Anchor Press/Doubleday, 1984) provides some useful information about women from Afghanistan to Zimbabwe. Though it is impossible for such a book to remain statistically up-to-date or even accurate, the background information on the kinds of laws and customs governing such institutions as marriage, divorce, prostitution, homosexuality, rape, contraception, employment rights, education and suffrage in each country are fascinating. The sections on "Herstory"—highlighting some of the important dates, movements and names pertaining to women in each country—and

"Mythography" are especially helpful in learning about the women of the world.

A Feminist Dictionary (Boston: Pandora Press, 1985) by Cheris Kramarae and Paula A. Treichler, is both fun and useful as a collection of witty feminist word play. One of my favorites is Joanna Russ's definition of an "understanding man"—"A figure who often appears in women's novels."

Three books of quotes that the feminist advocate of nonviolence shouldn't be without are *The Quotable Woman: 1800–On* (Garden City, NY: Anchor Press/Doubleday, 1978), compiled and edited by Elaine Partnow; *Seeds of Peace: A Catalogue of Quotations* (Philadelphia: New Society, 1987), compiled by Jeanne Larson and Madge Micheels-Cyrus; and *My Country Is the Whole World: An Anthology of Women's Work on Peace and War* (London: Pandora Press, 1984), compiled by the Cambridge Women's Peace Collective. This last is not really a book of quotations in the sense of the other two, but contains long passages from diaries, letters, speeches, poems, songs, political tracts and petitions, from Sappho to the women at Greenham Common Peace Camp.

> I have not placed reading before praying because I regard it as more important, but because, in order to pray aright, we must understand what we are praying for.
> —Angelina Grimké, 1836

CHRONOLOGY OF WOMEN'S NONVIOLENT ACTIONS

The following is a chronology of events mentioned in this book. It is not intended to be an exclusive list of women's nonviolent action, but to include the contents of this book.

1300 B.C.	**Egypt** Hebrew midwives disobey pharaoh.
1694 A.D.	**England** Early feminist Mary Astell writes *A Proposal to the Ladies.*
1792	**England** Mary Wollstonecraft writes *Vindication of the Rights of Woman.*
1818	**Valencia, Venezuela** Hospital laundresses strike to demand back pay.
1830 (ca.)	**Philadelphia** White Quaker sisters, Sarah and Angelina Grimke, sit with their black friend Sarah Douglass and her mother to protest the existence of a "colored" bench in the Quaker meeting house.
1832 (ca.)	**Boston** Maria Weston Chapman encourages the use of interracial walk-alongs after the Boston Female Anti-Slavery Society meetings.
1838	**Philadelphia** Black and white women in attendance at the second Anti-Slavery Convention of American Women so perturb racists by walking together that rioters burn the abolitionist's Pennsylvania Hall to the ground.
1849	**United States** Lydia Sayer Hasbrouck is denied admission to Seward Seminary for wearing the "Bloomer" outfit. She begins to lecture for feminism and dress reform, edits a feminist newsletter *Sibyl*, and becomes a tax resister.
1850s	**United States** Harriet Tubman is a conductor on the Underground Railroad.
1855	**United States** Lucy Stone and Henry Blackwell marry, using the wedding as an opportunity to challenge marriage laws. Stone keeps her own last name and other women, nicknamed "Lucy Stoners," follow her example.
1858	**Orange, NJ** Lucy Stone refuses to pay taxes, protesting women's taxation without suffrage rights.
	Newport, RI A white parishioner loses her right to sit in a church pew after inviting a black worshipper to sit with her. She returns the next week with a camp stool.

1868	**New York City** Jane Croly helps organize a women's club, Sorosis, after women are denied admission to the male Press Club.
1871	**Paris** Women block cannons and stand between Prussian and Parisian troops.
1873	**Worcester, MA** After hearing about the tax resistance of two sisters in Connecticut, Abby Kelly Foster and her husband become tax resisters to protest women's political inequality.
1876	**France** Hubertine Auclert founds the "Women's Rights Society" which meets in secret for several years, defying government orders to disband.
1877	**England** Annie Besant publishes a birth-control pamphlet and consequently loses custody of her daughter.
1878	**Shikoku, Japan** Kusunose Kita protests having to pay taxes while being denied the vote.
1880	**Paris** After trying to vote as full French citizens, Hubertine Auclert and twenty others declare a women's "tax strike" to protest the injustice of taxation without representation. **New Vienna, OH** Women temperance activists use singing as a nonviolent tactic.
1888	**London** Women match workers go on strike.
1889	**Netherlands** Wilhelmina (Mina) Elisabeth Drucker founds the Association of Free Women.
1890	**Iran** Royal harem women organize a tobacco strike to break the British monopoly.
1905	**India** Bengali Muslim Rokeya Sakhawat Hossein writes *Sultana's Dream* in which she envisions *reverse purdah*.
1907	**Greensburg, PA** Mary "Mother" Jones tells imprisoned wives of striking miners to "sing to the babies all night long." They sing their way out of jail.
1909	**New York City** 100 garment workers walk out of Leiserson's shop. Three days later, workers at the Triangle Waist Company go on strike. The women's actions set the stage for the "Uprising of the 20,000" women garment workers. **New York City** "Uprising of the 20,000" **New York City** The Women's Trade Union League organizes a march of 10,000 striking workers. **New York City** Mary "Mother" Jones addresses New York's Socialist Party meeting in support of the striking garment workers. **Philadelphia** Waistmakers join New York strikers.
1910	**New York City** Mass rally held in Carnegie Hall in support of the striking women. **New York City** Mary White Ovington calls for a meeting to address the role of black women in the garment workers' strike. **United States** Alice Duer Miller writes "Why We Oppose Votes for Men."
1911	**London** The Women's Tax Resistance League of London publishes *Why We Resist Our Taxes*.

1912   **Lawrence, MA** Women textile workers on strike carry banner "We Want Bread and Roses, Too!" and use singing extensively to raise morale.

1913   **South Africa** Indian women illegally cross state borders in civil disobedience campaign.

South Africa 600 women led by Charlotte Maxeke march in Bloemfontein to protest pass laws and return their unwanted passes to the mayor.

England Emily Wilding Davison throws herself beneath the King's horse at the Derby and dies a martyr to the suffrage cause.

London Suffrage activists disrupt opera at Covent Garden to address the King. Emmeline Pankhurst is in jail on a hunger strike.

1920s   **Zambia** Women working in solidarity with the nationalist movement for independence cut down trees to block roads used by government soldiers.

1923   **Shanghai, China** 20,000 women silk workers go on strike demanding a ten-hour day.

1929   **Nigeria** Ibo Women's War

1943   **South Africa** Three women chain themselves to a storefront to gain union recognition.

1946   **Massachusetts** Mary Bacon Mason becomes a war tax resister following the bombings of World War II.

1948   **Yellow Springs, Ohio** Caroline Urie gains national attention for her war tax resistance.

1950s   **South Africa** White women form Black Sash and protest outside government offices.

Johannesburg, South Africa 400 domestic workers go on strike.

Pretoria, South Africa 4000 women block streets.

Venterpost, South Africa 10,000 women sign petition against apartheid. 500 women deliver it to government officials.

Gopane Village, South Africa Women burn passes. When thirty-five women are arrested, two hundred step forward, volunteering to go to jail with their sisters.

Sanderton, South Africa 900 women arrested after illegal procession.

Motswedi and Braklaagte, South Africa Women desert villages in protest exodus.

Johannesburg, South Africa 2000 women arrested for defying pass laws.

Zambia Women block road leading to the airport to stop car carrying British colonial secretary.

1955   **Pretoria, South Africa** 2000 women protest pass laws.

1956   **Pretoria, South Africa** 20,000 women protest the pass laws and deliver petition with over 100,000 women's signatures to the prime minister. August 9 becomes South African Women's Day.

1957   **Santiago, Cuba** Over 1000 mourning women march in silent procession to city hall.

1958   **Johannesburg, South Africa** Winnie Mandela is arrested and jailed for the first time.

1959   **Philadelphia** Juanita Nelson is arrested for tax resistance and taken to court in her bathrobe.

          South Africa Miriam Makeba is exiled.

1960s   **Minnesota** Nancy Krody helps establish new attitudes about homosexuality by lecturing as a lesbian Christian.

1960   **Chicago** Eroseanna Robinson is arrested for tax resistance and begins a ninety-three-day fast.

1962   **Zimbabwe** 2000 jailed women disrupt prison by singing.

          United States Bernice Reagon becomes the leader of the Student Nonviolent Coordinating Committee Freedom Singers.

          United States Fannie Lou Hamer begins to work on voter registration in the black community of Ruleville, Mississippi.

1965   **United States** Joan Baez publicizes her war tax resistance.

1966   **Yellow Springs, OH** Doris Sargent proposes a new tactic—refusing to pay the telephone tax—to protest the US war in Vietnam.

1968   **Atlantic City, NJ** 200 women protest the Miss America Pageant.

1969   **Vietnam** Women political prisoners on Con Son Island use singing as an act of defiance.

1970   **Israel** Prime Minister Golda Meir suggests a curfew for men.

          Netherlands Feminists taking the name of "Dolle Mina" create consciousness-raising events—such as tying up men's public lavatories with pink ribbon to protest the lack of women's facilities.

          Japan 1000 riot police try to evict the Shibokusa women from their peace witness at the foot of Mount Fuji. The women remain.

          small town, United States Two young lesbians begin a campaign to address homophobia in their school.

          Philippines Women found MAKIBAKA (the Liberation Movement of New Women). The group pickets a national beauty contest.

          New Haven, CT Fifteen women at Yale Law School launch "Operation Hassle."

1971   **United States** Holly Near integrates her music and her politics performing in the "Free the Army" tour in the Pacific.

1972   **Naples, Italy** Department store cashiers go on a "smile strike."

          United States Meg Bowman writes a letter to the IRS justifying her war tax resistance.

          Auckland, New Zealand Maori feminist seeks support of lesbians and gay men, spurring formation of the first gay liberation group in the country.

1973   **Namibia** Women sing news to jailed husbands.

1974   **California** Women begin yearly protests of the Miss California Pageant.

          Israel Women collect 30,000 signatures on petition in favor of safe and legal abortion.

Sacramento, CA   Martha Tranquilli begins prison term for war tax resistance.

1975   **Haifa, Israel**   Women demonstrate in front of the Rabbinical Court.

Tel Aviv, Israel   200 women stage mock funeral for the civil rights bill.

Tel Aviv, Israel   Over 500 people march in candlelight procession for women's freedom.

1976   **Tel Aviv, Israel**   Eleven women infiltrate and disrupt the national convention of the Society of Gynaecologists and Obstetricians.

1977   **Buenos Aires, Argentina**   First public vigil by the Mothers of the Plaza.

Buenos Aires, Argentina   Mothers of the Plaza buy an advertisement in *La Prensa* publishing the names of mothers and pictures of 230 of "the disappeared."

1978   **Northampton, MA**   Feminists spray-paint anti-rape graffiti around the city.

Canberra, Australia   Twenty women attend Anzac Day Parade holding WOMEN AGAINST RAPE banner.

Seattle, WA   BettyJohanna and Jane Meyerding pour blood in the office of Save Our Moral Ethics, a group working to deny the civil rights of lesbians and gay men.

1979   **Olympia, WA**   "Women Warriors" paste STOP RAPE stickers on city's stop signs.

Buenos Aires, Argentina   After a year in hiding, the Mothers of the Plaza return to public vigils.

Madison, WI   The Madison Billboard Brigade defaces anti-choice billboards.

Rochester, NY   Following a speakout on rape, feminists post curfew notices for men on the RIT campus. Women in other cities—including Leeds, England and Toronto, Canada—use the same tactic.

1980s   **West Germany**   Feminists dress male statues in women's clothes.

Leeds, England   Women transform statues glorifying war into anti-cruise missile tableaus.

India   Editors of the feminist journal *Manushi* call for a nationwide boycott of dowry marriages.

1980   **Belo Horizonte, Brazil**   Feminists blanket city with graffiti to protest "defense of honor" plea.

Dublin, Ireland   Feminists spray-paint a papal cross with pro-abortion slogans.

Belfast, Ireland   An English activist joins women in Armagh prison in solidarity action and singing.

Poland   Women in Gdansk stare down tanks and hand out flowers and Solidarity bulletins. In Katowice, women block police from entering a worker-occupied steel mill.

Hartford, CT Three women pour blood on pornographic books in the Bare Facts store.

Washington, DC Women's Pentagon Action

1981

Jakarta, Indonesia Two lesbians publicly proclaim their love and exchange vows before 100 guests.

Ireland Women in Armagh jail smear menstrual blood on the walls of their cells.

Japan Women collect signatures on petition protesting increased militarization of Japan.

Japan Rally to Build Peace with Women's Votes

Japan Women's Symposium for Thinking of the Constitution

Japan Women's Rally Never to Allow an Undesirable Amendment of the Constitution

Tokyo Central Rally of Women for a Ban on Adverse Revision of the Japanese Constitution and for the Establishment of Peace

Canberra, Australia 300 women protest rape and seek to participate in Anzac Day parade. Sixty-one women are arrested.

Boston Future Moms for the MX Missile hold bake sale and distribute literature about the US military budget.

Santa Cruz, CA Seven rape survivors pour blood on the steps of the Civic Auditorium to protest the Miss California Beauty Pageant.

United States Women form a "Fired Lesbians Caucus" at the National Women's Studies Association convention.

Greenham Common, England Women arrive at Greenham airbase and decide to stay.

Washington, DC Women's Pentagon Action

Arlington, VA Women arrested at the Women's Pentagon Action stage sit-in in Arlington Jail.

Tokyo 2000 women march in remembrance of the bombing of Pearl Harbor and protest renewed militarization of Japan.

1982

Zimbabwe Women petition the government to withdraw support of beauty contests.

Netherlands Evelien Eshuis, elected to parliament, wears a pink triangle badge on her lapel as a public sign of her lesbian identity.

Lima, Peru Women disrupt beauty pageant.

Cleveland, OH Members of Ladies Against Women upstage Phyllis Schlafly with street theater.

Worldwide Women participate in the "International Shadow Project."

British Columbia, Canada Edith Adamson, coordinator of the Peace Tax Fund Committee, makes headlines with her war tax resistance.

Canberra, Australia 500 women participate in alternative Anzac Day ceremonies in remembrance of women who've been raped in war.

1983

Greenham Common, England At dawn on New Year's Day, forty-four women dance on top of the cruise missile silos.

Providence, RI Women post curfew notices for men.

San Francisco Constance Shepard Jolly marches with her husband in the San Francisco Lesbian and Gay Freedom Day Parade in public support of her daughter's choice to be a lesbian.

New York City Anti-pornography activist, Dorchen Leidholdt, is arrested for defacing *Penthouse* subway advertisement.

Philadelphia Feminists infiltrate and disrupt US-West German banquet to protest US deployment of US-made missiles.

Greenham Common, England 50,000 women encircle the base.

1984   **London** Eight feminists dismantle and deface the marquee of the Whitehall Theatre of War.

South Africa Albertina Sisulu, age sixty-eight, is sentenced to prison for singing freedom songs.

Philippines Women found umbrella organization GABRIELA (General Assembly Binding Women for Reforms, Integrity, Equality, Leadership and Action). Poet, teacher Mila Aguilar is imprisoned by Marcos regime. Hildegard Goss-Mayr conducts nonviolence training.

New York City Over 1000 women march in "Not In Our Name" demonstration in preparation for the next day's civil disobedience action on Wall Street.

1985   **British Columbia, Canada** During the "Take Back the Night" march in Vancouver, women spray-paint slogans and symbols along the march route.

New Haven, CT Spinsters Opposed to Nuclear Genocide disrupt Armed Forces Recruiting Station.

Columbus, OH Radical feminist members of the Sisters of Justice pour blood in a protest of Jerry Falwell's Moral Majority.

New York City Women's Tax Resistance Assistance performs street theater on steps of Federal Hall protesting the US military budget.

1986   **Stade, West Germany** West German women, inspired by Mary Daly's ideas, experiment with laughter as nonviolent action while touring power plant.

Philippines Women are in the forefront of the nonviolent People Power revolution. June Keithley plays a vital role in broadcasting from a clandestine radio station. Nuns lead the people in kneeling in prayer to block Marcos' tanks.

1987   **British Columbia, Canada** Jerilynn Prior issues a press release explaining progress with the test case to establish the legality of Peace Tax Fund.

Madrid Lesbians hold a "kiss-in" protesting arrest of two women jailed for kissing in public.

Brooklyn, NY Tax resister writes open letter to the IRS protesting the US war in Nicaragua.

Eurajoki, Finland Forty women protest at a nuclear power plant on Father's Day and deliver bag marked "Plutonium" to the mayor.

WOMEN AND WOMEN'S ORGANIZATIONS FOR PEACE AND JUSTICE

The following is a list of the women and women's organizations for peace and justice that are mentioned in this book. It is not intended to be an exclusive list of women and groups for peace and justice, but to include the contents of this book.

Sidney Abbott	co-authors *Sappho Was a Right-On Woman* with Barbara Love, 1972
Edith Adamson	war tax resistance in Canada, 1982
African National Congress Women's League	founded in 1919, South Africa
Mila Aguilar	Filipina poet jailed in 1984
Alliance of Women Towards Action and Reconciliation	founded in Philippines, 1984
Susan B. Anthony	advocates equal pay for equal work, mid-1800s
Corazon Aquino	participates in Philippines People Power revolution and advocates nonviolence; elected president, 1986
Mary Astell	England, writes *A Serious Proposal to the Ladies* (1666–1731)
Hubertine Auclert	French feminist organizer; in 1880 calls for women's tax strike (1848–1914)
Joan Baez	1965, United States, war tax resistance
Beguines	Twelfth- to fifteenth-century women-only ascetic/philanthropic communities
Alva Belmont	1909, supports shirtwaist workers' strike, New York City; sets up motorcade to transport picketers
Annie Besant	helps organize 1888 London "Matchgirls' Strike"
Clementina Black	Secretary of Women's Trade Union League, England

Black Sash	South African anti-apartheid organization founded by white women
Boston Female Anti-Slavery Society	1800s, society members—black women and white—leave meetings arm-in-arm
Meg Bowman	1972, United States, war tax resistance
BUGA UP	Billboard Utilising Graffitists Against Unhealthy Promotions
Leonie Caldecott	English author and activist, speaks in Japan at women's peace rally
Carrie Chapman Catt	US suffrage activist
Maria Weston Chapman	1800s, chairs Boston Female Anti-Slavery Society meetings and encourages interracial "walk-alongs"
Jane Croly	1868, United States, founds women-only club, Sorosis
COUGH IN	Campaign on Use of Graffiti for Health in Neighborhoods
COUGH UP	Citizens' Organisation Using Graffiti to Halt Unhealthy Promotions
Nikki Craft	California activist, leader of beauty pageant protests
Mary Daly	1980s, United States, encourages feminists to laugh at the patriarchs; authors *Beyond God the Father*, *Gyn/Ecology* and *Pure Lust*
Emily Wilding Davison	1913, dies a martyr to the suffrage cause in England
Barbara Deming	—ponders myth of the Gorgons —in essay "New Men, New Women," writes about power of the strike —advocates war tax resistance —writes essay "Two Perspectives on Women's Struggle" —writes about "coming out" to herself as a lesbian, 1930s
Azucena De Vicenti	rallies the Mothers of the Plaza in Argentina, becomes one of the "disappeared," 1977
Dolle Mina	twentieth-century organization of feminist activists in the Netherlands

Sarah Douglass	1800s, United States, black Quaker teacher protests "colored bench" in meeting house
Mary Dreier	president of New York Women's Trade Union League, arrested as supporter of shirtwaist strikers, 1909
Wilhelmina (Mina) Elisabeth Drucker	1889, Netherlands, founded the Association of Free Women
Andrea Dworkin	1980, called as expert witness to testify in trial of anti-pornography activists; authors *Woman Hating*, 1974
Evelien Eshuis	1982, Netherlands, elected to parliament, wears pink triangle signifying lesbian identity
FANG	Feminist Anti-Nuclear Graffiti
Federation of South African Women	founded in 1954 under the slogan "Forward to freedom, security, equal rights and peace for all"
Jane Fonda	1971, is joined by Holly Near in the "Free the Army" tour in the Pacific
Abby Kelly Foster	1838, tries to calm racist rioters outside Pennsylvania Hall and is inspired to join the anti-slavery lecture circuit; 1873, becomes tax resister
Marcia Freedman	Israel, women's movement leader elected to the Knesset in 1973; with ten other feminists, invades conference of gynecologists, 1976
Future Moms for the MX Missile	1981, Boston, group holds bake-sale and protests US military spending
GABRIELA	General Assembly Binding Women for Reforms, Integrity, Equality, Leadership and Action, founded in Philippines, 1984. Named in honor of eighteenth-century woman who led revolt against Spanish rule.
Kasturbai Gandhi	participates in anti-pass protests with Indians led by her husband Mohandas in South Africa, 1913
Charlotte Perkins Gilman	1915, writes *Herland*
Hildegard Goss-Mayr	1984, arrives in Philippines to conduct nonviolence-training workshops
Greenham Common	—women maintain "Cruise Watch" and protest deployment of missiles —1984, women from Greenham Common deface Whitehall Theatre of War marquee

	—a Greenham support group transforms war monuments into anti-war tableaus
Sarah and Angelina Grimké	1800s, sit with friend Sarah Douglass to protest "colored bench" in the Quaker meeting house; 1838, Angelina marries Theodore Weld; 1838, Angelina tries to calm racist rioters outside Pennsylvania Hall; 1838, Sarah proposes resolution for action by white abolitionist women
Martha Gruening	Bryn Mawr student jailed for action supporting striking shirtwaist workers, 1909, Philadelphia
Sarah Hagar	temperance activist and poet writes "Father, Won't You Stop Your Drinking?"
Fannie Lou Hamer	1962, United States, begins work on voter registration in black community
Linda Hand	1980, pours blood on pornography in Bare Facts store, Connecticut
Lydia Sayer Hasbrouck	1849, United States, denied admission to Seward Seminary for wearing "Bloomer" outfit; edits *Sibyl;* becomes tax resister
Rokeya Sakhawat Hossein	Bengali Muslim author of *Sultana's Dream* envisions *reverse purdah* (1880–1932)
Housewives Association	protests Japan's militarization
Japanese Women's Caucus Against War	protests Japan's militarization
Japan Women's Council	protests Japan's militarization
Betty Johanna	1978, pours blood in offices of Save Our Moral Ethics
Constance Shepard Jolly	1983, marches in support of lesbian daughter in San Francisco Lesbian and Gay Freedom Day parade
Mary "Mother" Jones	1907, Greensburg, Pennsylvania, encourages jailed women to sing to their babies; 1909, New York City, speaks in support of shirtwaist strikers
Helen Joseph	white activist, secretary of Federation of South African Women, participates in women's protests, 1955, 1956
Jossie and Bonnie	Indonesian lesbians publicly proclaim their love before 100 wedding guests

June Keithley	1986, Philippines, broadcasts vital information from clandestine radio station in support of People Power revolution
Madhu Kishwar	India, radical feminist writes about dowry system
Kusunose Kita	1878, Japan, protests having to pay taxes while being denied right to vote; called "Grandmother Popular Rights"
Nancy Krody	1960s, lectures in United States on being a lesbian Christian
Ladies Against Women	1982, upstages Phyllis Schlafly with street theater; founded in 1980 as all-woman faction of Plutonium Players' "Reagan for Shah" campaign
Little Sisters of Jesus	community of nuns in Manila instrumental in People Power revolution
Liz Lagrua	1980, uses songs for solidarity with other women in Ireland's Armagh prison
Dorchen Leidholdt	1983, arrested for defacing *Penthouse* advertisement in New York City subway
Clara Lemlich	1909, inspires thousands of shirtwaistmakers by calling (in Yiddish) for a general strike
Esther Lobetkin	participates in 1909 shirtwaist makers' strike, New York City
Barbara Love	co-authors *Sappho Was a Right-On Woman* with Sidney Abbott, 1972
Hien Luong	Vietnamese poet imprisoned with other women on Con Son Island, 1969
Madison Billboard Brigade	1979 impromptu group does graffiti action for reproductive rights
Miriam Makeba	1959, exiled from South Africa for opposing apartheid and singing freedom songs
MAKIBAKA	Liberation Movement of New Women, Philippines, 1970, pickets beauty pageants
Theresa Malkiel	participates in 1909 shirtwaist workers' strike, New York City
Winnie Mandela	South African activist, first arrested in 1958
Manushi	1980s, editors of feminist magazine call for boycott of dowry marriages
Mary Bacon Mason	Massachusetts war tax resister, 1946

Charlotte Maxeke	Mother of African Freedom (1874–1939)
Judith McDaniel	writes about "Fired Lesbians Caucus" at 1981 National Women's Studies Association annual convention
Donna Mehle	1987, United States, war tax resistance
Jane Meyerding	1978, pours blood in offices of Save Our Moral Ethics
Louise Michel	1871, France, nicknamed the "Red Virgin," participates in the Paris Commune; sent to prison colony for ten years
Alice Duer Miller	writes "Why We Oppose Votes For Men" between 1910 and 1920
Mitzi and Jackie	begin anti-homophobia campaign in their high school
Rahima Moosa	participates in South African women's protest, 1956
Anne Morgan	1909, supports shirtwaist workers' strike, New York City
Mrs. Henry Morgenthau	1909, supports shirtwaist workers' strike, New York City
Mothers of the Plaza	keep vigil for the "disappeared" in Argentina
Lucretia Mott	1838, active Quaker provides leadership at Second Anti-Slavery Convention of American Women, Philadelphia
Holly Near	1970s/1980s, United States, uses singing to entertain, educate, challenge and heal
Juanita Nelson	1959, United States, arrested for war tax resistance and taken to court in her bathrobe
Pauline Newman	participates in and organizes for 1909 shirtwaist workers' strike
New York Radical Women	1968, protest Miss America Pageant at Atlantic City, New Jersey
Lilian Ngoyi	participates in South African women's protest, 1956
Teurai Ropa Nhongo	1982, Zimbabwe Minister of Community Development and Women's Affairs, protests beauty pageants

Dr. Naomi Nhiwatiwa	1982, Zimbabwe, deputy minister, protests beauty pageants
Nwanyeruwa	1929, Nigeria, issues call for Ibo women to act against British, the "Women's War" begins in her name
Yoko Ono	proposes color war
Mary White Ovington	1910, founder of the National Association for the Advancement of Colored People, calls meeting in Brooklyn to address role of black women in shirtwaist workers' strike
Emmeline Pankhurst	England, leader of militant Women's Social and Political Union
Margaret Kineton Parkes	London suffragist, authors pamphlet on women's tax resistance, 1911
Philadelphia Women's Encampment	1983, radical feminists disrupt government banquet
Jill Posener	London-based photographer edits two books on political graffiti
Preying Mantis Women's Brigade	1981, pours blood on auditorium steps to protest California beauty pageant
Jerilynn Prior	1987, Canada, issues press release explaining her war tax resistance
Puah	1300 B.C., Hebrew midwife disobeys pharoah
Sarah Pugh	1838, Quaker schoolteacher offers schoolhouse as women's anti-slavery convention space after rioters burn Pennsylvania Hall to the ground
Jane Quinn	1980, pours blood on pornography in Bare Facts store, Connecticut
Bernice Reagon	1960s, makes lifetime commitment to being a freedom singer; later founds Sweet Honey in the Rock
Malvina Reynolds	folksinger, United States
Adrienne Rich	writes essay "Compulsory Heterosexuality and Lesbian Existence"
Eroseanna Robinson	1960, United States, arrested and jailed for war tax resistance; fasts for ninety-three days
Yetta Ruth	participates in 1909 shirtwaist workers' strike, New York City

SAMAKANA	organization of urban poor women in the Philippines
Doris Sargent	1966, United States, proposes war tax resistance tactic of refusing to pay phone tax
Rose Schneiderman	helps raise money for 1909 shirt-waist workers' strike, New York City
Shibokusa women	maintain peace vigil at foot of Mount Fuji
Shiphrah	1300 B.C., Hebrew midwife disobeys pharoah
Ann Simonton	United States, wears "meat dress" to protest beauty pageants
Sisters of Justice	1985, protest at meeting of Moral Majority, Ohio
Albertina Sisulu	1984, South Africa, arrested for singing freedom songs and working in the resistance to apartheid
Julia and Abby Smith	1873, Connecticut tax resisters
William Soler's mother	Cuba, 1957, leads procession of mourning mothers
Spinsters	Vermont feminist affinity group
Spinsters Opposed to Nuclear Genocide	1985, disrupts Connecticut Armed Forces Recruiting Station
Elizabeth Cady Stanton	1874, United States, sends words of encouragement to Abby Kelly Foster for tax resistance action
Lucy Stone	United States, 1855, keeps last name after marrying Henry Blackwell; 1858 becomes tax resister
Marjorie Swann	1960, United States, joins other members of Peacemakers in vigil for Eroseanna Robinson outside Alderson prison
Martha Tranquilli	1974, United States, jailed for war tax resistance
Harriet Tubman	1850s, works to liberate black people from slavery as a conductor on the Underground Railroad
Caroline Urie	1948, United States, war tax resister
Natalya Urosova	participates in 1909 shirtwaist workers' strike, New York City
Nghula Volkering	1972, New Zealand Maori feminist spurs formation of first gay liberation group in country

Shell Wildwomoon	1980, pours blood on pornography in Bare Facts store, Connecticut
Sophie Williams	participates in South African women's protest, 1956
Annie Wittenmyer	1882, US, writes *The History of the Women's Temperance Crusade*
Mary Wollstonecraft	1792, writes *Vindication of the Rights of Women*
Women Against Imperialism	1979, English women act in solidarity with women imprisoned in Ireland's Armagh prison on International Women's Day
Women's Bureau of the General Council of Trade Unions of Japan	protests Japan's militarization
Women's International League for Peace and Freedom	named as a "dependent" by Martha Tranquilli on tax withholding form
Women's Pentagon Action	1980, 1981 action of mourning, rage, empowerment and defiance by women protesting US war-making
Women's Rights Society	France, 1876, organized by Hubertine Auclert and forced to meet in secret
Women's Social and Political Union	England, militant suffrage group
Women's Suffrage Circle	France, 1880s, founded by Hubertine Auclert
Women's Tax Resistance Assistance	1985, New York, women perform street theatre to protest US military spending
Women's Tax Resistance League	London, 1911, publishes *Why We Resist Our Taxes*
Women's Trade Union League	United States, helps organize and support 1909 shirtwaist workers' strike, New York City; wealthy members form "Mink Brigade" to support picketers
Women Warriors	1979, paste STOP RAPE stickers on stop signs in Olympia, Washington
Women Workers Movement	1984, founded in the Philippines

PLACES WHERE WOMEN HAVE ACTED NONVIOLENTLY

The following is a listing of the places where women have acted nonviolently that are mentioned in this book. It is not intended to be an exclusive list of places of women's nonviolent action, but to include the contents of this book.

AFRICA

Namibia
1973, Women sing information to jailed husbands.

Nigeria
1929, Ibo Women's War

South Africa
1913, 600 women led by Charlotte Maxeke march in Bloemfontein and return their unwanted passes to the mayor.
1913, Indian women illegally cross state borders (Natal/Transvaal) in civil disobedience campaign.
1943, Three women chain themselves to storefront to win union recognition.
1950s
—Gopane Village: Women burn passes.
—Johannesburg:
400 domestic workers go on strike.
2000 women arrested for defying pass laws.
—Motswedi and Braklaagte: Women desert villages in protest exodus.
—Pretoria:
2000 women protest pass laws.
Black Sash women protest.
August 9, 1956: 20,000 women protest the pass laws and deliver petition with over 100,000 women's signatures to the Prime Minister.
4000 women block streets.
—Sanderton: 900 women arrested after illegal procession.
—Venterpost: 10,000 women sign petition against apartheid.
1958, Winnie Mandela arrested and jailed for the first time.
1959, Miriam Makeba, Empress of African Song, exiled from South Africa.
1984, Albertina Sisulu jailed for singing freedom songs.

Zambia

1920s, Women working for nationalist movement cut down trees to block roads used by government soldiers.

1950s, Women block road leading to Ndola Airport.

Zimbabwe

1962, (Rhodesia) 2000 women use singing to disrupt prison.

1982, Women petition the government to withdraw support of beauty contests.

ASIA

China

1923, 20,000 women silk workers go on strike.

India

1905, Bengali Muslim Rokeya Sakhawat Hossein writes *Sultana's Dream*.

1980s, Editors of the feminist journal *Manushi* call for a nationwide boycott of dowry marriages.

Japan

1878, Kusunose Kita protests having to pay taxes.

1970, 1000 riot police try to evict the Shibokusa women from their peace witness at the foot of Mount Fuji. The women remain.

1981

—Women collect two million signatures on petition protesting increased militarization.

—Rally to Build Peace with Women's Votes

—Women's Symposium for Thinking of the Constitution

—Women's Rally Never to Allow an Undesirable Amendment of the Constitution

—Central Rally of Women for a Ban on Adverse Revision of the Japanese Constitution and for the Establishment of Peace

—2000 women march in remembrance of the bombing of Pearl Harbor and protest renewed militarization of Japan.

Philippines

1970, Members of MAKIBAKA (the Liberation Movement of New Women) picket a national beauty contest.

1984

—GABRIELA (General Assembly Binding Women for Reforms, Integrity, Equality, Leadership and Action) founded.

—Poet Mila Aguilar imprisoned by Marcos' regime.

—Hildegard Goss-Mayr and her husband Jean lead seminars in nonviolence.

February 1986, June Keithley broadcasts from clandestine radio station and plays a key role in the People Power Revolution. Nuns provide leadership by kneeling in prayer before Marcos' tanks and guns.

Vietnam

1969, Women political prisoners on Con Son Island sing freedom songs in act of nonviolent solidarity and defiance.

CENTRAL and SOUTH AMERICA

Argentina
April 1977, First public vigil by Mothers of the Plaza.

Brazil
1980, Feminists blanket Belo Horizonte with graffiti.

Cuba
1957, 1000 mourning women march in silent procession.

Peru
1982, Women and disrupt the Miss Universe Pageant.

Venezuela
1818, Hospital laundresses strike.

EUROPE

England
1694, Early feminist Mary Astell writes *A Serious Proposal to the Ladies.*
1792, Mary Wollstonecraft writes *Vindication of the Rights of Women.*
1877, Annie Besant publishes a birth-control pamphlet.
1888, London "Matchgirl's Strike"
1911, The Women's Tax Resistance League of London publishes a pamphlet, *Why We Resist Our Taxes.*
1913
—Emily Wilding Davison throws herself beneath the King's horse at the Derby and dies a martyr to the suffrage cause.
—Suffrage activists disrupt the opera at Covent Garden to address the King. Emmeline Pankhurst is on a hunger strike.
September 1981, Women arrive at Greenham airbase and decide to stay.
1983
—At dawn on New Year's Day, January 1983, forty-four Greenham Common women dance on the cruise missile silos.
—50,000 Greenham Common women encircle the base in December.
1984, Eight feminists dismantle and deface the marquee of the Whitehall Theatre of War.
1980s, In Leeds, women transform statues glorifying war into anti-cruise missile tableaus.

Finland
1987, Forty women protest nuclear power on Father's Day.

France
1871, The housewives of Paris support the Paris Commune by blocking the Prussian troops.
1876, Hubertine Auclert founds the "Women's Rights Society" which meets in secret for several years.
1880, Hubertine Auclert and twenty others declare a women's "tax strike."

Ireland

1980, Feminists spray-paint a papal cross with pro-abortion slogans.

1981, Women in Armagh jail smear menstrual blood on the walls of their cells.

1980, English activist joins women in Armagh prison in solidarity action and singing.

Italy

1972, Department store cashiers go on a "smile strike."

Netherlands

1889, Wilhelmina (Mina) Elisabeth Drucker founds the Association of Free Women.

1970, Feminists taking the name of "Dolle Mina" create consciousness-raising events.

1982, Evelien Eshuis, elected to parliament, wears a pink triangle as a public sign of her lesbian identity.

Poland

1980

—Women in Gdansk stare down tanks while handing out flowers and Solidarity bulletins.

—In Katowice, women form blockade with their bodies, preventing the police from entering a worker-occupied steel mill.

Spain

1987, Lesbians in Madrid hold a "kiss-in."

West Germany

1980s, Feminists dress male statues in women's clothes.

1986, Women, inspired by Mary Daly's ideas, experiment with laughter as a nonviolent direct action.

MIDDLE EAST

Egypt

1300 B.C., Hebrew midwives disobey pharaoh.

Iran

1890, Royal harem women organize a tobacco strike.

Israel

1970, Golda Meir suggests a curfew for men.

1974, Women collect 30,000 signatures on petition in favor of safe and legal abortion.

1975, Women in Haifa demonstrate at Rabbinical Court.

1975, 200 women in Tel Aviv stage mock funeral for the civil rights bill.

1975, 500 people march in Tel Aviv in a candlelight procession for women's freedom.

1976, Eleven women in Tel Aviv disrupt the national convention of the Society of Gynaecologists and Obstetricians.

NORTH AMERICA

Canada

1982, Edith Adamson makes headlines with her tax resistance.

1985, During the "Take Back the Night" march in Vancouver, women spray-paint slogans and symbols along the march route.

1987, Jerilynn Prior issues a press release explaining progress with the test case she is bringing to establish the legality of Canada's Peace Tax Fund.

United States

CA   **1971,** Holly Near integrates her music and her politics in the "Free the Army" tour in the Pacific.

1974, Women begin yearly protests of the Miss California Pageant.

1974, Martha Tranquilli begins her prison term for war tax resistance.

1981, Seven Santa Cruz rape survivors use blood to protest the Miss California Beauty Pageant.

1983, Constance Shepard Jolly marches in the San Francisco Lesbian and Gay Freedom Day Parade in public support of her daughter.

CT   **1970,** Women at Yale Law School launch "Operation Hassle."

1980, Three Hartford feminists pour blood on pornographic books in the Bare Facts "lingerie shop."

1985, Spinsters Opposed to Nuclear Genocide disrupt the local Armed Forces Recruiting Station.

DC   **1980,** Women's Pentagon Action
1981, Women's Pentagon Action

GA   **1962,** Bernice Reagon becomes the leader of the Student Nonviolent Coordinating Committee Freedom Singers.

IL   **1960,** Chicago, Eroseanna Robinson is arrested for tax resistance and begins a ninety-three-day fast.

MA   **1830s,** Boston, Maria Weston Chapman encourages interracial walk-alongs.

1873, Abby Kelly Foster refuses to pay taxes.

1912, Lawrence, women textile workers go on strike.

1946, Mary Bacon Mason becomes a war tax resister following the bombings of World War II.

1978, Northampton, feminists spray-paint anti-rape graffiti.

1981, Boston, Future Moms for the MX Missile hold bake sale.

MN   **1960s,** Nancy Krody begins lecturing as a lesbian Christian.

MS   **1962,** Fannie Lou Hamer begins her work on voter registration.

NJ   **1858,** Orange, Lucy Stone refuses to pay taxes.
1968, Atlantic City, 200 women protest the Miss America Pageant.

NY   **1868,** Women's club, Sorosis, founded.

September 1909, Women garment workers walk out of Leiserson's and Triangle Waist Company shops.

November 1909, "Uprising of the 20,000"

December 1909, Women's Trade Union League organizes a march of 10,000 striking garment workers. Mary "Mother" Jones addresses New York's Socialist Party.

January 1910, Mass rally held in Carnegie Hall in support of the striking women.

1910, Mary White Ovington calls meeting to address the role of black women in garment strike.

1979, Rochester, feminists post curfew notices for men.

1987, Tax resister writes open letter to the IRS.

1983, Anti-pornography activist Dorchen Leidholdt is arrested for defacing a poster advertising *Penthouse* magazine.

November 1984, Over 1000 women march in "Not In Our Name" demonstration.

April 1985, Women's Tax Resistance Assistance performs street theater on the steps of Federal Hall.

OH   **ca. 1880,** Temperance activists sing to saloon owner.

1948, Yellow Springs, Caroline Urie gains national attention for her war tax resistance.

1966, Yellow Springs, Doris Sargent proposes phone tax resistance.

1982, Cleveland, members of Ladies Against Women upstage Phyllis Schlafly with their street theater.

1985, Columbus, Sisters of Justice pour blood in protest of Jerry Falwell's Moral Majority.

PA   **1830s,** White Quaker sisters, Sarah and Angelina Grimke, sit with their black friend Sarah Douglass and her mother to protest the existence of a "colored" bench in the meeting house.

1838, Philadelphia, black and white women attend second Anti-Slavery Convention of American Women. Rioters burn their meeting place to the ground.

1907, Mother Jones tells striking miners' wives in Greensburg jail to "Sing to the babies all night long."

1909, Philadelphia waistmakers join the New York strike.

1959, Juanita Nelson is arrested for tax resistance and taken to court in her bathrobe.

1983, Feminists infiltrate and disrupt United States-West German banquet to protest deployment of US-made cruise and Pershing II missiles.

RI   **1858,** White parishioner loses right to sit in a church pew after inviting a black worshipper to sit with her.

1983, Providence, women post curfew notices for men.

VA   **1981,** Women arrested at Women's Pentagon Action stage sit-in at Arlington Jail.

WA   **1978,** Seattle, BettyJohanna and Jane Meyerding pour blood in
        office of Save Our Moral Ethics, a group working to deny the civil
        rights off lesbians and gay men.
        1979, Olympia, "Women Warriors" paste STOP RAPE stickers on
        the city's stop signs.

WI   **1979,** Madison Billboard Brigade action

Other

1849, Lydia Sayer Hasbrouck is denied admission to Seward Seminary for
wearing the "Bloomer" outfit. She begins to lecture for feminism and dress
reform, edits a feminist newsletter, *Sibyl,* and becomes a tax resister.

1850s, Harriet Tubman, conductor on the Underground Railroad, uses songs
as secret codes.

1855, Lucy Stone and Henry Blackwell marry, using the wedding as an
opportunity to challenge marriage laws. Stone keeps her own last name.

1910, Alice Duer Miller writes "Why We Oppose Votes for Men."

1965, Joan Baez becomes an influential war tax resister.

1970s, Two young lesbians begin campaign to address homophobia in their
small town's high school.

1970, Meg Bowman writes a letter to the IRS justifying her war tax resistance.

1981, Women form a "Fired Lesbians Caucus" at the National Women's
Studies Association annual convention.

SOUTH PACIFIC

Australia

1978, Canberra, twenty women attend Anzac Day Parade holding banner,
WOMEN AGAINST RAPE.

1981, 300 women protest rape and seek to participate in Anzac Day parade
in Canberra.

1982
        —500 women participate in alternative Anzac Day ceremonies in
        Canberra.
        —Perth, Anzac Day protest.
        —Adelaide, Anzac Day protest.
        —Melbourne, Anzac Day protest.

Indonesia

1981, Two lesbians publicly proclaim their love and exchange vows of commitment before 100 wedding guests.

New Zealand

1972, Maori feminist Nghula Volkering seeks support of lesbians and gay
men and spurs formation of the first gay liberation group in the country.

WORLDWIDE

1982, Women participate in the global graffiti campaign called "The International Shadow Project."

INDEX

ABOUT THE AUTHOR

PAM McALLISTER IS THE EDITOR and author of several books in addition to *You Can't Kill the Spirit*. She edited the anthology, *Reweaving the Web of Life: Feminism and Nonviolence*, New Society Publishers, 1982 (now in its fifth printing), as well as coedited *The Bedside, Bathtub and Armchair Companion to Agatha Christie*, Frederick Ungar Publishers, 1979. Her one-act play, *Approaching the Apple*, about women and organized religion, won a national Religious Arts Guild drama award in 1978. She has also lectured widely on women and nonviolence.

McAllister's essays, stories, poems, book, art and theater reviews have been published in more than forty periodicals and anthologies including *Soho Weekly News, Maenad: A Women's Literary Journal, Woman Artist News, Radical America* and *The Ladies' Home Journal*.

She is currently under contract with New Society Publishers to write a series of books on women and active nonviolence. She also serves as the administrator of the Money for Women/Barbara Deming Memorial Fund, Inc., which provides small grants to feminists in the arts. McAllister resides in Brooklyn, New York.